USING
microsoft®
access® 2010

Alison Balter

800 East 96th Street, Indianapolis, Indiana 46240 USA

Using Microsoft® Access® 2010

Copyright © 2011 by Pearson Education, Inc.

ISBN-13: 978-0-7897-4289-6

ISBN-10: 0-7897-4289-6

Library of Congress Cataloging-in-Publication Data

Balter, Alison.

Using Microsoft Access 2010 / Alison Balter.

p. cm.

ISBN 978-0-7897-4289-6

1. Microsoft Access. 2. Relational databases. I. Title.

QA76.9.D3B3263 2010

005.75'65—dc22

2010023689

Printed in the United States of America

First Printing: July 2010

Trademarks

All terms mentioned in this book that are known to be trademarks or service marks have been appropriately capitalized. Que Publishing cannot attest to the accuracy of this information. Use of a term in this book should not be regarded as affecting the validity of any trademark or service mark.

Warning and Disclaimer

Every effort has been made to make this book as complete and as accurate as possible, but no warranty or fitness is implied. The information provided is on an "as is" basis. The author and the publisher shall have neither liability nor responsibility to any person or entity with respect to any loss or damages arising from the information contained in this book.

Bulk Sales

Que Publishing offers excellent discounts on this book when ordered in quantity for bulk purchases or special sales. For more information, please contact

U.S. Corporate and Government Sales
1-800-382-3419
corpsales@pearsontechgroup.com

For sales outside of the U.S., please contact

International Sales
international@pearson.com

Editor-in-Chief
Greg Wiegand

Acquisitions Editor
Loretta Yates

Development Editor
The Wordsmithery LLC

Managing Editor
Kristy Hart

Project Editor
Betsy Harris

Copy Editor
Keith Cline

Indexer
Erika Millen

Proofreader
Williams Woods Publishing

Technical Editor
Peter Vogel

Publishing Coordinator
Cindy Teeters

Multimedia Developer
John Herrin

Interior Designer
Anne Jones

Cover Designer
Anna Stingley

Compositor
Jake McFarland

Contents at a Glance

Media Table of Contents

To register this product and gain access to the Free Web Edition and the audio and video files, go to **quepublishing.com/using**.

Table of Contents

About the Author

Alison Balter is the president of InfoTech Services Group, Inc., a computer consulting firm based in Newbury Park, California. Alison is a highly experienced independent trainer and consultant specializing in Windows applications training and development. During her 25 years in the computer industry, she has trained and consulted with many corporations and government agencies. Since Alison founded InfoTech Services Group, Inc. (formerly Marina Consulting Group) in 1990, its client base has expanded to include major corporations and government agencies such as Cisco, Shell Oil, Accenture, Northrop, the U.S. Drug Enforcement Administration, Prudential Insurance, Transamerica Insurance, Fox Broadcasting, the U.S. Navy, and others.

Alison is the author of more than 300 internationally marketed computer training videos and CD-ROMs, including 18 Access 2000 videos, 35 Access 2002 videos, 15 Access 2003 videos, 14 Access 2007 User Videos, and 18 Access 2007 Developer Videos. Alison travels throughout North America giving training seminars on Microsoft Access, Microsoft SQL Server, and Visual Basic for Applications. She is also featured in several live satellite television broadcasts for National Technological University.

Alison is also author of 13 books published by Sams Publishing: *Alison Balter's Mastering Access 95 Development, Alison Balter's Mastering Access 97 Development, Alison Balter's Mastering Access 2000 Development, Alison Balter's Mastering Access 2002 Desktop Development, Alison Balter's Mastering Access 2002 Enterprise Development, Alison Balter's Mastering Microsoft Access Office 2003, Teach Yourself Microsoft Office Access 2003 in 24 Hours, Access Office 2003 in a Snap, Alison Balter's Mastering Access 2007 Development*, three e-books on Microsoft Access 2007, and *Teach Yourself SQL Express 2005 in 24 Hours*. Alison is a co-author of three Access books published by Sams Publishing: *Essential Access 95, Access 95 Unleashed*, and *Access 97 Unleashed*.

An active participant in many user groups and other organizations, Alison is a past president of the Independent Computer Consultants Association of Los Angeles and of the Los Angeles Clipper Users' Group. She served as president of the Ventura County Professional Women's Network for two years.

Alison's firm, InfoTech Services Group, Inc., is available for consulting work and onsite training in Microsoft Access, Visual Studio .NET, and SQL Server, as well as for Windows Server 2003, Windows 2000, Windows NT, Windows Vista, Windows XP, PC networking, and Microsoft Exchange Server. You can contact Alison by email at Alison@CallInfoTech.com, or visit the InfoTech Services Group website at http://www.CallInfoTech.com.

Dedication

Many people are important in my life, but there is no one as special as my husband, Dan. I dedicate this book to Dan. Thank you for your ongoing support, for your dedication to me, for your unconditional love, and for your patience. Without you, I'm not sure how I would make it through life. Thank you for sticking with me through the good times and the bad! There's nobody I'd rather spend forever with than you.

I also want to thank God for giving me the gift of gab, a wonderful career, an incredible husband, two beautiful children, a spectacular area to live in, a very special home, and an awesome life. Through your grace, I am truly blessed.

Acknowledgments

Authoring training videos is not an easy task. Special thanks go to the following wonderful people who helped make these videos possible and, more important, who give my life meaning:

Dan Balter (my incredible husband), for his ongoing support, love, encouragement, friendship, and, as usual, patience with me while I authored this book. Dan, words cannot adequately express the love and appreciation I feel for all that you are and all that you do for me. You treat me like a princess! Thank you for being the phenomenal person you are, and thank you for loving me for who I am and for supporting me during the difficult times. I enjoy not only sharing our career successes, but even more I enjoy sharing the lives of our beautiful children, Alexis and Brendan. I look forward to continuing to reach highs we never dreamed of.

Alexis Balter (my daughter and confidante), for giving life a special meaning. Your intelligence, compassion, caring, and perceptiveness are far beyond your years. Alexis, you make all my hard work worth it. No matter how bad my day, when I look at you, sunshine fills my life. You are such a special gift to me. Even in these difficult teenage years your wisdom and inner beauty shine through. Finally, thanks for being my walking partner. I love the conversations that we have as we walk many miles each day.

Brendan Balter (my adorable son and little actor and athlete), for showing me the power of persistence. Brendan, you are small, but, boy, are you mighty! I have never seen such tenacity and fortitude in such a little person. You are able to tackle people twice your size just through your incredible spirit and your remarkable athletic ability. Your imagination and creativity are amazing! Thank you for your sweetness, your sensitivity, and your unconditional love. I really enjoy our times together, especially all of the cuddling. Most of all, thank you for reminding me how important it is to have a sense of humor.

Charlotte and Bob Roman (Mom and Dad), for believing in me and sharing in both the good times and the bad. Mom and Dad, without your special love and support, I never would have become who I am today. Without all your help, I could never get everything done. Words can never express how much I appreciate all that you do!

Al Ludington, for helping me slow down and experience the shades of gray in the world. You somehow walk the fine line between being there and setting limits, between comforting me and confronting me. Words cannot express how much your unconditional love means to me. Thanks for always being there for me and for showing me that a beautiful mind is not such a bad thing after all.

Roz, Ron, and Charlie Carriere, for supporting my endeavors and for encouraging me to pursue my writing. It means a lot to know that you guys are proud of me for what I do. I enjoy our times together as a family. Charlie, I am very proud of you for all of your successes.

Herb and Maureen Balter (my honorary dad and mom), for being such a wonderful father-in-law and mother-in-law. Although our paths were rocky at the beginning, I want you to know how special you are to me. I appreciate your acceptance and your warmth. I also appreciate all you have done for Dan and me. I am grateful to have you in my life.

Reverend Molly, for advancing me spiritually in ways that I can't even describe. You are an amazing woman and are my mentor. I love you dearly. Thanks also to all my church friends: Ed, Zach, Brynn, Gail, Diana, Martha, Marti, Dominic, Bobbi, Ivette, Gary, Heather, Jim, Sheryl, John, Rick, Janie, Sherry, Cory, Mildred, Opal, Suemary, Susan, Beth, Xina, Peter, Shannon, Twila, Karon, Stacy, Juan, Lucy, Sylvia, David, Maria, Steve, Susie, Evelyn, and everyone I am forgetting to mention, for all of your love and support.

Dr. William Cipriano for helping to add balance to my life and for being a good listener. I appreciate your time and your dedication.

Sue and Bob Lopez, for their friendship, and for being godparents to Alexis and Brendan. Sue, you are the best friend that I could possibly ask for. Thank you for your unconditional love, and for all of the great times that we have had together. Bob, thanks for taking care of my best friend. And, to both of you, thanks for making me comfortable knowing that you are there for Alexis and Brendan if they need you.

All of my friends at BNI for supporting me every Friday, and for sharing in my joy about writing so many books: Paula, Bob, Deby, Debbie, Terri, Grace, Scott, Wendi, Paul, Larry, Tracy, Forrest, Amir, Dave, Jane, Steve (Stevil), Anita, Emily, Aaron, John, Tom, Dennis, Eric, Rod, Kathy, and Vern.

All of my friends at DBSA for your ongoing support, unconditional love, and for your encouragement while I wrote this book: Vince, Rachel, Jeff, Dawn, Debbie, Bobby, Roger, Pearl, Phyllis, Anjali, Amanda, Terri, Andrea, Jamaal, Stephanie, Dale, Gail, Harold, and all the rest of my friends.

Ross Pimentel for being so understanding as I completed this book. I so much enjoy working with you, and have fun on both on our programming ventures, and at our lunches. Thank you also for your contribution to this book. I can't tell you how much I appreciate your hard work on the podcasts. You gave it your all, and it shows. You're awesome! Give my love to Hannah for all of her patience while you were busy helping me to support all my endeavors.

Philip and Sharyn Ochoa for giving me the opportunity to work at such a special company. I appreciate all of the work, as well as the friendships that I have been able to make. Thanks for all of your faith in me.

Chris Sabihon, Melisa Beneville, Rachael Chambers, and Elaine Grahek for being clients that have uniquely touched my life. Each of you has made a difference in my life in your own exceptional way. Chris, you have changed my spiritual life forever and will always occupy a special place in my heart. Melisa, I really enjoy working with you. I appreciate the work, but most of all I appreciate the friendship that we have developed, and having a client that values my work. Rachael, you are another client that I particularly value having in my life. You are lots of fun, the work is exciting, and I very much appreciate the relationship that we have developed. Elaine, although we don't directly work together, I want you to know that our walks and talks have made my days at FDI more enjoyable and less taxing.

Ivette Saiz and Diane Dennis for being two extraordinary friends to me. Ivette, I relish our long walks and talks. You are a very unique person with so much to offer. I appreciate the special difference you have made in Alexis's life. Diane, we have known each other since kindergarten! You have the dubious title of having been my friend for the longest. You need to remember how very special you are and to take care of yourself accordingly.

Loretta Yates and Peter Vogel, for making my book-writing experience such a positive one. Loretta, I can't tell you how much I have enjoyed working with you over the past several years. You are very easy to work with, and I enjoy the personal relationship that we have developed as well. I look forward to working together for years to come. Peter, I appreciate all your work tech editing this book, and I look forward to working with you on many books to come!

We Want to Hear from You!

As the reader of this book, *you* are our most important critic and commentator. We value your opinion and want to know what we're doing right, what we could do better, what areas you'd like to see us publish in, and any other words of wisdom you're willing to pass our way.

As an associate publisher for Que Publishing, I welcome your comments. You can email or write me directly to let me know what you did or didn't like about this book—as well as what we can do to make our books better.

Please note that I cannot help you with technical problems related to the topic of this book. We do have a User Services group, however, where I will forward specific technical questions related to the book.

When you write, please be sure to include this book's title and author as well as your name, email address, and phone number. I will carefully review your comments and share them with the author and editors who worked on the book.

Email: feedback@quepublishing.com

Mail: Greg Wiegand
Associate Publisher
Que Publishing
800 East 96th Street
Indianapolis, IN 46240 USA

Reader Services

Visit our website and register this book at quepublishing.com/register for convenient access to any updates, downloads, or errata that might be available for this book.

Introduction

Who Should Read This Book

This book is for anyone comfortable using a personal computer who needs to collect and manipulate information. Experience with Microsoft Access 2010 or an earlier version of Access is helpful, but not necessary. The book takes the user from the basic techniques on how to use Microsoft Access 2010 to a strong intermediate level. After reading this book, you should be comfortable creating and working with databases and the objects that they contain.

How This Book Is Organized

This book starts by covering the basics of working with Microsoft Access. You learn the basics of working with databases, tables, queries, forms, and reports. After learning the basics, you are ready to move to more advanced features, where you learn how to build your own databases and tables and how to relate the tables within your database. You are then ready to embark on a journey through power query, form, and report techniques. Finally, you learn about three exciting aspects of Access 2010. You learn how to create macros, how to share data with other applications, and how to build a database that runs in a browser.

Requirements, Editions, and Features

Microsoft hasn't dramatically increased the hardware requirements for Access 2010 compared to those for earlier versions of Access. In fact, if anything, you'll find Access 2010 runs on existing hardware as well as or even better than earlier versions of Access.

To be sure you can run Access 2010, here's a look at the basic hardware and operating system requirements:

- 500MHz or faster 32-bit or 64-bit processor
- 256MB of RAM
- 2GB available hard disk space (32-bit) or 20GB (64-bit)
- 1024x768 resolution monitor
- Windows XP with Service Pack 3, Windows Vista with SP1, Windows Server 2003 R2 with MXXML 6.0, Windows Server 2008 (32-bit or 64-bit), Windows 7, or later operating systems

Let's take a peek at some of the techniques for using Access 2010 that you'll be learning about:

- **Manipulating data**—After you learn about relational databases, and what Microsoft Access 2010 has to offer, Chapter 1, "Manipulating Data with Databases and Tables," shows you how to open a database and modify the data within it. You will also learn how to filter table data.

- **Retrieving the data you need**—Chapter 2, "Using Queries to Retrieve the Data You Need," shows you all the basics of working with queries. You learn techniques such as how to select fields, apply criteria, and order the query result.

- **Displaying data with forms**—Chapter 3, "Using Forms to Enter and Edit Table Data," shows you how to manipulate table data from within a form. It also covers the process of using a Form Wizard to create a form.

- **Printing data with reports**—Chapter 4, "Using Reports to Print Information," first shows you how to open, view, and print an existing report. You then learn how to build your own reports.

- **Building databases and tables**—Chapter 5, "Creating Your Own Databases and Tables," covers both the process of creating new databases, and of creating new tables. In this chapter, you learn important techniques such as how to work with field properties.

- **Relating the data in your database**—Chapter 6, "Relating the Information in Your Database," shows you how to relate the tables that you build. After this chapter provides you with a crash course on database design, you learn how to establish relationships, and how to enforce referential integrity.

- **Working with queries**—Chapter 7, "Enhancing the Queries That You Build," enhances what you learned about queries in Chapter 2. In this chapter, you learn how to build queries based on multiple tables, how to add calculations to the queries that you build, how to run parameter queries when you don't know the criteria at design time, how to use action queries to update your table data, and how and why to work with outer joins.

- **Working with forms**—Chapter 8, "Building Powerful Forms," enhances what you learned about forms in Chapter 3. In this chapter, you learn how to work with form controls, how to apply conditional formatting, and how to modify form properties. You also learn how to work with combo boxes, the Command Button Wizard, how to build forms based on more than one table, and how to work with subforms.

- **Working with reports**—Chapter 9, "Building Powerful Reports," enhances what you learned about reports in Chapter 4. In this chapter you learn how to work with report bands, work with controls, build multi-table reports, work with subreports, add sorting and grouping, and take advantage of report properties.

- **Using macros to automate your database**—Chapter 10, "Automating Your Database with Macros," shows you how to automate the databases that you build. In this chapter, you learn important techniques such as how to create and run macros, how to control the flow of the macros that you build, and how to create submacros. You also learn how to take advantage of Access 2010's new features such as embedded macros, data macros, and drillthrough macros. You learn how to work with variables and error handling, and finally, you learn how to take advantage of a very special macro, the AutoExec macro.

- **Sharing data with other applications**—One of Access's greatest strengths is its ability to share data with other applications. In Chapter 11, "Sharing Data with Other Applications," you learn how to export data to and import data from Excel, text files, and other Access databases. You learn how to link to data in other databases, and how to use a powerful tool called the Linked Table Manager to manage the links that you create. As a special bonus, you learn how to link to data in a SQL Server database, so that you can take advantage of Access's strong ability to participate in a client/server environment.

- **Running your application in a web browser**—Chapter 12, "Working with Web Databases," shows you how to take your database to the Web. In this chapter, you learn about web databases and what they are. You are introduced to application parts, and you learn how to create server objects. Finally, you witness your completed application running in a web browser.

Whether it's the new and exciting macro environment, or the ability to easily take Access data to the Web, it won't take long for you to get to know this new and exciting version of Microsoft Access. Access 2010 is fast, stable, and extremely packed with new and thrilling features. *Using Access 2010* is your personal guide to learning how to use Access 2010 and how to get the most out of what it has to offer.

Using This Book

This book allows you to customize your own learning experience. The step-by-step instructions in the book give you a solid foundation in using Access 2010, while rich and varied online content, including video tutorials and audio sidebars, provide the following:

- Demonstrations of step-by-step tasks covered in the book

- Additional tips or information on a topic

- Practical advice and suggestions

- Direction for more advanced tasks not covered in the book

Here's a quick look at a few structural features designed to help you get the most out of this book.

- **Chapter objective:** At the beginning of each chapter is a brief summary of topics addressed in that chapter. This objective enables you to quickly see what is covered in the chapter.

- **Notes:** Notes provide additional commentary or explanation that doesn't fit neatly into the surrounding text. Notes give detailed explanations of how something works, alternative ways of performing a task, and other tidbits to get you on your way.

 LET ME TRY IT tasks are presented in a step-by-step sequence so you can easily follow along.

 SHOW ME video walks through tasks you've just got to see—including bonus advanced techniques.

 TELL ME MORE audio delivers practical insights straight from the experts.

Special Features

More than just a book, your USING product integrates step-by-step video tutorials and valuable audio sidebars delivered through the **Free Web Edition** that comes with every USING book. For the price of the book, you get online access anywhere with a web connection—no books to carry, content is updated as the technology changes, and the benefit of video and audio learning.

About the USING Web Edition

The Web Edition of every USING book is powered by **Safari Books Online**, allowing you to access the video tutorials and valuable audio sidebars. Plus, you can search the contents of the book, highlight text and attach a note to that text, print your notes and highlights in a custom summary, and cut and paste directly from Safari Books Online.

To register this product and gain access to the Free Web Edition and the audio and video files, go to **quepublishing.com/using**.

Using Access 2010, you use databases and tables to manipulate data.

1

Manipulating Data with Databases and Tables

In this chapter, you will learn what a relational database is. You will then discover some of the exciting things you can do with Microsoft Access. With that information under your belt, you will begin working with existing Access databases. You will learn both how to navigate the data in a table and how to edit the data that you are viewing. Finally, you'll learn how to search for specific data that you want to work with.

What Is a Relational Database?

The term *database* means different things to different people. For many years, in the world of xBase (that is, dBASE, FoxPro, CA-Clipper, and other older database technologies), *database* was used to describe a collection of fields and records. (Access refers to this type of collection as a *table*.) In a client/server environment, *database* refers to all the data, schema, indexes, rules, triggers, and stored procedures associated with a system. In Access terms, a *database* is a collection of all the tables, queries, forms, reports, macros, and modules that compose a complete system. *Relational* refers to concepts based on set theory. These concepts are covered in Chapter 6, "Relating the Information in Your Database."

A Preview of the Database Components

As mentioned previously, tables, queries, forms, reports, macros, and modules combine to comprise an Access database. Each of these objects has a special function. The following sections take you on a tour of the objects that make up an Access database.

Tables: A Repository for Data

Tables are the starting point for an application. Whether data is stored in an Access database or you are referencing external data by using linked tables, all the other objects in a database either directly or indirectly reference tables.

To view all the tables that are contained in an open database, you select Tables from the list of objects available in the database (see Figure 1.1). A list of available tables appears (see Figure 1.2).

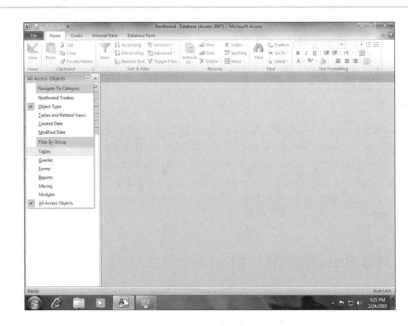

Figure 1.1   *To view the tables in a database, select Tables from the list of available objects.*

To view the data in a table, double-click the name of the table you want to view. (You can also right-click the table and then select Open.) Access displays the table's data in a datasheet that includes all the table's fields and records (see Figure 1.3). You can modify many of the datasheet's attributes and even search for and filter data from within the datasheet; these techniques are covered later in this chapter.

If the table is related to another table (such as the Northwind database's Customers and Orders tables), you can also expand and collapse the sub-datasheet to view data stored in child tables (see Figure 1.4).

As an Access user, you will often want to view the table's design, which is the blue-print or template for the table. To view a table's design (see Figure 1.5), right-click the table name in the Navigation Pane, and then select Design View. In Design view, you can view or modify all the field names, data types, and field and table properties. Access gives you the power and flexibility you need to customize the design of tables. Chapter 5, "Creating Your Own Databases and Tables," covers these topics.

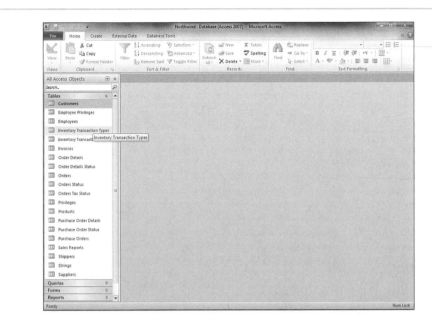

Figure 1.2   *You can view the tables contained in a database.*

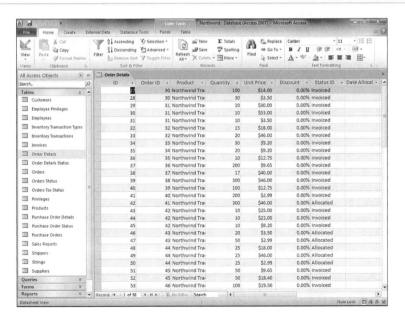

Figure 1.3   *A table's datasheet contains fields and records.*

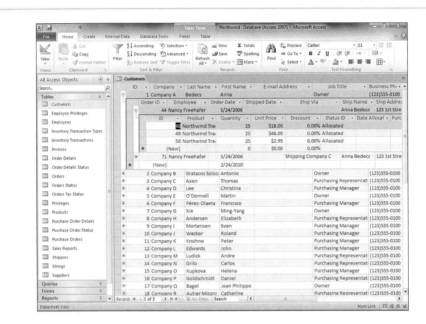

Figure 1.4   *Datasheet view of the Customers table in the Northwind database.*

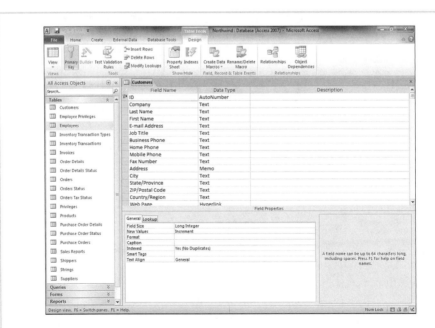

Figure 1.5   *The design of the Customers table.*

Relationships: Tying the Tables Together

To properly maintain data's integrity and ease the process of working with other objects in a database, you must define relationships among the tables in a database. You accomplish this by using the Relationships window. To view the Relationships window, select Relationships from the Database Tools tab of the Ribbon. The Relationships window appears. In this window, you can view and maintain the relationships in the database (see Figure 1.6). If you or a fellow user or developer have set up some relationships, but you don't see any in the Relationships window, you can select All Relationships in the Relationships group on the Design tab of the Ribbon to unhide any hidden tables and relationships.

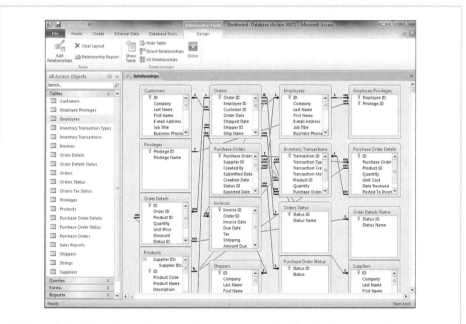

Figure 1.6   *The Relationships tab, where you view and maintain the relationships in a database.*

Notice that many of the relationships in Figure 1.6 have join lines between tables and show a number 1 on one side of the join and an infinity symbol on the other. This indicates a one-to-many relationship between the tables. If you double-click a join line, the Edit Relationships dialog box opens (see Figure 1.7). In this dialog box, you can specify the exact nature of the relationship between tables. The relationship between the Customers and Orders tables in Figure 1.7, for example, is a one-to-many relationship with referential integrity enforced. This means that the user cannot add orders for customers who don't exist. Notice in Figure 1.7 that the

Cascade Update Related Fields check box is selected. This means that if the user updates a CustomerID field, Access updates all records containing that CustomerID value in the Orders table. Because Cascade Delete Related Records is not checked in Figure 1.7, the user cannot delete from the Customers table customers who have corresponding orders in the Orders table.

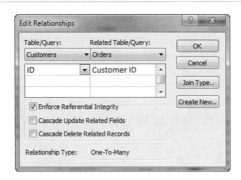

Figure 1.7   *The Edit Relationships dialog box, which lets you specify the nature of the relationships between tables.*

Chapter 6, "Relating the Information in Your Database," extensively covers the process of defining and maintaining relationships. For now, you should remember that you should establish relationships both conceptually and literally as early in the design process as possible. Relationships are integral to successfully designing and implementing your application.

Queries: Stored Questions or Actions You Apply to Data

Queries in Access are powerful and multifaceted. A query retrieves data from your database based on criteria you specify. An example is a query that retrieves all employees who live in Florida. Select queries allow you to view, summarize, and perform calculations on the data in tables. Action queries let you add to, update, and delete table data. To run a query, you select Queries from the Objects list and then double-click the query you want to run, or you can click in the list of queries to select the query you want to run and then right-click and select Open. When you run a Select query, a datasheet appears, containing all the fields specified in the query and all the records meeting the query's criteria (see Figure 1.8). When you run an Action query, Access runs the specified action, such as making a new table or appending data to an existing table. In general, you can update the data in a query result because the result of a query is actually a dynamic set of records, called a *dynaset*, that is based on the tables' data. A dynaset is a subset of data on which you can base a form or report.

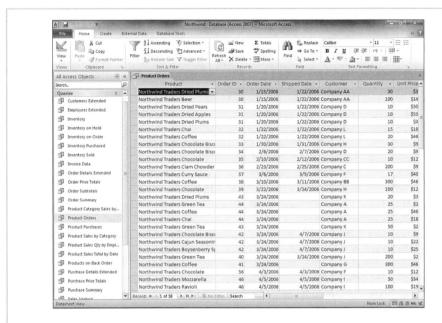

Figure 1.8　*The result of running the Product Orders query.*

When you store a query, Access stores only the query's definition, layout, or formatting properties in the database. Access offers an intuitive, user-friendly tool that helps you design queries: the Query Design window (see Figure 1.9). To open this window, select Queries from the Objects list in the Navigation Pane, choose the query you want to modify, right-click, and select Design View.

The query pictured in Figure 1.9 selects data from the CustomersExtended query and the Orders and Order Details tables. It displays several fields, including the ProductID, Quantity, Unit Price, and Discount fields from the Order Details table, and the OrderID, Order Date, Shipped Date, and CustomerID fields from the Orders table. The query's output displays the data in order by order date. It displays only records with order dates within a specific date range. This special type of query is called a *parameter query*. It prompts for criteria at runtime, using the criteria entered by the user to determine which records it includes in the output. Chapter 2, "Using Queries to Retrieve the Data You Need," and Chapter 7, "Enhancing the Queries That You Build," both cover the process of designing queries. Because queries are the foundation for most forms and reports, they are covered throughout this book as they apply to other objects in the database.

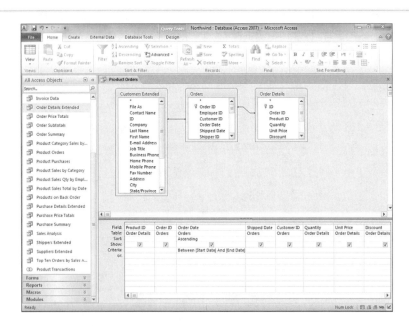

Figure 1.9   *The design of a query that displays data from the Customer Extended query, Orders table, and Order Details table.*

Forms: A Means of Displaying, Modifying, and Adding Data

Although you can enter and modify data in a table's Datasheet view, you can't control the user's actions very well, nor can you do much to facilitate the data-entry process. This is where forms come in. Access forms can have many traits, and they're very flexible and powerful.

To view a form, you select Forms from the Objects list. Then you double-click the form you want to view or right-click in the list of forms to select the form you want to view and then click Open. Figure 1.10 illustrates a form in Form view. This Customer Details form is actually two forms in one: one main form and one subform. The main form displays information from the Customers table, and the subform displays information from the Orders table (a table that is related to the Customers table). As the user moves from customer to customer, the form displays the orders associated with that customer. When the user clicks to select an order, the form displays the entire order.

Like tables and queries, you can also view forms in Design view. The Design view provides tools you may use to edit the layout of your form. To view the design of a

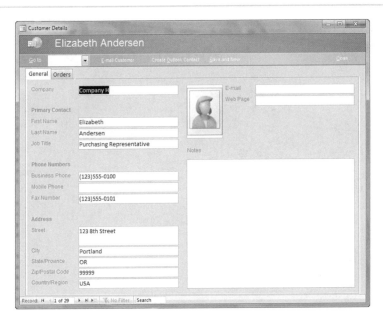

Figure 1.10 *The Customer Details form, which includes customer, order, and order detail information.*

form, you select Forms from the Objects list, choose the form whose design you want to modify, and then right-click and select Design View. Figure 1.11 shows the Customer Details form in Design view. Chapter 3, "Using Forms to Enter and Edit Table Data," and Chapter 8, "Building Powerful Forms," cover forms in more detail.

Reports: Turning Data into Information

Forms allow you to enter and edit information, but with reports, you can display information, usually to a printer. Figure 1.12 shows a report in Preview mode. To preview any report, you select Reports from the Objects list. You double-click the report you want to preview or right-click the report you want to preview from the list of reports in the Navigation Pane, and then you click Open. Notice the chart in the report in Figure 1.12. Like forms, reports can be elaborate and exciting, and they can contain valuable information.

As you may have guessed, you can view reports in Design view, as shown in Figure 1.13. To view the design of a report, you select Reports from the Objects list, select the report you want to view, and then right-click and select Design View. Figure 1.13 illustrates a report with many sections; in the figure you can see the Page Header, Order ID Header, Detail section, Order ID Footer, and Page Footer (just a

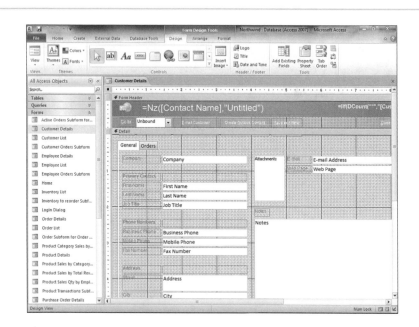

Figure 1.11   *The design of the Customer Details form, showing two subforms.*

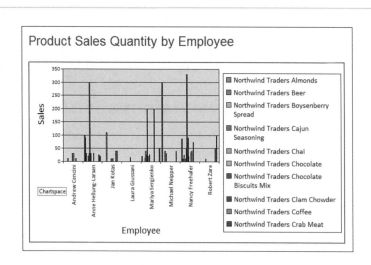

Figure 1.12   *A preview of the Product Sales Quantity by Employee report.*

few of the many sections available on a report). Just as a form can contain sub-forms, a report can contain subreports. Chapter 4, "Using Reports to Print Information," and Chapter 9, "Building Powerful Reports," cover the process of designing reports.

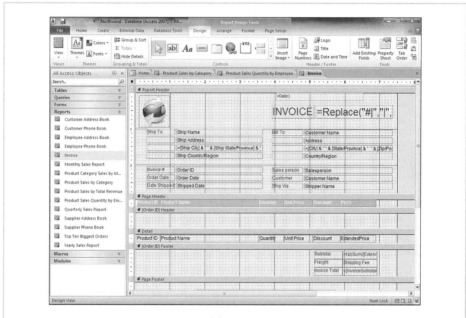

Figure 1.13 *Design view of the Invoice report.*

Macros: A Means of Automating a System

Macros in Access aren't like the macros in other Office products. You can't record them, as you can in Microsoft Word or Excel, and Access does not save them as Visual Basic for Applications (VBA) code. With Access macros, you can perform most of the tasks that you can manually perform from the keyboard, Ribbon, and Quick-Access toolbar. Macros allow you to build logic in to your application flow.

To run a macro, select Macros from the Objects list, and then double-click the macro you want to run (or you can right-click the macro and click Run). Access then executes the actions in the macro. To view a macro's design, you select Macros from the Objects list, select the macro you want to modify, right-click and select Design View to open the Macro Design window (see Figure 1.14). The macro pictured in

Figure 1.14 performs one action, the MessageBox action. The MessageBox action accepts four arguments: Message, Beep, Type, and Title.

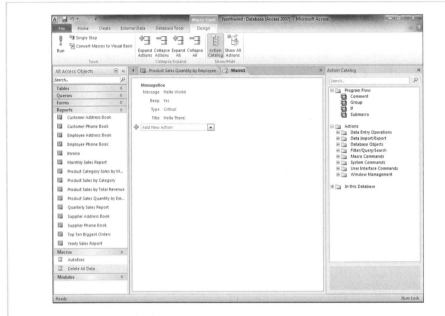

Figure 1.14   *The design of a macro containing the MessageBox action.*

Modules: The Foundation of the Application Development Process

Modules, the foundation of any complex Access application, let you create libraries of functions that you can use throughout an application. You usually include subroutines and functions in the modules that you build. A function always returns a value; a subroutine does not. By using code modules, you can do just about anything with an Access application. Figure 1.15 shows an example of a module.

What Types of Things Can I Do with Microsoft Access?

I often find myself explaining exactly what types of applications you can build with Microsoft Access. Access offers a variety of features for different database needs. You can use it to develop five general types of applications:

- Personal applications
- Small-business applications

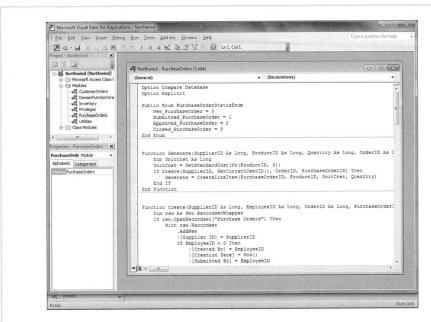

Figure 1.15 *The global code module in Design view, showing the General Declarations section and the Generate and Create functions.*

- Departmental applications

- Corporation-wide applications

- Front-end applications for enterprise-wide client/server databases

Access as a Development Platform for Personal Applications

At a basic level, you can use Access to develop simple personal database-management systems. I know people who automate everything from their wine collections to their home finances. The one thing to be careful of is that Access is deceptively easy to use. Its wonderful built-in wizards make Access look like a product that anyone can use. After answering a series of questions, you have finished application switchboards that allow you to easily navigate around your application, data-entry screens, reports, and the underlying tables that support them. In fact, when Microsoft first released Access, many people asked whether I was concerned that my business as a computer programmer and trainer would diminish because Access seemed to let absolutely anyone write a database application. Although it's true that you can produce the simplest of Access applications without any thought for design and without any customization, most applications require at least some design and customization.

If you're an end user and don't want to spend too much time learning the intricacies of Access, you'll be satisfied with Access as long as you're happy with a wizard-generated personal application. After reading this text, you can make some modifications to what the wizards have generated, and no problems should occur. It's when you want to substantially customize a personal application without the proper knowledge base that problems can happen.

Access as a Development Platform for Small-Business Applications

Access is an excellent platform for developing an application that can run a small business. Its wizards let you quickly and easily build the application's foundation. The ability to create macros and to build code modules allows power users and developers to create code libraries of reusable functions, and the ability to add code behind forms and reports allows them to create powerful custom forms and reports.

The main limitation of using Access for developing a custom small-business application is the time and money involved in the development process. Many people use Access wizards to begin the development process but find they need to customize their applications in ways they can't accomplish on their own. Small-business owners often experience this problem on an even greater scale than personal users. The demands of a small-business application are usually much higher than those of a personal application. Many doctors, attorneys, and other professionals have called me in after they reached a dead end in the development process. They're always dismayed at how much money it will cost to make their application usable. An example is a doctor who built a series of forms and reports to automate her office. All went well until it came time to produce patient billings, enter payments, and produce receivable reports. Although at first glance these processes seem simple, on further examination the doctor realized that the wizard-produced reports and forms did not provide the sophistication necessary for her billing process. Unfortunately, the doctor did not have the time or programming skills to add the necessary features. So, in using Access as a tool to develop small-business applications, it is important that you be realistic about the time and money involved in developing anything but the simplest of applications.

Access as a Development Platform for Departmental Applications

Access is perfect for developing applications for departments in large corporations. Most departments in large corporations have the development budgets to produce well-designed applications.

Fortunately, most departments also usually have a PC guru who is more than happy to help design forms and reports. This gives the department a sense of ownership because it has contributed to the development of its application. If complex form or report design or coding is necessary, large corporations usually have on-site resources available that can provide the necessary assistance. If the support is not available within the corporation, most corporations are willing to outsource to obtain the necessary expertise.

Access as a Development Platform for Corporation-wide Applications

Although Access might be best suited for departmental applications, you can also use it to produce applications that you distribute throughout an organization. How successful this endeavor is depends on the corporation. There's a limit to the number of users who can concurrently share an Access application while maintaining acceptable performance, and there's also a limit to the number of records that each table can contain without a significant performance drop. These numbers vary depending on factors such as the following:

- How much traffic already exists on the network.
- How much RAM and how many processors the server has.
- How the server is already being used. For example, are applications such as Microsoft Office being loaded from the server or from local workstations?
- What types of tasks the users of the application are performing. For example, are they querying, entering data, running reports, and so on?
- Where Access and Access applications are run from (the server or the workstation).
- What network operating system is in place.

My general rule of thumb for an Access application that's not client/server based is that poor performance generally results with more than 10 to 15 concurrent users and more than 100,000 records. Remember that these numbers vary immensely depending on the factors mentioned, and on what you and the other users of the application define as acceptable performance. If you go beyond these limits, you should consider using Access as a front end to a client/server database such as Microsoft SQL Server—that is, you can use Access to create forms and reports while storing tables and possibly queries on the database server.

Access as a Front End for Enterprise-wide Client/Server Applications

A client/server database, such as Microsoft SQL Server or Oracle, processes queries on the server machine and returns results to the workstation. The server software itself can't display data to the user, so this is where Access comes to the rescue. Acting as a front end, Access can display the data retrieved from the database server in reports, datasheets, or forms. If the user updates the data in an Access form, the workstation sends the update to the back-end database. You can accomplish this process either by linking to these external databases so that they appear to both you and the user as Access tables or by using techniques to access client/server data directly.

Working with an Existing Database

Before we dive right into creating our own databases, we're going to start by working with an existing database. To work with an existing database, you must first open it.

 **LET ME TRY IT**

Open an Existing Database

To open an existing database:

1. From File tab of the Ribbon (see Figure 1.16) select one of the recently opened databases, or click Open to view additional files. If you click Open, the Open dialog appears (see Figure 1.17).

2. Locate the file you want to open and then click Open. Access opens the file, and the desktop appears as in Figure 1.18.

Your desktop might not look exactly like the figure. This is because Access remembers the state of the Navigation Pane when you last had the database open. For example, if you had the list of tables expanded the last time the database was

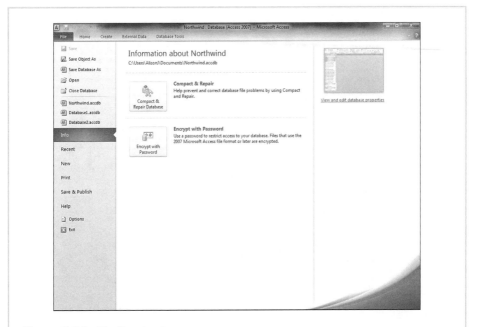

Figure 1.16 *The Opening Access screen.*

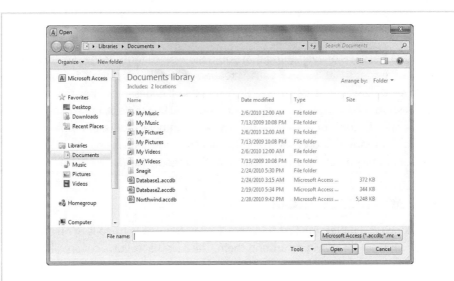

Figure 1.17 *The Open dialog.*

open, Access will show the list of tables in the Navigation Pane the next time that you open the database. In fact, you can collapse the Navigation Pane entirely by using the Shutter Bar Open/Close Button at the top of the Navigation Pane.

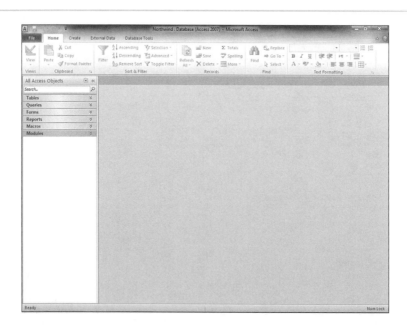

Figure 1.18   *The Access desktop.*

Working with Table Data

Tables are the basis of everything that you do in Access. Most of the data for your database resides in tables. So if you're creating an employee payroll database, your employee data will be stored in a table, your payroll codes might be stored in a table, and your past payroll records could be stored in a table. A table contains data about a specific topic or subject (for example, customers, orders, or employees). Tables are arranged in rows and columns, similar to a spreadsheet. The columns represent the fields, and the rows represent the records (see Figure 1.19).

Open an Access Table

In working with tables, the first thing you'll want to be able to do is open them in Datasheet view and navigate around them. The text that follows covers all the basics of working with tables in Datasheet view.

To open a table in Datasheet view, follow these steps:

1. Select Tables in the list of objects in the Navigation Pane.

2. Select the table you want to open and click the Open button in the Navigation Pane or double-click the table you want to open.

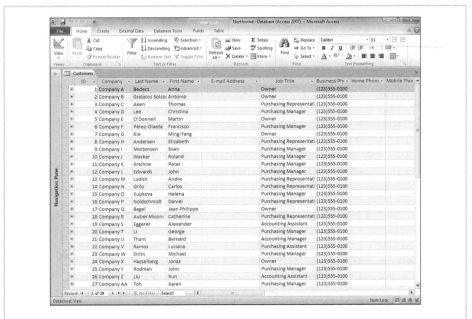

Figure 1.19   *A table composed of columns and rows associated with customers.*

Navigating Around a Table

You can move around a table by using the keyboard or mouse. When you are editing or adding records, your hands are on the keyboard, and you might find it easiest to move around a table by using the keyboard. However, if you are looking for a specific record, you might find it most convenient to use the mouse.

Table 1.1 shows the keyboard and mouse actions for moving around a table and their resulting effects. As you can see, Microsoft Access provides numerous keyboard and mouse alternatives for moving around a table.

The insertion point does not change locations just because you move your mouse, only the mouse pointer moves when you move your mouse. You need to click *within* a field before you begin typing; otherwise, the changes occur in the original mouse location.

The tab displaying the data includes tools that enable you to scroll through the fields and records, move from record to record, expand and collapse to show and hide related records, and more. Figure 1.20 illustrates these features. Table 1.2 provides a list of these features and provides a description of each.

Table 1.1   Keyboard and Mouse Actions to Move Around a Table

Keyboard Action	Mouse Action	Effect
Tab or right arrow	Click the right arrow on the bottom scrollbar.	Moves one field to the right of the current field
Shift+Tab or left arrow	Click the left arrow on the bottom scrollbar.	Moves one field to the left of the current field
Down arrow	Click the next record button.	Moves down one record
Up arrow	Click the previous record button.	Moves up one record
Page Down	No equivalent mouse action	Moves down one screen of records
Page Up	No equivalent mouse action	Moves up one screen of records
Home	No equivalent mouse action	Selects the first field of the current record
End	No equivalent mouse action	Selects the last field of the current record
Ctrl+Home	Click the first record button.	Moves to the first record of the table
Ctrl+End	Click the last record button.	Moves to the last record of the table
F2	Click and drag within a field.	Selects the text in the field

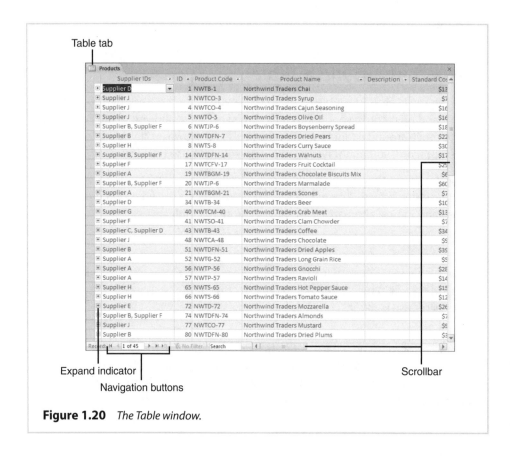

Figure 1.20   *The Table window.*

Table 1.2 The Components of the Table Window

Table Component	Description
Table tab	Allows you to easily select the open table.
Scrollbar	You can use the scrollbars to move up and down and right and left in the table.
Navigation buttons	These icons enable you to select the first record, last record, next record, or previous record in the table.
Expand indicator	The expand indicator enables you to view the data hierarchy by showing you any subdata records that are linked to the main record.

SHOW ME   Media 1.1—Viewing and Navigating Table Data
Access this video file through your registered Web Edition at
my.safaribooksonline.com/9780132117128/media.

Closing a Table

When you are finished working with a table, you need to close it. To close a table, you choose File, Close or click the close button in the upper-right corner of the Table tab.

Access often prompts you as you close a table, asking if you want to save changes to the layout of the table. It is important that you understand that Access is *not* asking whether you want to save changes to the data. As you'll learn in a moment, Access saves changes to data the moment you move off a record. When you close a table and Access prompts you, it is asking whether you want to save formatting changes, such as changes to column width, to the look of the datasheet, and so on.

Editing Table Data

You can change the data in a table any time that you are in Datasheet view of a table, the result of a query, or Form view of a form. Access saves changes you make to a record as soon as you move off the record.

 **LET ME TRY IT**

Edit Existing Records

One task you might want to perform is to simply modify table data. Here's the process:

1.   Select the record you want to change by using any of the techniques listed in Table 1.2.

2.   Select the field you want to change by clicking the field or using the arrow keys.

3.   Type to make the necessary changes to the data. Once you move off the record, Access saves your changes.

Undoing Changes

There are different options available when undoing changes to a field or to a record. The options differ depending on whether you are still within a field, have left the field, or have left the record. The sections that follow explore the various options available to you.

Undoing Changes Made to the Current Field

When you are in the process of making changes to a field, you might realize that you really didn't want to make changes to that field or to that record. To undo changes to the current field, you can either click the Undo tool on the QuickAccess toolbar or press the Esc key once. For example, if you mean to change the contact first name from Alison to Sue, but realize that you are accidentally typing Sue in the Customer field, you can press the Esc key once, or click the Undo tool on the Quick-Access toolbar, to undo your change.

Undoing Changes After You Move to Another Field

The process of undoing changes after you move to another field is identical to that of the process of undoing changes made to the current field. You can either click the Undo tool on the QuickAccess toolbar or press the Esc key once. For example, if you mean to change the contact first name from Alison to Sue, but realize that you accidentally typed Sue in the Customer field, and then moved to another field, you could click the Undo tool on the QuickAccess toolbar, or press the Esc key once, to undo your change.

Undoing Changes After You Save a Record

When you make changes to a field and then move to another record, Access saves all changes to the modified record. So long as you do not begin making changes to another record, you can still undo the changes you made to the most recently modified record. To do this, you can either click the Undo tool on the QuickAccess toolbar or press the Esc key twice. For example, if you mean to change the contact first name from Alison to Sue, but realize that you accidentally typed Sue in the Customer field, and then moved to another record, you either click the Undo tool on the QuickAccess toolbar or press the Esc key twice to undo your change.

 SHOW ME   Media 1.2—Editing Existing Records
Access this video file through your registered Web Edition at
my.safaribooksonline.com/9780132117128/media.

If Access is unable to undo a change, the Undo tool appears dimmed.

After you have made changes to a record and then have gone on to make changes to another record, you cannot undo the changes that you made to the first record.

Adding Records to a Table

Access adds records to the end of a table, regardless of how you add them to the table.

 LET ME TRY IT

Add Records to a Table

To add records, follow these steps:

1. Select the table to which you want to add information.

2. Click the New Record Navigation button at the bottom of the Datasheet window.

3. Add the necessary information to the fields within the record. When you move off the record, Access saves the new record.

You can use Ctrl + " to repeat the data in the field directly above the current field.

It is also important to note that Access always displays one blank record at the end of a table. When entering data, pressing the Tab key at the end of a record that you just added allows you to continue to add additional records.

SHOW ME   Media 1.3—Adding Records to a Table
Access this video file through your registered Web Edition at
my.safaribooksonline.com/9780132117128/media.

Deleting Records

Before you can delete records, you must select them. The following sections cover the process of selecting records and then the process of deleting records.

Selecting One or More Records

To select one record, you just click the gray record selector button to the left of the record within the datasheet.

To select multiple records, you click and drag within the record selector area. Access selects the contiguous range of records in the area over which you click and drag. As an alternative, you can click the gray selector button for the first record you want to select, hold down the Shift key, and then click the gray selector button of the last record that you want to select. When you do this, Access selects the entire range of records between them. Figure 1.21 shows the Customers table with three records selected.

If you want to select a single record when the cursor is within the record, you can simply choose Select from the Find group on the Home tab, and then choose Select. To select all records, choose Select from the Find group on the Home tab, and then choose Select All.

LET ME TRY IT

Deleting Records

When you know how to select records, deleting them is quite simple. You just follow these steps:

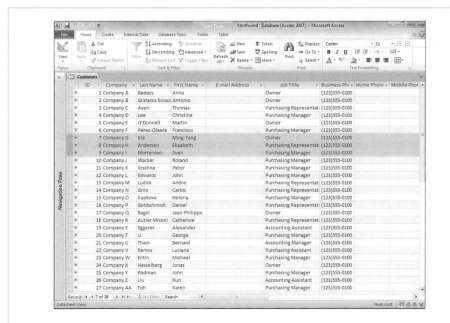

Figure 1.21 *The Customers table with three records selected.*

1. Select the records you want to delete.

2. Press the Delete key. The dialog box in Figure 1.22 appears, asking whether you're sure you want to delete the records.

3. Click the Yes button. Access deletes the records.

The process of deleting a record is not so simple if you have established referential integrity between the tables in a database and the row that you are attempting to delete has child rows. Chapter 6 covers relationships and referential integrity. For now, you can think about the fact that customers generally have orders associated with them, and those orders have order detail records associated with them. The relationship between the Customers table and the Orders table prohibits the user from deleting customers who have orders. Here's how you delete a customer who has orders:

1. Select the records you want to delete.

2. Press the Delete key. The dialog box in Figure 1.23 appears, telling you that the records cannot be deleted because the table includes related records.

3. Click OK to close the dialog box.

Figure 1.22   *Access asks if you want to delete the selected records.*

Figure 1.23   *Access notifying you that you cannot delete the selected records.*

Access provides a *referential integrity* option with which you can cascade a deletion down to the child table (a table related to a parent table, such as orders related to customers). This means, for example, that if you attempt to delete an order, Access deletes the associated order detail records. If you establish referential integrity with the cascade delete option, the deletion process works like this:

1. Select the records you want to delete.

2. Press the Delete key. The dialog box in Figure 1.24 appears, asking if you're sure you want to delete the records.

3. Click Yes to complete the deletion process.

After you have selected records, they appear in black, and you can copy them, delete them, or modify them as a group. Remember that deleting records is a permanent process. You cannot undo record deletion.

 SHOW ME   **Media 1.4—Selecting and Deleting Records**
Access this video file through your registered Web Edition at
my.safaribooksonline.com/9780132117128/media.

Figure 1.24   *Access asking if you want to delete the parent row and the associated child records.*

Finding and Replacing Records

When you are working with records in a large data table, you often need a way to locate specific records quickly. By using the Find feature, you can easily move to specific records within a table. After you have found records, you can also replace the text within them.

 LET ME TRY IT

Find a Record That Meets Specific Criteria

The Find feature enables you to search in a datasheet for records that meet specific criteria. Here's how it works:

1. Select the field containing the criteria for which you are searching.

2. Click the Find button in the Find group on the Home tab of the Ribbon. The Find and Replace dialog box appears (see Figure 1.25).

3. Type the criteria in the Find What text box.

4. Use the Look In drop-down list box to designate whether you want to search only the current field or all fields in the table.

5. Use the Match drop-down list box to designate whether you want to match any part of the field you are searching, the whole field you are searching, or the start of the field you are searching. For example, if you type **Federal** in the Find What text box and you select Whole Field in the Match drop-down list box, you find only entries where Ship Via is set to Federal. If you select Any Part of Field, you find Federal Shipping, Federal Express, United Federal Shipping, and so on. If you select Start of Field, you find Federal Shipping and Federal Express, but you do not find United Federal Shipping.

Figure 1.25   *The Find tab of the Find and Replace dialog box, which you can use to search for values in a datasheet.*

6. Use the Search drop-down list box to designate whether you want to search only up from the current cursor position, only down, or in all directions.

7. Use the Match Case check box to indicate whether you want the search to be case sensitive.

8. Use the Search Fields as Formatted check box to indicate whether you want to find data only based on the display format (for example, 17-Jul-96 for a date).

9. Click the Find Next button to find the next record that meets the designated criteria.

10. To continue searching after you close the dialog box, use the Shift+F4 keystroke combination.

Replacing Data in a Table

There may be times when you want to update records that meet specific criteria. You can use the Replace feature to automatically insert new information into the specified fields. Here's how:

1. Click within the field that contains the criteria you are searching for.

2. Click the Replace button in the Find group on the Home tab of the Ribbon. The Find and Replace dialog box appears.

3. Select the Replace tab (see Figure 1.26).

4. Type the criteria in the Find What text box.

5. Type the new information (the replacement value) in the Replace With text box.

6. Choose values for the Look In drop-down list box, Match drop-down list box, Search drop-down list box, Match Case check box, and Search Fields as Formatted check box, as described in the "Find a Record That Meets Specific Criteria" section of this chapter.

7. Click the Find Next button. Access locates the first record that meets the criteria designated in the Find What text box.

8. Click the Replace button. Access replaces the text for the record and finds the next occurrence of the text in the Find What text box.

Figure 1.26   *The Replace tab of the Find and Replace dialog, within which you can replace table data.*

9. Repeat step 8 to find all occurrences of the value in the Find What text box and replace them. As an alternative, you can click the Replace All button to replace all occurrences at once.

You should use Replace All with quite a bit of caution. Remember that the changes you make are *permanent*. Although Replace All is a viable option, when you use it you need to make sure you have a recent backup and that you are quite certain of what you are doing. In fact, I usually do a few replaces to make sure that I see what Access is doing *before* I click Replace All.

10. Click Cancel when you've finished.

If you are searching a very large table, Access can find a specific value in a field fastest if the field you are searching on is the primary key or an indexed field. Chapter 5 covers primary keys and indexes.

When using either Find or Replace, you can use several wildcard characters. A wildcard character is a character you use in place of an unknown character. Table 1.3 describes the wildcard characters.

Table 1.3 Wildcard Characters You Can Use When Searching

Wildcard Character	Description
*	Acts as a placeholder for multiple characters
?	Acts as a placeholder for a single character
#	Acts as a placeholder for a single number

Filtering Table Data

In a table, you can apply filters to fields to limit what records you view. This is very helpful if you want to view just the data associated with a subset of the records. For example, you may want to view just the data associated with Sales Managers.

 **LET ME TRY IT**

Filtering by Selection

The Filter by Selection feature allows you to select text and then filter the data in the table to that selected text. To use the Filter by Selection feature, follow these steps:

1. Open a table in Datasheet view.

2. Select the record and field in the table that contain the value on which you want to filter.

3. Click the Filter by Selection button. The data is filtered to only the specified rows. For example, in Figure 1.27, the data shows only orders associated with Jan Kotas.

Removing Filters

After you have applied filters, you might want to remove them so that you can once again view all rows or apply a different filter. The process is simple. You just click the Toggle Filter button in the Sort & Filter group on the Home tab of the Ribbon.

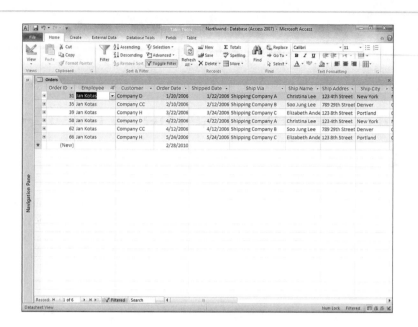

Figure 1.27   *Data filtered to show orders for Jan Kotas.*

SHOW ME   Media 1.5—Filtering by Selection
Access this video file through your registered Web Edition at
my.safaribooksonline.com/9780132117128/media.

TELL ME MORE   Media 1.6—What's Stored in a Database?
Access this audio recording through your registered Web Edition at
my.safaribooksonline.com/9780132117128/media.

Using Access 2010 queries, you can view the data you want when you want to view it.

2

Using Queries to Retrieve the Data You Need

In this chapter, you will learn what queries are and why they are important. You'll learn how to work with queries in both Datasheet view and Design view. We'll explore the basics of working with queries such as selecting fields, ordering the query result, and using basic criteria. Finally, you'll see the real power of queries when we work with queries based on data in multiple tables.

What Is a Query and When Should You Use One?

A Select query is a stored question about the data stored in a database's tables. Select queries are the foundation of much of what you do in Access. They underlie most forms and reports, and they enable you to view the data you want, when you want. You use a simple Select query to specify the tables and fields whose data you want to view and to specify the criteria that limits the data the query's output displays. A Select query is a query of a table or tables that just displays data; the query doesn't modify data in any way. An example is a query that allows you to view customers who have placed orders in the last month. You can use more advanced Select queries to summarize data, supply the results of calculations, or cross-tabulate data. You can use Action queries to add, edit, or delete data from tables, based on selected criteria, but this chapter covers Select queries. Chapter 7, "Enhancing the Queries That You Build," covers other types of queries, including Action queries.

Opening a Query

When you're working with an existing query, you need to be able to open it in Datasheet view or in Design view. Datasheet view allows you to view the results of running the query, whereas Design view allows you to view the blueprint, or design of the query.

LET ME TRY IT

Open a Query in Datasheet View

Here are the steps involved in working with a query in Datasheet view:

1. Select Queries in the list of objects in the Navigation Pane.

2. Click to select the query that you want to run, and then right-click and select Open or double-click the query to run it. The result of the query appears in Datasheet view (see Figure 2.1).

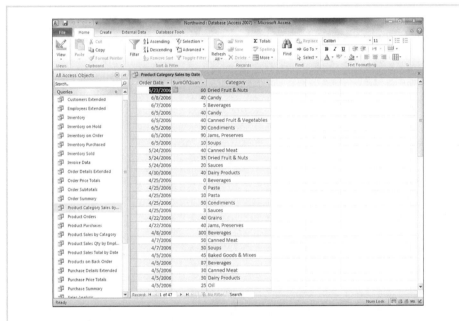

Figure 2.1 *The Product Category Sales by Date query in Datasheet view.*

A query has an underlying design, which you can think of as the *blueprint* for the query. This blueprint—not the result of running the query—is what Access stores in the database when you save a query. The text that follows explores the various methods that you can use to view a query in Design view.

LET ME TRY IT

Viewing the Design of a Query from the Navigation Pane

It is not necessary to first run a query to view its design. You can go directly into Design view of a query from the Database window. Here's how:

1. Select the query whose design you want to view.

2. Right-click the query, and then select Design. The query appears in Design view (see Figure 2.2).

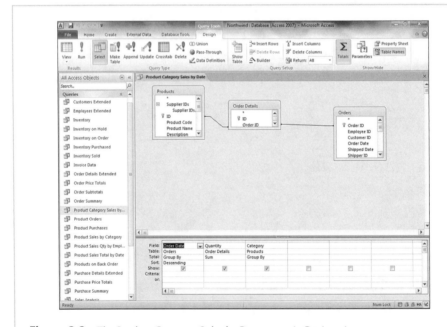

Figure 2.2   *The Product Category Sales by Date query in Design view.*

Viewing the Design of a Query While in Datasheet View

It is easy to toggle back and forth between Datasheet view and Design view. You accomplish this by using the View tool in the Results group of the Design tab of the

Ribbon. Notice in Figure 2.3 that the View tool enables you to toggle between the various views available for a query. This makes it easy for you to switch from Design view to Datasheet view and back as needed.

Figure 2.3   *The View tool, which enables you to toggle between views.*

Adding and Removing Fields

When viewing a query in Design view, you might decide to modify the fields that you want to include in the query's output. In other words, you might want to add fields to or remove fields from the query grid. You would do this if you have an existing query and you realize that it is missing fields, if you have a new query and are adding fields for the first time, or are working with an existing query and realize that you no longer want to include a field in the query.

Adding a Field Between Other Fields

There are times when you need to insert a field between two existing fields. To do so, you just drag the field from the field list to the grid and drop it where you want it to appear. The fields already included in the query then move over to the right. For example, your query already contains City and Zip, and you have decided to add the State field and place it between the City and the Zip fields. You would drag the State field from the field list to add it to the query.

Adding a Field to the End of the Query Grid

Sometimes you want to add a field to the end of the list of existing fields. Fortunately, the process is extremely easy. You just double-click in the field list on the field that you want to add. Access adds the field at the end of the existing field list. This is the technique that I use to add fields to a new query as I build it. I generally double-click each field that I want to add to the query. Access simply adds each field to the query grid in the order that I select each field.

 LET ME TRY IT

Adding a Group of Contiguous Fields to the Query Grid

It would be very tedious if you had to add each field, one field at a time, to add a contiguous group of fields from the field list to the query grid. Fortunately, Access allows you to add the fields as a group. The process is simple: This is a great technique to use when you are lucky because several of the fields you want to include in the query appear together in the field list:

1. Click the first field that you want to add to the query.

2. Scroll through the field list until you can see the last field that you want to add to the query.

3. Hold down the Shift key as you click the last field that you want to add to the query.

4. Drag the fields as a group to the query grid. The fields are placed on the query grid at the position where you dropped them.

 LET ME TRY IT

Adding a Group of Noncontiguous Fields to the Query Grid

The process for adding a noncontiguous group of fields from the field list to the query grid is much simpler than adding the fields one at a time. You would add a noncontiguous list of fields when there are several fields that you want to add to the query, but they do not appear together in the field list. Here's what you do:

1. Click the first field that you want to add.

2. Hold down the Ctrl key as you click each additional field that you want to add.

3. Drag the fields to the query grid by clicking any of the selected fields and dragging them to the query grid. Access adds the selected fields to the query grid at the position at which you drop them.

 SHOW ME   Media 2.1—Selecting Fields

Access this video file through your registered Web Edition at ***my.safaribooksonline.com/9780132117128/media.***

Modifying the Sort Order of a Query

You might want to modify the sort order designated by the designer of a query. As described in the following sections, you can sort on a single field or you can sort on multiple fields and you can sort in ascending order or you can sort in descending order. For example, you may want to sort in ascending order by company name in a company table, but in descending order by sales amount in a sales table so that the highest sales amount appears first. An example where you may want to sort on multiple fields is employee last name combined with employee first name.

Sorting on a Single Field

Sorting on a single field is a simple process. It works like this:

1. Open the desired query in Design view.

2. Click in the Sort row of the field you want to sort by.

3. Click the drop-down arrow button to display the choices for the sort order (see Figure 2.4).

4. Select the sort order:

   • **Ascending**—A to Z or 0 to 9

   • **Descending**—Z to A or 9 to 0

   • **Not Sorted**—No sorting

5. Click the Run button. The data appears in the designated sort order.

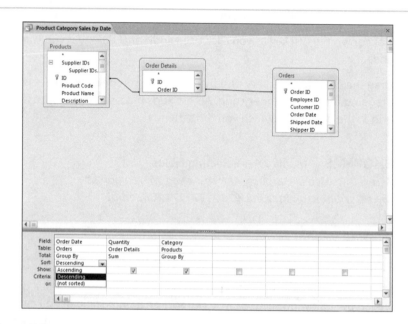

Figure 2.4 *Selecting the sort order of a query.*

Sorting on More Than One Field

The process for sorting on more than one field is slightly more complicated than the process of sorting on one field. It works like this:

1. Repeat steps 1–4 in the previous section, "Sorting on a Single Field," for the first field that you want to sort by.

2. Click in the Sort row of the second field that you want to sort by.

3. Click the drop-down arrow button to display the choices for sort order.

4. Select the sort order.

5. Click the Run button.

Moving a Field on the Query Grid

Access sorts the data in the query grid from left to right, meaning that if the first name field appears on the query grid before the last name field (see Figure 2.5), the data appears in order by first name and then within first name by last name (see Figure 2.6). Because you probably want the data in order by last name and then by first name, you need to move the Last Name field so that it appears before the First Name field.

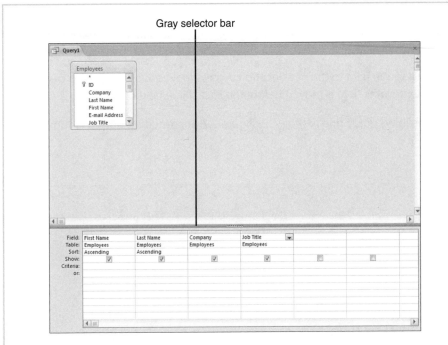

Figure 2.5   *The query grid with the First Name field before the Last Name field.*

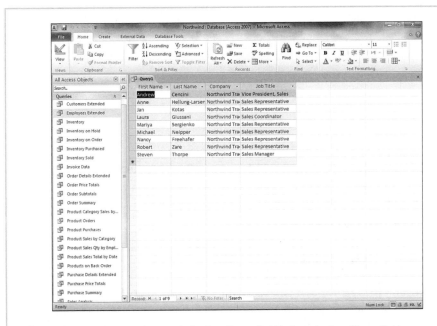

Figure 2.6   *Datasheet view with the First Name field before the Last Name field.*

Use these steps to move a field on a query grid:

1. Click the gray selector bar that contains the field name. This selects the entire column.

2. Drag the field to the new location. Access moves the field. (In this case, the Last Name field is moved before the First Name field.)

The resulting query grid is shown in Figure 2.7. The resulting output is shown in Figure 2.8.

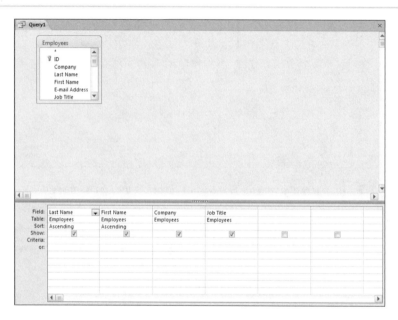

Figure 2.7   *The query grid with the Last Name field before the First Name field.*

 SHOW ME   **Media 2.2—Ordering the Query Result**
Access this video file through your registered Web Edition at
my.safaribooksonline.com/9780132117128/media.

Working with Simple Criteria

You can limit the records that you see in the result of a query by adding criteria to the query. For example, you might want to see just the customers in California, or you may just want to view the orders with sales greater than $500. You can also

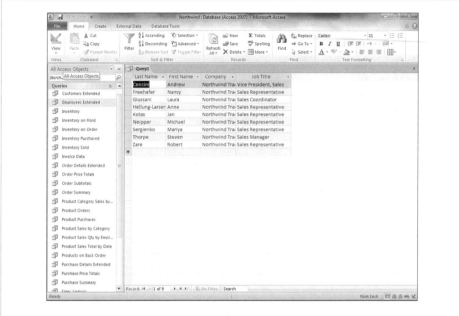

Figure 2.8   *Datasheet view with the Last Name field before the First Name field.*

view sales that occurred within a specific date range. Using criteria, you can easily accomplish any of these tasks, and many, many more!

 **LET ME TRY IT**

Using an Exact Match Query

An exact match query locates data only when there is an exact match with the criteria that you enter. Here's how you run an exact match query:

1. Open the desired query in Design view.

2. Select the cell on the Criteria row below the field for which you want to add the condition.

3. Type the criteria you want to apply for that field. For example, type **Sales Representative** in the Job Title field (see Figure 2.9).

Click the Run button. The results of this query are shown in Figure 2.10.

Although Access is not case sensitive, and you therefore can enter criteria in either upper- or lowercase, the criteria you enter must follow specific rules. These rules vary depending on the type of field the criteria applies to (see Table 2.1).

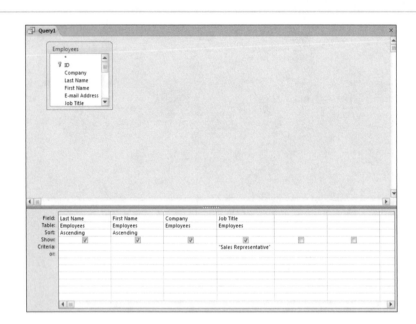

Figure 2.9   *Entering simple criteria.*

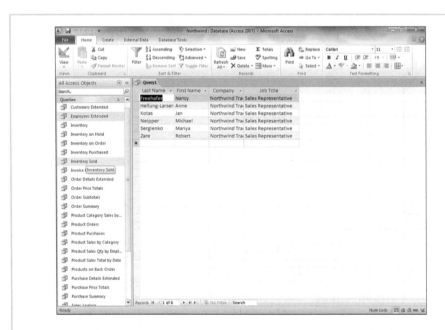

Figure 2.10   *Records with Sales Representative in the Job Title field.*

Table 2.1   Rules for Criteria, Based on Type of Field

Type of Field	Description
Text	After you type the text, Access puts quotes around the text entered.
Number/Currency	You type the digits, without commas or dollar signs but with decimals, if applicable.
Date/Time	You enter any date or time format.
Counter	You type the digits.
Yes/No	For yes, you type **yes** or **true**. For no, you type **no** or **false**.

Creating Criteria Based on Multiple Conditions

Sometimes you might want to create a query that contains two or more conditions. You would do this, for example, if you want only records in the state of California that had sales within a certain date range to appear in the output. The And *condition* is used to indicate that *both* of two conditions must be met for the row to be included in the resulting recordset. You can use the And condition in the same field or on multiple fields.

 **LET ME TRY IT**

Use the And **Condition on Multiple Fields**

By placing criteria for multiple fields on the *same* line of the query grid, you create an And condition. This means that *both* conditions must be true for the records to appear in the result. An example of an And condition on two fields is State Field = 'TX' And Credit limit >=5000. Here's how you create an And condition:

1. Open the desired query in Design view.

2. Select the cell on the Criteria row below the field that contains the first condition you want to enter.

3. Type the first criterion you want to enter. For example, you can type **Sales Representative** as the criterion for Job Title.

4. Select the cell on the Criteria row below the field that contains the second condition you want to apply.

5. Type the second criterion you want to apply. Figure 2.11 shows USA as the criterion for the Country.

6. Click the Run button to run the query. Only rows that meet both conditions appear in the query result (see Figure 2.12).

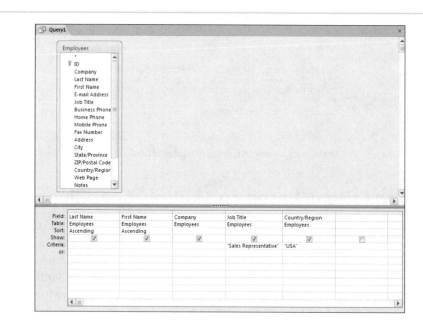

Figure 2.11   *The design of a query with criteria for Job Title and Country.*

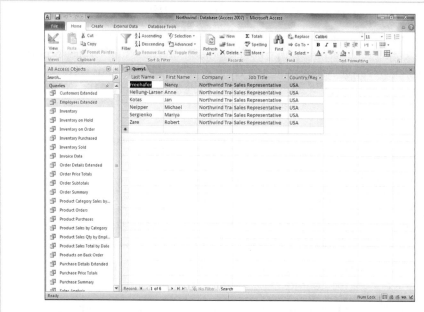

Figure 2.12   *The Result Includes All Sales Representatives in the USA.*

LET ME TRY IT

Use the And **Condition in a Single Field**

In only a few situations would you use an And condition on the same field. This is because in most situations using the And condition on the same field would yield a recordset with no results. For example, the criteria State = TX and State = CA would yield no results because the state cannot be equal to both values at the same time. On the other hand, HireDate > 7/1/2001 and HireDate < 6/30/2002 would return all employees hired in that date range. Here's how you would enter this sort of criteria:

1. Open the desired query in Design view.

2. Select the cell on the Criteria row below the field that contains the condition you want to add.

3. Type the first criterion you want to add (for example, **HireDate > 7/1/2001**).

4. Type the keyword **And**.

5. Type the second criterion (for example, **HireDate < 6/30/2002**).

6. Click the Run button. Access runs the query.

You need to make sure when you are adding the criteria to each field that you remain on the same row of the query grid.

 **LET ME TRY IT**

Use Wildcards in a Query

You can use wildcards to select records that follow a pattern. However, you can use the wildcard characters only in Text or Date/Time fields. You use the * to substitute for multiple characters, and the ? to substitute for single characters. To practice using wildcards in a query, follow these steps:

1. Open the desired query in Design view.

2. Select the cell on the Criteria row below the field that contains the condition.

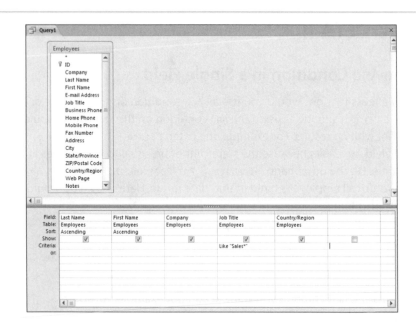

Figure 2.13   *Example that contains Sales* as the Criteria for the Job Title.*

3. Type the criteria, using a wildcard in the desired expression. In Figure 2.13, the expression Like Sales* is entered for the Job Title field. This expression returns all rows where the Job Title begins with Sales.

4. Click the Run button. The results of the query are shown in Figure 2.14, and show all the records where the contact title begins with Sales.

Table 2.2 provides examples of how to use wildcards.

Table 2.2   Examples of Using Wildcards

Expression	Results
Sm?th	Finds Smith or Smyth.
L*ng	Finds any record that starts with *L* and ends in *ng*.
*th	Finds any record that ends in *th* (for example, 158th or Garth).
on	Finds any record that has *on* anywhere in the field.
*/2000	Finds all dates in 2000.
6/*/2000	Finds all dates in June 2000.

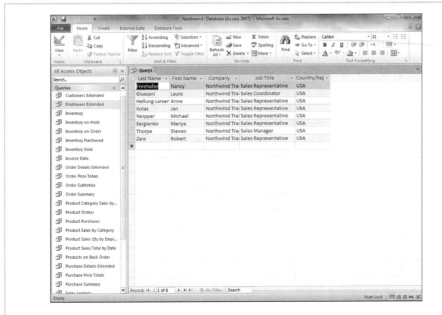

Figure 2.14   *The result of running a query with criteria that contains the wildcard *.*

Access displays the word *Like* in the criteria cell before a wildcard criteria. It is not necessary to type the word *Like* in the criteria cell before the criteria.

 **LET ME TRY IT**

Use Comparison Operators in a Query

Sometimes you want to select records in a table that fall within a range of values. You can use comparison operators (=, <, >, <=, >=) to create criteria based on the comparison of the value contained in a field to a value that you specify in your criteria. Each record is evaluated, and only records that meet the condition are included in the recordset. To practice using comparison operators in your queries, follow these steps:

1. Open the desired query in Design view.

2. Select the cell on the Criteria row below the field for which you want to apply the condition.

3. Type a comparison operator and the criteria you want the query to apply (for example, > **100**).

4. Click the Run button. The result of the query appears in Datasheet view.

Table 2.3 gives an example of comparison operators used for a field called Sales. It shows the operators, provides an example of each, and discusses the records that Access would include in the output.

You can use the word *Not* in place of the <> symbols.

Table 2.3   Comparison Operators Used to Compare Against a Field Called Sales

Operator	Indicates	Example	Includes Records Where
>	Greater than	>7500	Sales are greater than 7500
>=	Greater than or equal to	>=7500	Sales are 7500 or more
<	Less than	<7500	Sales are less than 7500
<=	Less than or equal to	<=7500	Sales are 7500 or less
<>	Does not equal	<>7500	Sales are not 7500
Between	Range of values	Between 5000 and 7500	Sales are between 5000 and 7500

 LET ME TRY IT

Use the Or Condition on a Single Field

The Or *condition* states that *either* condition of two conditions should be met for the record to appear in the result set. You can use the Or condition on a single field or on more than one field. To practice using an Or condition on a single field, follow these steps:

1. Open the desired query in Design view.

2. Select the cell on the Criteria row below the field that contains the condition.

3. Type the first criterion you want the query to apply. For example, you could type **Sales Manager** as criterion for the Job Title field.

4. Select the cell below the current cell (this is the Or row).

5. Type the second criterion you want the query to apply. For example you could type **Sales Agent** as criterion for the Job Title field (see Figure 2.15).

6. Click the Run button. The result of this query is shown in Figure 2.16. Notice that the result contains all the sales managers, sales agents, sales representatives, and owners.

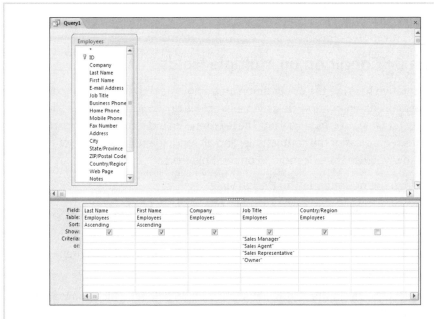

Figure 2.15 *Using an* Or *condition on the Job Title field.*

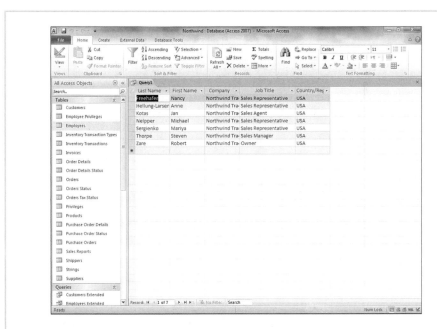

Figure 2.16 *The result contains all the records that contain sales manager, sales agent, sales representative, or owner in the Job Title field.*

 **LET ME TRY IT**

Use the Or Condition on Multiple Fields

An alternative to using the Or condition on a single field is to use the Or condition to create criteria on multiple fields. An example is City equals Bellevue or Contact Title equals Sales Agent. These criteria would return all companies in Bellevue, regardless of the contact title, and all sales agents, regardless of the city. Here's how you use the Or condition on multiple fields:

1. Open the desired query in Design view.

2. Select the cell on the Criteria row below the field for which you want to apply the first condition.

3. Type the first criterion you want the query to apply (from the criteria mentioned in the intro to the steps).

4. Select the cell in the Or row below the second field for which you want to apply the criterion.

5. Type the second criterion you want the query to apply (see Figure 2.17).

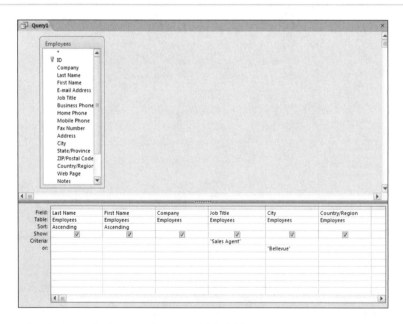

Figure 2.17   *Using the Or condition on multiple fields.*

6. Click the Run button. The result of this query is shown in Figure 2.18. Notice that the output contains all rows where the city is Bellevue or the contact title is sales agent.

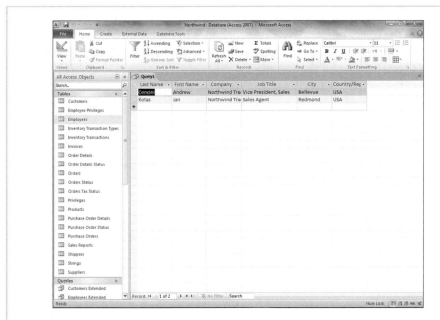

Figure 2.18 *The result contains the rows where the city is Bellevue or the job title is sales agent.*

When you use two fields in an Or condition, you need to make sure the criteria are listed on two separate lines. If not, they will combine as an And condition.

You need to use the Or condition to find dates or numbers that fall outside a range (for example, before 6/1/2006 or after 1/1/2007).

You can use the word *In* and list the multiple criteria, separated by commas, in parentheses (for example, In ('USA', 'France', 'Canada')).

SHOW ME   Media 2.3—Refining Queries with Criteria
Access this video file through your registered Web Edition at
my.safaribooksonline.com/9780132117128/media.

Modifying the Datasheet View of a Query

Just as you can modify the Datasheet view of a table, you can modify the
Datasheet view of a query. You can change things such as the font, the column
order, the column widths, and the attributes of the datasheet itself (such as background color). When you close the query, if you have made no changes to the
design of the query but you have made changes to the layout of the datasheet,
Access prompts you with the dialog box displayed in Figure 2.19. In this dialog box,
Access asks whether you want to change the layout changes that you made. If you
click Yes, Access remembers the layout changes. If you click No, Access will use the
old layout the next time that you view the query.

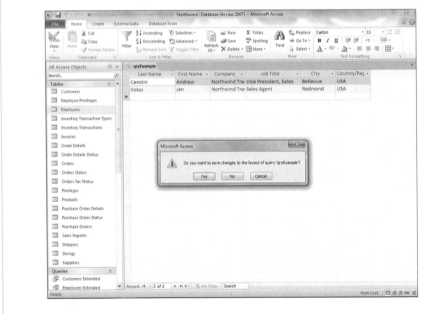

Figure 2.19   *Saving the layout of a query.*

Saving a Query

To save a query, you click the Save button on the toolbar. The Save As dialog box
appears (see Figure 2.20). After you provide a name and click OK, Access saves the
SQL (Structured Query Language) statement underlying the query. It does not save
the result of the query.

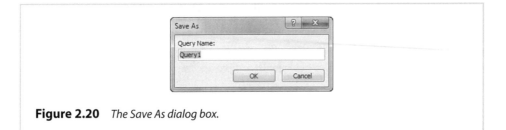

Figure 2.20 *The Save As dialog box.*

The industry standard for naming queries is to prefix the name with *qry*.

Printing Query Results

It is easy to print query results. Although not as elegant as a printed report, printed query results are often sufficient to meet people's needs. Here's how you print query results:

1. Run the query whose results you want to print.

2. Click the File tab.

3. Select Print. Your screen should appear as in Figure 2.21.

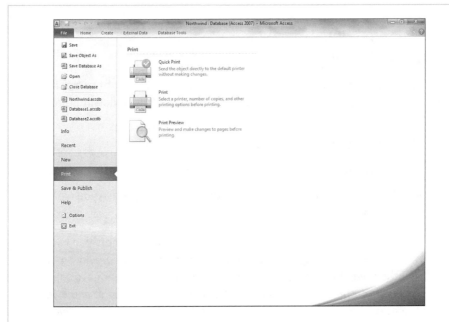

Figure 2.21 *After selecting Print, three print options are available.*

4. Click Print Preview. The results will appear as in Figure 2.22.

Figure 2.22   *The Print Preview option enables you to preview query results.*

Closing a Query

You close a query using the close button (the X) in the upper-right corner of the Query Design tab. How Access responds depends on the following three conditions:

- Whether you previously named and saved the query
- Whether you made design changes to the query
- Whether you made changes to the layout of the query while you were in Datasheet view

If you did not previously name and save the query, Access prompts you with the Save As dialog box when you attempt to close the query. If you previously named and saved the query but did not make any design or layout changes to the query, Access provides no prompts. If you made design changes or design and layout changes, Access asks whether you want to save those design changes. If you made *only* layout changes, Access asks if you want to save the layout changes.

Designing a Query Based on Multiple Tables

If you have properly normalized your table data, you probably want to bring the data from your tables back together by using queries. Fortunately, you can do this quite easily by using Access queries.

The query in Figure 2.23 joins the Customers, Orders, and Order Details tables, pulling fields from each. Notice in the figure that I have selected the ID and Company fields from the Customers table, the Order ID and Order Date fields from the Orders table, and the Unit Price and Quantity fields from the Order Details table. After you run this query, you should see the results shown in Figure 2.24. Notice that you get a record in the query's result for every record in the Order Details table. In other words, there are 2,155 records in the Order Details table, and that's how many records appear in the query output. By creating a multitable query, you can look at data from related tables, along with the data from the Order Details table.

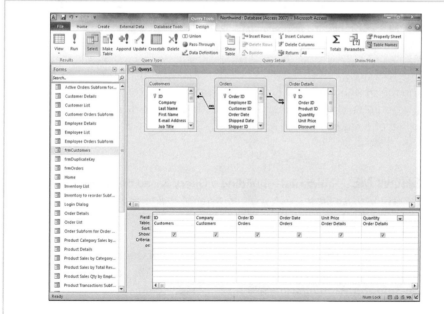

Figure 2.23   *A query joining the Customers, Orders, and Order Details tables.*

To remove a table from a query, you click anywhere on the table in the top half of the query design grid and then press the Delete key. You can add tables to the query at any time by clicking the Show Table button in the Query Setup

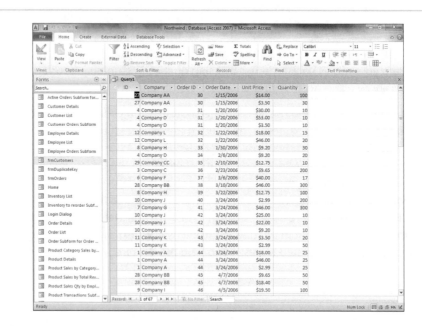

Figure 2.24 *The results of querying multiple tables.*

group on the Design tab of the Ribbon. If you prefer, you can show the Navigation Pane and then click and drag tables directly from the Navigation Pane to the top half of the query design grid.

SHOW ME   Media 2.4—Building a Query Based on Multiple Tables
Access this video file through your registered Web Edition at
my.safaribooksonline.com/9780132117128/media.

TELL ME MORE   Media 2.5—Updatability of Query Results
Access this audio recording through your registered Web Edition at
my.safaribooksonline.com/9780132117128/media.

Using Access 2010 forms, you can easily enter and edit the data in your database.

3

Using Forms to Enter and Edit Table Data

In this chapter, you will learn what forms are and why they are important. You'll learn how to work with forms in both Form view and Design view. We'll explore the basics of working with forms such as opening an existing form, working with data, finding, sorting, and filtering. Finally, you'll learn the basics of working with the design of a form, and how to close a form when you are finished working with it.

Opening an Existing Form

 LET ME TRY IT

Open a Form

Before you can work with a form, you must first open it. Here are the steps involved:

1. Click Forms in the list of objects.

2. Right-click the form you want to open, and then select Open from the context-sensitive menu. Access opens the selected form.

Working with Data in a Form

After you have opened a form, you probably want to work with the data you have bound it to. You most likely want to move from record to record, edit data, add new records, delete records, and copy records. The process of editing data includes learning important techniques such as how to select records, delete field contents, undo changes, search and replace, and more. The following sections cover all these techniques.

Moving from Record to Record in a Form

The Navigation Bar appears at the bottom of the Form tab (see Figure 3.1). It allows you to move from record to record. The first button on the Navigation Bar moves you to the first record in the form, and the second button moves you to the record that precedes the record you're currently viewing. Between the second and third navigation button is a record indicator. By typing a record number in the record indicator box, you can quickly move to a desired record. To the right of the record indicator are the next record button, the last record button, and the new record button.

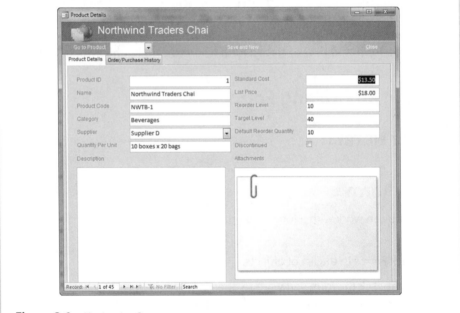

Figure 3.1   *Navigation Bar.*

You can also you use keystrokes to move from record to record. Pressing Page Down moves you forward through the records, one record at a time. Pressing Page Up moves you backward through the records, one record at a time. Pressing Ctrl+End moves you to the last record, and pressing Ctrl+Home moves you to the first record. Finally, Ctrl++ (plus sign) moves you to a new record.

 **LET ME TRY IT**

Edit the Data Underlying a Form

You can modify the table data from within a form. For example, you may want to change a customer's company name or address. Here's how:

1. Select the record you want to change by using any of the techniques covered in the previous section, "Moving from Record to Record in a Form."

2. Select the field you want to change by clicking the field or using the directional keys.

3. Type to make the necessary changes to the data.

 LET ME TRY IT

Delete Field Contents Within a Form

Now that you know how to modify the contents of a field, let's talk about how to delete the contents of a field. In following along with this section, make sure that you understand that we are not deleting records, we are simply deleting the contents of an individual field *within* a record. You would do this, for example, if you entered a region for a company and then realized that it was located in a country that did not have regions. The process is simple:

1. Select the field contents you want to delete.

2. Press the Delete key.

A couple of items are important to note. First, if you press the Esc key twice, Access cancels all changes you made to that record. Second, it is important to recognize that Access saves the record you are working with as soon as you move off of it onto another record.

Undoing Changes Made Within a Form

There are many times when you need to undo changes that you made to a control or to a record. An example is when you started making changes to the incorrect control, or even to the incorrect record. Undo comes to the rescue! You have several different options for how to do this, depending on whether you are still within a control, have left the control, or have left the record. You can use the Undo feature only to undo the last change made to a control or changes made to the most recently modified record.

Undoing Changes Made to the Current Control

When you are in the process of making changes to a field, you might realize that you really didn't want to make changes to that field or to that record. To undo changes to the current control, you can either click the Undo tool on the QuickAccess toolbar, select Edit, Undo Typing, or press the Esc key once.

Undoing Changes After You Move to Another Control

The process of undoing changes after you move to another control is from the same as the process of undoing changes made to the current control. You can either click the Undo tool on the QuickAccess toolbar or press the Esc key once.

It is important to understand that once you make changes to more than one control in a record, you can only undo those changes by undoing the changes to the entire record. This requires select Undo twice on the QuickAccess toolbar.

Undoing Changes After You Save the Record

When you make changes to a field and then move to another record, Access saves all changes to the modified record. So long as you do not begin making changes to another record, you can still undo the changes you made to the most recently modified record. To do this, you can either click the Undo tool on the toolbar or press the Esc key twice.

If Access is unable to undo a change, the Undo tool appears dimmed.

 LET ME TRY IT

Use a Form to Add New Records to a Table

Access adds records to the end of a table, regardless of how you add them to the table. To use a form to add new records to a table:

1. Click the New Record tool on the Navigation Bar at the bottom of the form.

2. Type the data for the new record (see Figure 3.2).

3. Press Tab to go to the next control.

4. Repeat steps 2 and 3 to enter all the data for the record.

5. Press Tab to move to another new record. Access saves the record.

Figure 3.2 *Adding a new record.*

Access always displays one blank record at the end of a table. This blank record is ready to act as the new record. Also, you can press the Tab key to add a record when you are on the last field of the last record in the table.

Using a Form to Delete Records from a Table

Before you can delete records, you must first select them. I therefore cover the process of selecting records before I cover the process of deleting records.

To select a record, you just click the gray record selector button to the left of a record within a form (see Figure 3.3). Access selects the record.

To select multiple records (when the form is in Continuous Forms view or Datasheet view), you click and drag within the record selector area. Continuous Forms view enables you to view multiple rows of data in a form at a time. Access selects the contiguous range of records in the area over which you click and drag. As an alternative, you can click the selector button for the first record you want to select, hold down the Shift key, and then click the selector button of the last record that you want to select. Access selects the entire range of records between the two selector buttons. Figure 3.4 shows the Orders table, with three records selected.

Gray selector button

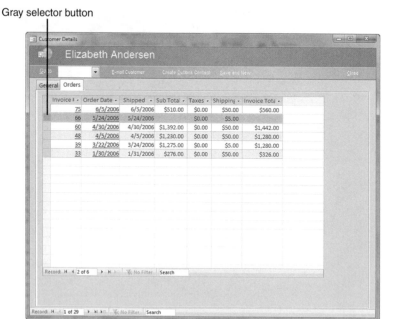

Figure 3.3 *The gray selector button.*

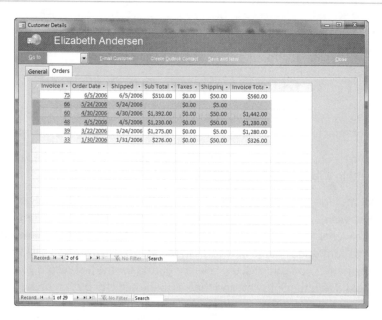

Figure 3.4 *The Orders table, with three records selected.*

If you want to select a single record when the cursor is within the record, you can simply choose Select from the Find group on the Home tab of the Ribbon. Then choose Select from the drop-down menu.

LET ME TRY IT

Delete a Record

When you know how to select records, deleting them is quite simple. The process is almost identical to that of deleting records in a datasheet:

1. Select the record you want to delete.

2. Press the Delete key. A dialog box appears, asking whether you're sure you want to delete the records (see Figure 3.5).

Figure 3.5   *A dialog box that asks if you want to delete the selected records.*

3. Click the Yes button.

LET ME TRY IT

Delete Records from Tables with Referential Integrity

The process of deleting a record is not so simple if you have established referential integrity between the tables in a database and the row that you are attempting to delete has child rows. Chapter 6, "Relating the Information in Your Database," covers relationships and referential integrity. For now, you can think about the fact that customers generally have orders associated with them, and those orders have order detail records associated with them. The relationship between the Customers table and the Orders table prohibits the user from deleting customers who have orders. Here's how you delete a customer who has orders:

1. Select the records you want to delete.

2. Press the Delete key. A dialog box appears, saying that the record cannot be deleted or changed because the table includes related records (see Figure 3.6).

Figure 3.6   *Access notifying you that you cannot delete the selected records.*

3. Click OK to close the dialog box.

Access provides a referential integrity option with which you can cascade a deletion down to the child table. This means, for example, that if you attempt to delete an order, Access deletes the associated order detail records. If you establish referential integrity with the cascade delete option, the deletion process works like this:

1. Select the records you want to delete.

2. Press the Delete key. A dialog box appears, asking whether you are sure you want to delete the records (see Figure 3.7).

Figure 3.7   *Access asking whether you want to delete the parent row and the associated child records.*

3. Click Yes to complete the deletion process.

Copying Records Within a Form

LET ME TRY IT

Copy Entire Records

At times, you want to copy an entire record. This generally occurs because you are creating a new record and the new record is very similar to an existing record. For example, you might have two contacts at the same company who share similar information. You can copy the existing record and then make the necessary changes to the new record. Here's the process:

1. Select the record you want to copy. You can select the record by clicking the gray record selector or by choosing Select from the Find group on the Home tab of the ribbon and then choosing Select from the drop-down menu.

2. Select Copy in the Clipboard group on the Home tab of the Ribbon.

3. Select Paste in the Clipboard group on the Home tab of the Ribbon, and then choose Paste Append from the drop-down. Access copies the original record and places you in the new record (the copy).

Copying a record often results in what is called a *referential integrity error*. This occurs, for example, when copying a record would cause a duplicate primary key (that is, unique record identifier). In such a situation, you see an error message such as that displayed in Figure 3.8. You can either change the data in the field or fields that constitute the duplicate key or you can press the Escape key to cancel the process of appending the new row. For example, in the example shown in Figure 3.8, you can modify the company name.

Figure 3.8   *Error that appears when copying a record results in a referential integrity error.*

SHOW ME   Media 3.1—Working with Data
Access this video file through your registered Web Edition at
my.safaribooksonline.com/9780132117128/media.

Finding a Record That Meets Specific Criteria

If you are editing records in a form, you need to find specific records quickly. The same procedure used in Datasheet view helps you to quickly locate data in a form:

1. Select the field that contains the criteria for which you are searching (in this case, Salesperson).

2. Click the Find button in the Find group on the Home tab of the Ribbon. The Find and Replace dialog box appears (see Figure 3.9).

Figure 3.9   *The Find tab of the Find and Replace dialog box, where you search for values in a datasheet.*

3. Type the criteria in the Find What text box. For this example, type **Nancy Freehafer**.

4. Use the Look In drop-down list box to designate whether to search only the current field or all fields in the table. For this example, designate that you want to search only the current field.

5. Use the Match drop-down list box to designate whether to match any part of the field you are searching, the whole field you are searching, or the start of the field you are searching. For example, if you type the word **Federal** in the Find What text box and you select Whole Field in the Match drop-down list box, you find only entries where Ship Via is set to Federal. If you select Any Part of Field, you find Federal Shipping, Federal Express, United Federal Shipping, and so on. If you select Start of Field, you find Federal Shipping and Federal Express, but you do not find United Federal Shipping. For this example, designate that you want to match the whole field.

6. Use the Search drop-down list box to designate whether to search only up from the current cursor position, only down, or in all directions. For this example, designate that you want to search in all directions.

7. Use the Match Case check box to indicate whether you want the search to be case sensitive.

8. Use the Search Fields as Formatted check box to indicate whether you want to find data only based on the display format (for example, 17-Jul-96 for a date).

9. Click the Find Next button to find the next record that meets the designated criteria.

10. To continue searching after you close the dialog box, use the Shift+F4 keystroke combination or select Find again from the Ribbon.

 LET ME TRY IT

Replace Data in the Table Underlying a Form

Sometimes you might want to update records that meet specific criteria. You might want to do this, for example, if a company changes its name or you realize that you have improperly entered an employee's social security number. The Replace feature automatically inserts new information into the specified fields. Here's the process:

1. Click within the field that contains the criteria you are searching for (Job Title for this example).

2. Click the Replace button in the Find group on the Home tab of the ribbon. The Find and Replace dialog box appears.

3. Select the Replace tab (see Figure 3.10).

Figure 3.10   *The Replace tab of the Find and Replace dialog box, where you can replace table data.*

4. Type the criteria in the Find What text box. Type **Owner** for this example.

5. Type the new information (the replacement value) in the Replace With text box. Type **CEO** for this example.

6. Choose values for the Look In drop-down list box, Match drop-down list box, Search drop-down list box, Match Case check box, and Search Fields as Formatted check box, as described in the "Finding a Record That Meets Specific Criteria" section of this chapter.

7. Click the Find Next button. Access locates the first record that meets the criteria designated in the Find What text box.

8. Click the Replace button.

9. Repeat steps 7 and 8 to find all occurrences of the value in the Find What text box and replace them. As an alternative, you can click the Replace All button to replace all occurrences simultaneously.

You should use Replace All with quite a bit of caution. Remember that the changes you make are *permanent*. Although Replace All is a viable option, when you use it, you need to make sure you have a recent backup and that you are quite certain of what you are doing. In fact, I usually do a few replaces to make sure that I see what Access is doing *before* I click Replace All.

10. Click Cancel when you've finished.

If you are searching a very large table, Access can find a specific value in a field fastest if the field you are searching on is the primary key or an indexed field. Chapter 5, "Creating Your Own Databases and Tables," covers primary keys and indexes.

When using either Find or Replace, you can use several wildcard characters. A *wildcard character* is a character you use in place of an unknown character. Table 3.1 describes the wildcard characters.

Table 3.1   Wildcard Characters You Can Use When Searching

Wildcard Character	Description
*	Acts as a placeholder for multiple characters
?	Acts as a placeholder for a single character
#	Acts as a placeholder for a single number

Sorting Records

You can change the order of records by using sort buttons. You use this feature when you want to view your records in a particular order. For example, you may want to first view the records in order by company name, and later view them in order by most recent order date. The wonderful thing is that with this easy-to-use feature, changing the sort order involves a simple mouse click.

 **LET ME TRY IT**

Sort Records on a Single Field

To sort on a field, follow these steps:

1. Click anywhere within the field.

2. Click the Ascending button or click the Descending button. These buttons are found in the Sort & Filter group on the Home tab of the Ribbon. Access reorders the form data by the designated column.

Another way to do this is to right-click a field and then choose Sort A to Z or Sort Z to A. (Options will differ for numeric and date fields.)

Filtering the Data Underlying a Form

From the Form view, you can apply a filter to view a select group of records. You do this when you want to focus on a select group of records. For example, you may just want to work with the records in the Customers table where the contact title is owner. You can use the filter by form feature to accomplish this task. Once you learn how to use the filter by form feature, you will need to know how to remove filters, and how to work with multiple filter criteria.

 **LET ME TRY IT**

Use the Filter by Form Feature

The Filter by Form feature is a wonderful feature that is built in to Access 2010. It enables you to easily implement filtering while viewing data within a form. Here's how you use it:

1. Open the form whose data you want to filter.

2. Choose the Advanced drop-down from the Sort & Filter group on the Home tab of the Ribbon. Select Filter by Form from the drop-down. The Filter by Form feature appears.

3. Click in the field whose data you want to use as the filter criteria.

4. Select the field data to filter on from the drop-down list (see Figure 3.11).

5. Choose the Advanced drop-down from the Sort & Filter group on the Home tab of the Ribbon. Select Apply Filter/Sort from the drop-down. Access filters the data to just the designated rows.

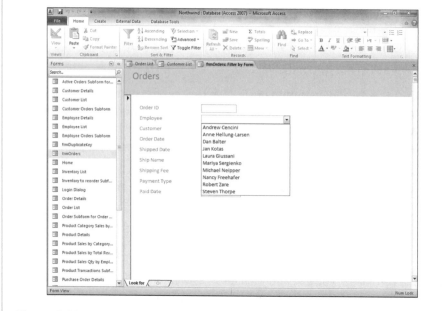

Figure 3.11   *The Filter by Form feature.*

Removing a Filter

To remove a filter, you just select the Toggle Filter button in the Sort & Filter group on the Home tab of the Ribbon. Access then displays all the records in the record source underlying the form.

LET ME TRY IT

Use Multiple Filter Criteria

So far in this chapter you have learned how to apply a single filter criterion for a single field. The following steps describe how to apply multiple filter criteria for multiple fields or multiple filter criteria for a single field. The process is similar to that of applying a single filter criterion for a single field:

1. Open the form whose data you want to filter.

2. Choose the Advanced drop-down from the Sort & Filter group on the Home tab of the Ribbon. Select Filter by Form from the drop-down. The Filter by Form feature appears.

3. Click in the first field you want to filter by.

4. Select the field data to filter on from the drop-down list that automatically appears when you click the Filter by Form tool and then click in a text box.

5. Select the Or tab.

6. Click in the next field you want to filter by. A drop-down list appears for that field.

7. Select the field data to filter on from the drop-down list.

8. Repeat steps 5 through 7 to apply as many additional filter options as desired.

9. Choose the Advanced drop-down from the Sort & Filter group on the Home tab of the Ribbon. Select Apply Filter/Sort from the drop-down. Access applies the designated filter.

You can filter by right-clicking a field and selecting from one of the available filter options. Figure 3.12 shows the filtering options available for a text field. Appropriate options are available for numeric and date fields.

If you create multiple filters by using the Or tab, the records that meet either condition appear in the output.

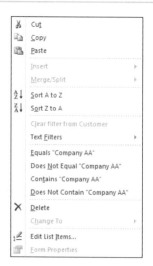

Figure 3.12   *Filtering options available when you right-click a text field.*

SHOW ME   Media 3.2—Filtering Form Data
Access this video file through your registered Web Edition at
my.safaribooksonline.com/9780132117128/media.

Viewing the Design of a Form

You can use the View tool on the Ribbon to toggle back and forth between Design view and Form view. Figure 3.13 shows a form in Design view. When you are in Design view, you can modify the underlying blueprint of the form. You can move and size controls, and you can add and remove controls. In fact, you can change the entire look, feel, and functionality of the form. Chapter 8, "Building Powerful Forms," covers form design techniques.

SHOW ME   Media 3.3—Viewing the Design of a Form
Access this video file through your registered Web Edition at
my.safaribooksonline.com/9780132117128/media.

Closing a Form

To close a form, click the close button (the X) in the upper-right corner of the form. If you try to close a form without having made any *design changes*—that is, changes that you make to the design of the form—Access does not prompt you to

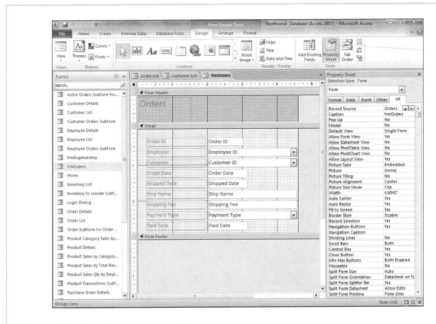

Figure 3.13   *A form in Design view.*

save. This is because Access saves all data changes as you move from row to row. If you close a form and save design changes, those changes are permanent for all users of the form.

The AutoForm Feature

You can quickly build forms by using the AutoForm feature. The AutoForm feature gives you absolutely no control over how a form appears, but it provides you with an instantaneous means of data entry.

 **LET ME TRY IT**

Create a Form by Using the AutoForm Feature

Creating a form by using the AutoForm feature is amazingly easy. Here's how it works:

1. Select the table or query on which you want to base the new form. Select the Customers table for this example.

2. Select Form in the Forms group on the Create tab of the Ribbon. Access creates a form based on the selected table or query (see Figure 3.14).

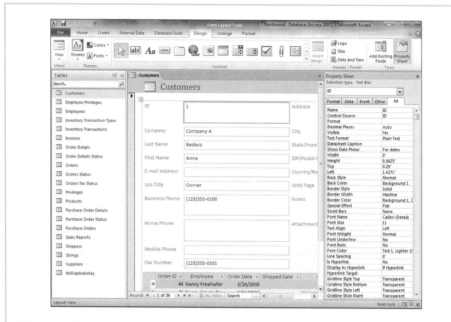

Figure 3.14 *Access creating a form based on the selected table or query.*

Saving a Form

Although Access automatically saves all the data changes that you make to a form, it is up to you to save all the design changes that you make to the form. As you work with the design of a form, you should periodically click the Save tool on the QuickAccess toolbar to save changes. When you close the form, Access prompts you to once again save your changes. Here's the process:

1. Click the close button (the X). A dialog box appears, asking whether you want to save your changes.

2. Click the Yes button.

3. If you have not yet named the form, Access prompts you with the Save As dialog box, asking you to provide a name for the form.

4. Enter a form name and click OK.

Naming standards suggest that you use the *frm* prefix to name every form.

The name of a form can be up to 64 characters and can contain text, numbers, and spaces.

Sub-datasheets are available within forms, just as they are in datasheets.

Using the Form Wizard to Build a Form

 LET ME TRY IT

Build a Form with the Form Wizard

Using the Form Wizard gives you more flexibility than using the AutoForm feature to create forms. It also requires more knowledge on your part. Here's how you use it:

1. Select Form Wizard in the Forms group on the Create tab of the Ribbon. The Form Wizard appears (see Figure 3.15).

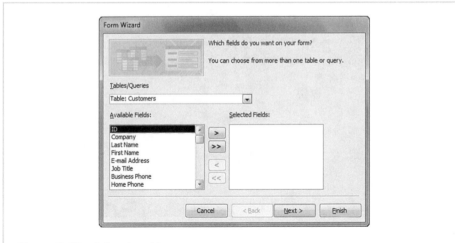

Figure 3.15 *Select the table or query.*

2. Select the table or query on which you want to base the form.

3. Select the fields you want to include on the form (see Figure 3.16).

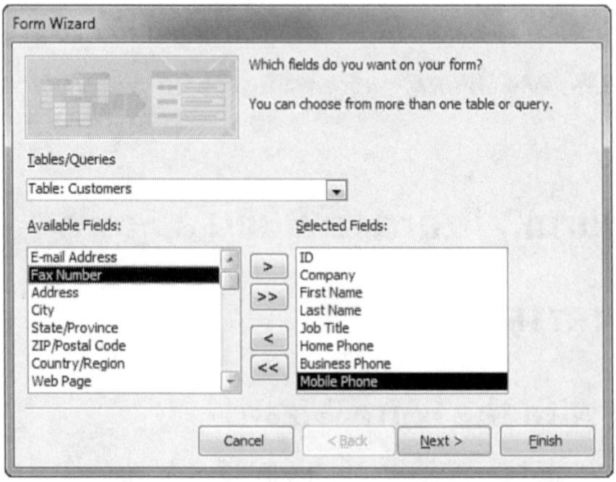

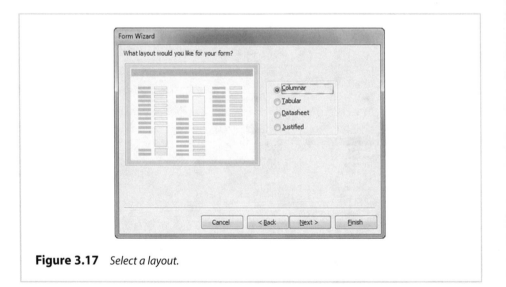

Figure 3.16   *Select the fields.*

4. Click Next. Select a layout for the form (see Figure 3.17).

Figure 3.17   *Select a layout.*

5. Click Next. Provide a title for the form (see Figure 3.18).

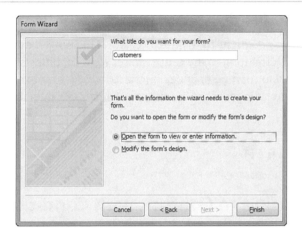

Figure 3.18   *Provide a title.*

6. Click Finish.

If you create a form by clicking the More Forms button in the Forms group of the Create tab of the Ribbon, you have choices about what kind of form you want to create:

- The Multiple Items option creates a form that shows multiple records at once.

- The Datasheet option displays multiple records in a datasheet.

- The Split Form option creates a form that includes a datasheet in the upper section and a data entry form in the lower section. You enter information into the form section.

- Using the Modal Dialog option, you can quickly and easily create dialogs that you use in your application. An example is a form used to gather criteria for the printing of a report.

- The PivotChart option assists you in creating a form that contains a graph.

- The PivotTable option assists you in creating a form that contains an embedded Excel pivot table.

SHOW ME   Media 3.4—Using a Form Wizard
Access this video file through your registered Web Edition at
my.safaribooksonline.com/9780132117128/media.

Using the Conditional Formatting Feature of a Form

At some point you might need to have a control stand out if it meets certain criteria. You can add formatting to the control to set what condition should be met for a particular type of formatting to appear in the record. An example is for the inventory amount to appear in red if the inventory amount is less than the reorder amount.

 LET ME TRY IT

Add Formatting to Controls with Conditional Formatting

Here's how you use this Conditional Formatting feature:

1. Open the form that you want to format in Design view.

2. Click in the control that will contain the conditional formatting.

3. Choose Conditional Formatting from the Control Formatting group on the Format tab of the Ribbon. The Conditional Formatting dialog box appears (see Figure 3.19).

Figure 3.19   *The Conditional Formatting dialog box.*

4. Select the condition (equal to, greater than, and so on).

5. Type the appropriate criteria.

6. Select the desired formatting.

7. Click OK. Access applies the conditional formatting expression.

You can click the Add button to specify a second condition for a field.

 SHOW ME   Media 3.5—Taking Advantage of Conditional Formatting
Access this video file through your registered Web Edition at
my.safaribooksonline.com/9780132117128/media.

 TELL ME MORE   Media 3.6—Uses for Forms
Access this audio recording through your registered Web Edition at
my.safaribooksonline.com/9780132117128/media.

Using Reports to Print Information

In this chapter, you will learn how to work with existing reports, and how to create your own reports. You will begin by opening and viewing an existing report. You will see how easy it is to print the data displayed on the report. Then you'll launch into the exciting world of creating your own reports. You will learn how to use both the AutoReport and Report Wizard features, and how to view the design of a report so that you can modify the reports that you build. Finally, you'll explore the types of reports available in Access 2010.

Opening and Viewing a Report

Microsoft Access provides an excellent means of working with existing reports. You can either send a report directly to the printer or you can first preview a report that you want to work with.

 LET ME TRY IT

Preview a Report

Let's begin by taking a look at the process of previewing a report:

1. Click the Reports list of objects in the Navigation Pane (see Figure 4.1).

2. Double-click the report you want to open or right-click the report, and then select Open from the context-sensitive menu. The report appears in Preview mode.

Moving from Page to Page

A report is a way to present the data from a table or query in a formatted document. Although you can print datasheets, reports control how you present and summarize the data. When you open a report, you can use the navigation buttons

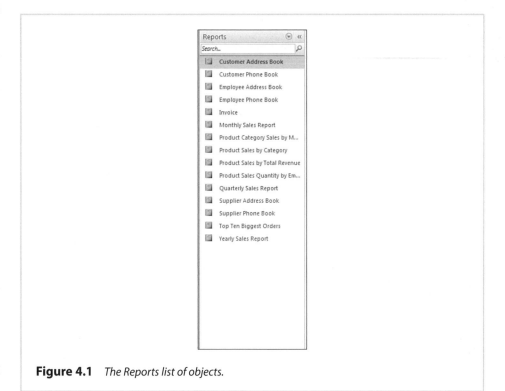

Figure 4.1   *The Reports list of objects.*

to easily move from page to page. You accomplish this by using the page navigation buttons at the bottom of the report window (see Figure 4.2). By using these
buttons, you can easily navigate to the first page of the report, the previous page,
the next page, or the last page of the report. By typing a number into the text box
on the navigation bar, you can easily navigate to any page in the report.

Zooming In and Out

When previewing reports, you can change the amount of text (and the size of the
text) that you see onscreen in a report. You do this by zooming in and out of the
report page. There are two different techniques that you can use to set the zoom
level. Here's the first technique:

1. Place the mouse pointer over the report so that it appears as a magnifying
   glass.

2. Click the mouse. The page zooms in.

3. Click the mouse again. The page zooms out.

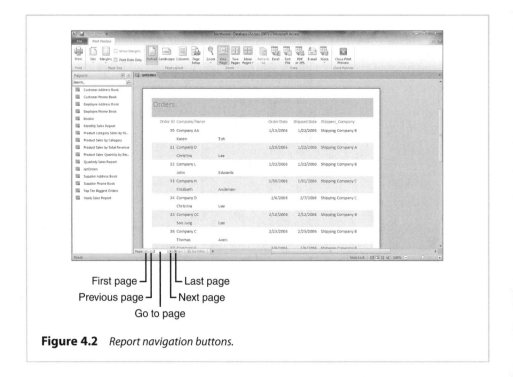

First page — Last page
Previous page — Next page
Go to page

Figure 4.2   *Report navigation buttons.*

Here's the second technique:

1. Click the Zoom drop-down list box in the Zoom group on the Print Preview tab of the Ribbon (see Figure 4.3).

2. Select a size. The report zooms to the designated level.

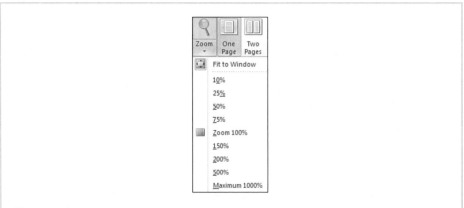

Figure 4.3   *The Zoom drop-down list box, which allows you to select a zoom level.*

You may wonder what the Fit option is within the Zoom drop-down. The Fit option fits the report within the available screen real estate of the report window.

Viewing Multiple Pages

While you're previewing an Access report, you can preview more than one page at a time. To view two pages, you click the Two Pages button in the Zoom group on the Print Preview tab of the Ribbon. To view multiple pages, you click the Multiple Pages button and select how many pages you want to view (see Figure 4.4).

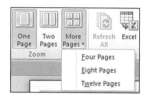

Figure 4.4   *Selecting how many pages you want to view.*

SHOW ME   Media 4.1—Opening and Viewing a Report
Access this video file through your registered Web Edition at
my.safaribooksonline.com/9780132117128/media.

Printing a Report

Before you print your report, you can change the report margins, orientation, paper size, and several other important options. You accomplish this using the Page Setup feature.

LET ME TRY IT

Use Page Setup

Here's how Page Setup works:

1. While previewing the report, click the Page Setup button in the Page Layout group on the Print Preview tab of the Ribbon. The Page Setup dialog box appears (see Figure 4.5).

Figure 4.5   *The Page Setup dialog box, where you select report settings.*

2. The Print Options tab allows you to modify the margins. The Page tab allows you to customize important settings such as the orientation, paper size and source, and the printer you want to use. The Columns tab allows you to designate column size and other information applicable for multi-column reports. Select the desired options.

3. Click OK to accept your changes.

If you prefer, you can use the appropriate Ribbon buttons to designate the settings available in the Page Setup dialog box. For example, you can easily switch from portrait to landscape using the Landscape tool available in the Page Layout group of the Print Preview tab of the Ribbon.

Sending Reports to the Printer

You can print the reports you create by using the context-sensitive menu. You can just right-click the report that you want to print, and then select Print. You can also print from Print Preview mode. You just click the Print button in the Print group on the Print Preview tab of the Ribbon. To print a report by using the context-sensitive menu, follow these steps:

1. Click Reports in the list of objects in the Navigation Pane.

2. Right-click the report you want to print.

3. Choose Print.

4. Complete the dialog box, entering information such as the number of copies that you want to print, the printer you want to print to, and so on.

5. Click OK to complete the process.

The process of printing a report by using the Print button while previewing the report works like this:

1. Click Reports in the list of objects in the Database window.

2. Right-click the report you want to print, and then select Preview.

3. Click the Print tool in the Print group on the Print Preview tab of the Ribbon. Once again the Print dialog appears, prompting you for additional information.

SHOW ME   Media 4.2—Printing a Report

Access this video file through your registered Web Edition at
my.safaribooksonline.com/9780132117128/media.

The AutoReport Feature and the Report Wizard

To help you create reports, Access provides the Report Wizard. The Report Wizard asks questions about the report and then creates the report based on your answers.

Using the AutoReport Feature

Using the AutoReport feature is the quickest and easiest way to create a report. Access creates a report via the AutoReport feature without asking you any questions. Although you can create this type of report effortlessly, as you will see, it is not very flexible in that it does not ask you *any* questions.

LET ME TRY IT

Create a Report with AutoReport

Here's how AutoReport works:

1. Select Tables or Queries in the list of objects in the Navigation Pane.

2. Select the table or query on which you want to base the report.

3. Click the Create tab (see Figure 4.6).

Figure 4.6   *The Create tab allows you to quickly and easily create a report based on a table or query.*

4. Select Report. Access creates a report based on the selected table or query.

 LET ME TRY IT

Create a Report by Using the Report Wizard

Although the AutoReport feature is great at producing a quick report, it does not offer much in terms of flexibility. The Report Wizard asks a series of questions and then better customizes the report to your needs. Let's take a look at how it works:

1. Select the Create tab.

2. Click the Report Wizard tool in the Reports group.

3. In the first step of the wizard, you select the table or query on which you want to base the report.

4. Select the fields you want to include in the report (see Figure 4.7). You can add any type of field to a report. You can also add as many fields or as few fields as you'd like. In fact, you can even include fields from more than one table! Click Next.

5. If you base the report on data from more than one table, the second step of the wizard prompts you to designate how you want to view your data (see Figure 4.8).

6. In the third step the wizard prompts you to select any fields that you want to group by (see Figure 4.9). Click Next.

7. In the fourth step of the wizard you select the desired sort order (see Figure 4.10). You can select either ascending or descending. In Figure 4.10, I selected ascending. Click Next.

8. In the fifth step of the wizard you select the desired layout for the report (see Figure 4.11). The layout you select is a matter of personal preference,

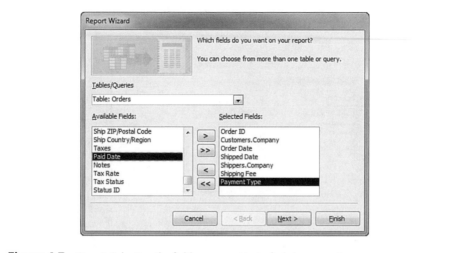

Figure 4.7   *Step 1: Selecting the fields you want to include in a report.*

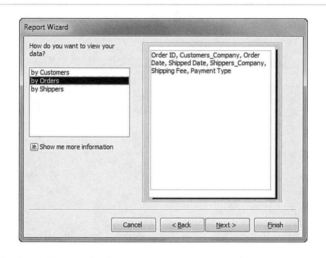

Figure 4.8   *Step 2: Designating how you want to view your data.*

and which layout will work best with the data you selected for the report. Click Next.

9. The sixth step of the wizard prompts you to type the report title.

10. Click the Finish button. Access creates the report and places you in Preview mode.

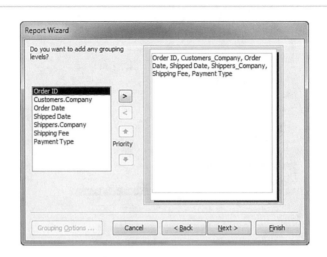

Figure 4.9   *Step 3: Selecting the fields that you want to group by.*

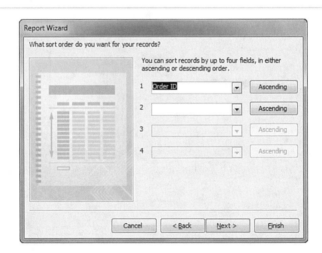

Figure 4.10   *Step 4: Selecting a sort order for a report.*

As you can see, the Report Wizard offers quite a bit more flexibility than the AutoReport feature. Using the Report Wizard, you can designate the fields you want to include on the report, the data groupings you want to add to the report, the sort order for the report, the layout for the report, and a style for the report. I find that the Report Wizard can generally do most of the work for me. It's then up to me to add those finishing touches.

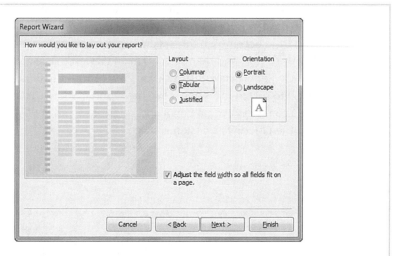

Figure 4.11   *Step 5: Selecting a layout for a report.*

SHOW ME   Media 4.3—AutoReports and the Report Wizard

Access this video file through your registered Web Edition at
my.safaribooksonline.com/9780132117128/media.

Closing a Report

When you have finished working with a report, you need to close it. Access first prompts you and asks whether you want to save changes to the report. You should click Yes. If you have not yet provided a name for the report, Access prompts you to name the report.

Naming standards suggest that you use the *rpt* prefix to name a report (for example, rptCustomers).

Viewing the Design of a Report

AutoReports are limiting because they create such generic reports. But once you create such a rather-dull, generic report the easy way using the AutoReport feature, you then can begin to make modifications using the Design view. Access does the basics, and then you add bells and whistles to make the report more individual and better suited to your specific application. Furthermore, although the Report Wizard gives you many choices, you still may want to customize many of the options that it set.

After you have created a report by using the AutoReport feature or the Report Wizard, you will probably want to customize the report. You must switch to Design view of the report to accomplish this task. While previewing the report, you must first right-click the report and then select Design View from the context-sensitive menu. Or, while in Report view, just click the View tool on the Print Preview toolbar (see Figure 4.12) to switch to Design view. The report is shown in Design view in Figure 4.13. You can easily toggle between Design view and Preview mode, to view the report and then modify its design.

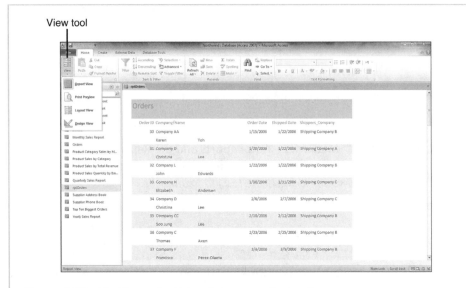

Figure 4.12   *The View tool, which switches you to Design view.*

 SHOW ME   Media 4.4—Viewing the Design of a Report
Access this video file through your registered Web Edition at
my.safaribooksonline.com/9780132117128/media.

 TELL ME MORE   Media 4.5—Types of Reports Available
Access this audio recording through your registered Web Edition at
my.safaribooksonline.com/9780132117128/media.

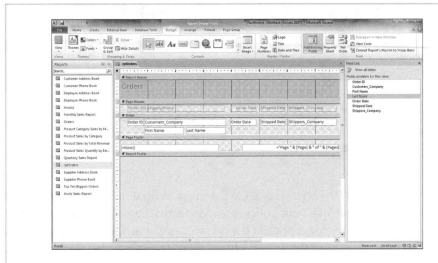

Figure 4.13   *The report in Design view.*

Using Access 2010 you can create your own
databases and tables.

5

Creating Your Own Databases and Tables

It is useful to think of the process of table design as being similar to the process of building a foundation for a house. Just as a house with a faulty foundation will fall over, an application with a poor table design will be difficult to build, maintain, and use. This chapter covers all the ins and outs of table design in Access 2010. After reading this chapter, you will be ready to build the other components of an application, knowing that the tables you design provide the application with a strong foundation.

Types of Databases Available

Access 2010 sports two types of databases: a standard database, and a web database. The standard database is consistent with that of all the previous versions of Access. A standard database can house all the tables, queries, forms, reports, macros, and modules that comprise your application. Microsoft designed it for use on a single machine or on your computer network. The web database is new to Access 2010. With a web database, your tables are stored on the Internet. Furthermore, you can create queries, forms, and reports, all of which reside on the Internet, rather than within the ACCDB file. Access 2010 is the first version of Access that allows for true web development.

Creating a New Database

 **LET ME TRY IT**

Create a New Database

To create a new blank database, follow these steps:

1. Select New from the File tab.

2. Select Blank Database or Blank Web Database from the list of options on the right side of the screen (see Figure 5.1).

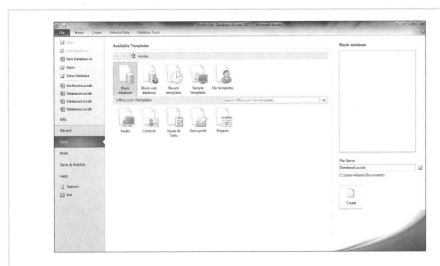

Figure 5.1   *Creating a new database.*

3. Select a drive/folder where you will place the database.

4. Type a filename for the database.

5. Click the OK button.

Access creates an empty database file. It is your responsibility to add the necessary tables, queries, forms, reports, macros, and modules that comprise a functional application.

Database filenames must follow these rules:

- Database names can contain up to 255 characters.
- Database names can contain spaces, but you should avoid special characters such as asterisks.
- Access assigns the extension .ACCDB to a databases that you create.

Most of what this book covers applies to both standard databases and web databases. Chapter 12, "Working with Web Databases," covers the specifics of working with web databases.

SHOW ME   Media 5.1—Creating a Database
Access this video file through your registered Web Edition at
my.safaribooksonline.com/9780132117128/media.

Building a New Table

You can add a new table to an Access 2010 database in several ways: You can design the table from scratch, build the table from a *datasheet* (a spreadsheet-like format), import the table from another source, or link to an external table. This chapter discusses the processes of building a table from a datasheet and designing a table from scratch. Chapter 11, "Sharing Data with Other Applications," covers the processes of importing and linking.

Regardless of which method you choose, you should start building a new table by selecting the Create tab. The icons that appear enable you to create a table in Design view or to create a table by entering data (see Figure 5.2).

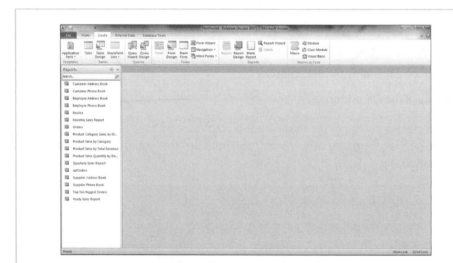

Figure 5.2   *Creating a new table.*

LET ME TRY IT

Building a Table from a Datasheet

Building a table from a datasheet was very limited in earlier versions of Access. With Access 2010, you can do quite a bit while in Datasheet view. To use the datasheet method, follow these steps:

1. Select the Create tab on the Ribbon.

2. Click the Table button from the Tables group. A new datasheet appears, ready for you to design your table (see Figure 5.3).

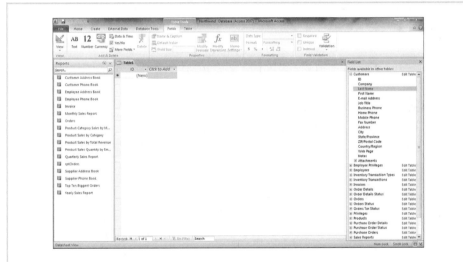

Figure 5.3 *Building a table from a datasheet.*

3. Click to add a column. A drop-down appears with a list of the available field types (see Figure 5.4). Select the appropriate field type from the list.

4. Enter a name for the field. Press Enter. The focus appears on the next field. At any time, you can refine the properties associated with a field. You accomplish the task with the buttons on the Fields tab of the Ribbon. For example, you can designate a field as Required or Unique (see Figure 5.5).

5. After you have added all the columns and data you want, click the Save button on the QuickAccess toolbar. Access prompts you for a table name. Enter a table name and click OK.

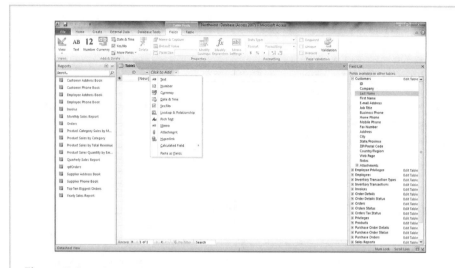

Figure 5.4 *Selecting the appropriate field type.*

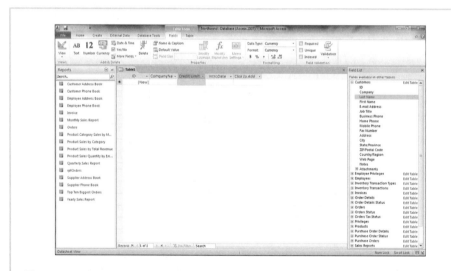

Figure 5.5 *Refining the properties of the fields in the table.*

6. After the save operation is complete, click the View button on the Ribbon to look at the design of the resulting table.

7. If you'd like, you can add a description to each field to help make the table self-documenting. Your table design should look something like Figure 5.6.

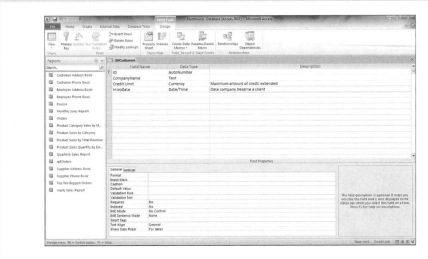

Figure 5.6 *The table design results from building a table with the datasheet method.*

 SHOW ME Media 5.2—Designing a Table from a Datasheet
Access this video file through your registered Web Edition at
my.safaribooksonline.com/9780132117128/media.

Adding descriptions to table, query, form, report, macro, and module objects goes a long way toward making an application self-documenting. Such documentation helps you, or anyone who modifies an application, perform any required maintenance on the application's objects.

 **LET ME TRY IT**

Designing a Table from Scratch

Many people believe that designing tables from scratch offers flexibility and encourages good design principles. Although it requires some knowledge of database and table design, it gives you more control and precision than designing a table from datasheet view. It allows you to select each field name and field type, and to define field properties. To design a table from scratch, you select Tables from the list of objects and double-click the Create Table in Design View icon. The Table Design view window appears.

When the Table Design view window appears, follow these steps to design a table:

1. Define each field in the table by typing its name in the Field Name column.

2. Tab to the Data Type column. Select the default field type, which is Text, or use the drop-down combo box to select another field type. You can find details on which field type is appropriate for data in the "Selecting the Appropriate Field Type for Data" section, later in this chapter. Note that if you use the Field Builder, it sets a data type value for you that you can modify.

If you forget a field and need to insert it later, you can right-click the column heading to the right of where you want to insert the new column and then select Insert Field from the context menu. Access inserts a column that you can rename by double-clicking the column heading. You can then use the Fields tab of the Ribbon to set properties of the field.

3. Tab to the Description column and enter a description for the data. What you type in this column appears on the status bar when the user is entering data into the field. This column is also great for documenting what data is actually stored in the field.

4. Continue entering fields. If you need to insert a field between two existing fields, click the Insert Rows button in the Tools group of the Design tab of the Ribbon. Access inserts the new field above the field you were on. To delete a field, select it and click the Delete Rows button.

5. To save your work, click the Save tool on the QuickAccess toolbar. The Save As dialog box, shown in Figure 5.7, appears. Enter a table name and click OK. A dialog box appears, recommending that you establish a primary key. Every table should have a primary key. Primary keys are discussed in the section "The All-Important Primary Key," later in this chapter.

Figure 5.7   *The Save As dialog box.*

SHOW ME   Media 5.3—Designing a Table from Scratch
Access this video file through your registered Web Edition at
my.safaribooksonline.com/9780132117128/media.

Field names can be up to 64 characters long. For practical reasons, you should try to limit them to 10–15 characters, which is enough to describe the field without making the name difficult to type.

Access supplies default names for the tables that you create (for example, Table1, Table2). I suggest that you supply a more descriptive name. I generally follow the industry-wide naming convention of prefixing all my table names with *tbl*.

Field names can include any combination of letters, numbers, spaces, and other characters, excluding periods, exclamation points, accents, and brackets. I recommend that you stick to letters. Spaces in field names can be inconvenient when you're building queries, modules, and other database objects. You shouldn't be concerned that users will see the field names without the spaces. The Caption property of a field allows you to designate the text that Access displays for users.

A field name cannot begin with leading spaces. As mentioned previously, field names shouldn't contain any spaces, so the rule to not begin a field name with spaces shouldn't be a problem. Field names also cannot include ASCII control characters (ASCII values 0–31).

You should try not to duplicate property names, keywords, function names, or the names of other Access objects when naming fields (for example, naming a field Date). Although the code might work in some circumstances, you might get unpredictable results in others.

To make a potential move to the client/server platform as painless as possible, you should be aware that not all field types are supported by every back-end database. Furthermore, most back-end databases impose stricter limits than Access does on the length of field names and the characters that are valid in field names. To reduce the number of problems you'll encounter if you migrate tables to a back-end database server, you should consider these issues when you're naming the fields in Access tables.

Selecting the Appropriate Field Type for Data

The data type you select for each field can greatly affect the performance and functionality of an application. Several factors can influence your choice of data type for each field in a table:

- The type of data that's stored in the field

- Whether the field's contents need to be included in calculations

- Whether you need to sort the data in the field

- The way you want to sort the data in the field

- How important storage space is to you

The type of data you need to store in a field has the biggest influence on which data type you select. For example, if you need to store numbers that begin with leading zeros, you can't select a Number field because leading zeros entered into a Number field are ignored. This rule affects data such as zip codes (some of which begin with leading zeros) and department codes.

If the contents of a field need to be included in calculations, you must select a Number or Currency data type. You can't perform calculations on the contents of fields defined with the other data types. The only exception to this rule is Date data type fields, which you can include in date/time calculations.

If it is unimportant that leading zeros be stored in a field and you just need them to appear on forms and reports, you can accomplish this by using the **Format** property of the field.

You must also consider whether you will sort or index the data in a field. You can't sort the data in OLE Object and Hyperlink fields, so you shouldn't select these field types if you must sort or index the data in the field. Furthermore, you must think about the *way* you want to sort the data. For example, in a Text field, a set of numbers would be sorted in the order of the numbers' leftmost character, then the second character from the left, and so on (that is, 1, 10, 100, 2, 20, 200) because data in the Text field is sorted as characters rather than numbers. On the other hand, in a Number or Currency field, the numbers would be sorted in ascending value order (that is, 1, 2, 10, 20, 100, 200). You might think you would never want data sorted in a character sequence, but sometimes it makes sense to sort certain information, such as department codes, in this fashion. Access 2003 introduced the ability to sort or group based on a Memo field, but Access performs the sorting or grouping only based on the first 255 characters. Finally, you should consider how important disk space is to you. Each field type takes up a different amount of storage space on a hard disk, and this could be a factor when you're selecting a data type for a field.

Nine field types are available in Access: Text, Memo, Number, Date/Time, Currency, AutoNumber, Yes/No, OLE Object, and Hyperlink. Table 5.1 briefly describes the appropriate uses for each field type and the amount of storage space each type needs.

Table 5.1   Appropriate Uses and Storage Space for Access Field Types

Field Type	Appropriate Uses	Storage Space
Text	Data containing text, a combination of text and numbers, or numbers that don't need to be included in calculations. Examples are names, addresses, department codes, and phone numbers.	Based on what's actually stored in the field; ranges from 0 to 255 bytes.
Memo	Long text and numeric strings. Examples are notes and descriptions.	Ranges from 0 to 65,536 bytes.
Number	Data that's included in calculations (excluding money). Examples are ages, codes (such as employee IDs), and payment methods.	1, 2, 4, or 8 bytes, depending on the field size selected (or 16 bytes for replication ID).
Date/Time	Dates and times. Examples are date ordered and birth date.	8 bytes.
Currency	Currency values. Examples are amount due and price.	8 bytes.
AutoNumber	Unique sequential or random numbers. Examples are invoice numbers and project numbers.	4 bytes (16 bytes for replication ID).
Yes/No	Fields that contain one of two values (for example, yes/no, true/false). Sample uses are indicating bills paid and tenure status.	1 bit.
OLE Object	Objects such as Word documents or Excel spreadsheets. Examples are employee reviews and budgets.	0 bytes to 1GB, depending on what's stored within the field.
Hyperlink	Text or a combination of text and numbers, stored as text and used as a hyperlink for a Web address (uniform resource locator [URL]) or a universal naming convention (UNC) path. Examples are Web pages and network files.	0 to 2,048 bytes for text for each of the three parts that compose the address (up to 64,000 characters total).

The most difficult part of selecting a field type is knowing which type is best in each situation. The following detailed descriptions of each field type and when you should use them should help you with this process.

Although Microsoft loosely considers Lookup Wizard a field type, it is really not its own field type. You use it to create a field that allows the user to select a value from another table or from a list of values via a combo box that the wizard helps define for you. As far as storage, it requires that same storage size as the primary key for the lookup field.

Text Fields: The Most Common Field Type

Most fields are Text fields. Many developers don't realize that it's best to use Text fields for any numbers that are not used in calculations. Examples of such numbers are phone numbers, part numbers, and zip codes. Although the default size for a Text field is 50 characters, you can store up to 255 characters in a Text field. Because Access allocates disk space dynamically, a large field size doesn't use hard disk space, but you can improve performance if you allocate the smallest field size possible. You can control the maximum number of characters allowed in a Text field by using the `FieldSize` property.

The Hyperlink field type contains a hyperlink object. The hyperlink object consists of three parts. The first part is called the *display text*; it's the text that appears in the field or control. The second part is the actual *file path* (UNC path) or *page* (URL) the field is referring to. The third part is the *subaddress*, a location within the file or page.

Memo Fields: For Long Notes and Comments

A Memo field can store up to 65,536 characters of text, meaning that it can hold up to 16 pages of text for each record. Memo fields are excellent for any types of notes you want to store with table data. Remember that in Access 2010 you can sort by a Memo field.

Number Fields: For When You Need to Calculate

You use Number fields to store data that you must include in calculations. If currency amounts are included in calculations or if calculations require the highest degree of accuracy, you should use a Currency field rather than a Number field.

The Number field is actually several types of fields in one because Access 2010 offers seven sizes of numeric fields. Byte can store integers from 0 to 255, Integer can hold whole numbers from –32768 to 32767, and Long Integer can hold whole numbers ranging from less than –2 billion to just over 2 billion. Although all three of these sizes offer excellent performance, each type requires an increasingly large amount of storage space. Two of the other numeric field sizes, Single and Double, offer floating decimal points and, therefore, much slower performance than integer and long integer. Single can hold fractional numbers to 7 significant digits; Double extends the precision to 14 significant digits. Decimal, a numeric data type that was introduced with Access 2002, allows storage of very large numbers and provides decimal precision up to 28 digits!

Date/Time Fields: For Tracking When Things Happened

You use the Date/Time field type to store valid dates and times. Date/Time fields allow you to perform date calculations and make sure dates and times are always sorted properly. Access actually stores the date or time internally as an 8-byte floating-point number. Access represents time as a fraction of a day.

Currency Fields: For Storing Money

The Currency field is a number field that is used when currency values are being stored in a table. A Currency field prevents the computer from rounding off data during calculations. It holds 15 digits of whole dollars, plus accuracy to one-hundredth of a cent. Although very accurate, this type of field is quite slow to process.

Any date and time settings you establish in the Windows Control Panel are reflected in your data. For example, if you modify Short Date Style in Regional Settings within the Control Panel, your forms, reports, and datasheets will immediately reflect those changes.

AutoNumber Fields: For Unique Record Identifiers

The AutoNumber field in Access 2010 automatically generates AutoNumber field values when the user adds a record. In Access 2.0, counter values have to be sequential. The AutoNumber field type in Access 2010 can be either sequential or random. The random assignment is useful when several users are adding records offline because it's unlikely that Access will assign the same random value to two records.

Any changes to the currency format made in the Windows Control Panel are reflected in your data. Of course, Access doesn't automatically perform any actual conversion of currency amounts. As with dates, if you modify the currency symbol in Regional Settings within the Control Panel, your forms, reports, and datasheets will immediately reflect those changes.

You should note a few important points about sequential AutoNumber fields. If a user deletes a record from a table, its unique number is lost forever. Likewise, if a user is adding a record but cancels the action, the unique counter value for that record is lost forever. If this behavior is unacceptable, you can generate your own counter values.

Yes/No Fields: For When One of Two Answers Is Correct

You should use Yes/No fields to store a logical true or false. What Access actually stores in the field is -1 for yes, 0 for no, or Null for no specific choice. The display format for the field determines what the user actually sees (normally Yes/No, True/False, On/Off, or a third option [Null] if you set the `TripleState` property of the associated control on a form to True). Yes/No fields work efficiently for any data that can have only a true or false value. Not only do they limit the user to valid choices, but they also take up only 1 bit of storage space.

OLE Object Fields: For Storing Just About Anything

OLE Object fields are designed to hold data from any OLE server application that is registered in Windows, including spreadsheets, word processing documents, sound, and video. There are many business uses for OLE Object fields, such as storing resumes, employee reviews, budgets, or videos. However, in many cases, it is more efficient to use a Hyperlink field to store a link to the document rather than store the document itself in an OLE Object field.

Hyperlink Fields: For Linking to the Internet

Hyperlink fields are used to store uniform resource locator addresses, which are links to web pages on the Internet or on an intranet, or UNC paths, which are links to a file location path. The Hyperlink field type is broken into three parts:

- What the user sees
- The URL or UNC
- A subaddress, such as a range name or bookmark

After the user places an entry in a Hyperlink field, the entry serves as a direct link to the file or page it refers to.

Using Indexes to Improve Performance

Indexes improve performance when you're searching, sorting, or grouping on a field or fields. Primary key indexes are used to maintain unique values for records. For example, you can create a single-field index that does not allow a duplicate order number or a multiple-field index that does not allow records with the same first and last names.

LET ME TRY IT

Create an Index Based on a Single Field

To create an index based on a single field (from Design view), follow these steps:

1. Select the field to be indexed.

2. Click the Indexed row of the Field Properties pane.

3. Select the desired index type—No, Yes (Duplicates OK), or Yes (No Duplicates). The Yes (Duplicates OK) option means that you are creating an index and that you will allow duplicates within that field. The Yes (No Duplicates) option means that you are creating an index and you will *not* allow duplicate values within the index. If the index is based on company name and you select Yes (Duplicates OK), you can enter two companies with the same name. If you select Yes (No Duplicates), you cannot enter two companies with the same name.

LET ME TRY IT

Create an Index Based on Multiple Fields

To create an index based on multiple fields (from Design view), follow these steps:

1. Select Indexes from the Show/Hide group on the Design tab of the Ribbon. The Indexes window appears (see Figure 5.8).

2. Type the index name in the Index Name column.

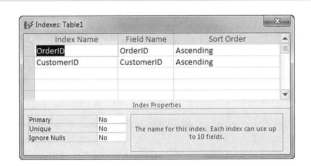

Figure 5.8 *The Indexes window enables you to manage the indexes associated with a table.*

3. From the Field Name column, select the desired fields to include in the index.

4. Select the desired index properties.

5. Close the Indexes window if desired.

 SHOW ME   Media 5.4—Creating Indexes
Access this video file through your registered Web Edition at
my.safaribooksonline.com/9780132117128/media.

The All-Important Primary Key

A primary key is a field or a combination of fields in a table that uniquely identifies each row in the table (for example, the OrderID). The most important index in a table is called the *Primary Key index*; it ensures uniqueness of the fields that make up the index and also gives the table a default order. You must set a primary key for the fields on the one side of a one-to-many relationship. To create a Primary Key index, you select the fields you want to establish as the primary key and then click the Primary Key button in the Tools group of the Design tab on the Ribbon.

Figure 5.9 shows the tblOrders table with a Primary Key index based on the OrderID field. Notice that the index name of the field designated as the primary key of the table is called PrimaryKey. Note that the `Primary` and `Unique` properties for this index are both set to Yes (true).

Indexes: tblOrders			
Index Name	**Field Name**	**Sort Order**	
OrderID	OrderID	Ascending	
CustomerID	CustomerID	Ascending	
PrimaryKey	OrderID	Ascending	

Index Properties		
Primary	Yes	
Unique	Yes	The name for this index. Each index can use up to 10 fields.
Ignore Nulls	No	

Figure 5.9   *A Primary Key index based on the OrderID field.*

Working with Field Properties

After you have added fields to a table, you need to customize their properties. Field properties let you control how Access stores data and what data the user can enter into a field. The available properties differ depending on which field type you select. You can find a comprehensive list of properties under the Text data type (see Figure 5.10). The following sections describe the various field properties. Notice that the lower portion of the Design view window in Figure 5.10 is the Field Properties pane. This is where you can set properties for the fields in a table.

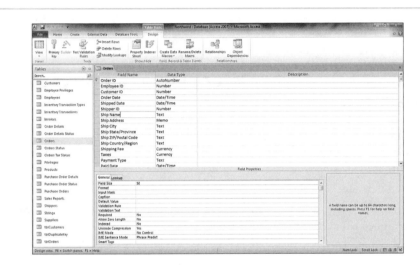

Figure 5.10 *Using the Field Properties pane of the Design view window to set the properties of a field.*

 **LET ME TRY IT**

The `Field Size` Property: Limiting What the User Enters into a Field

The `Field Size` property is available for Text and Number fields only. It's best to set the `Field Size` property to the smallest value possible. For Number fields, a small size means lower storage requirements and faster performance. The same is true for Text fields. To modify the `Field Size` property, follow these steps:

1. Select the desired field name from the top pane of the Design view window.

2. Click the `Field Size` property text box in the Field Properties pane.

3. Type the desired field size. In Figure 5.10 I've typed 50 as the field size of the Ship Name field.

It's important to note that for Number fields, you should select the smallest `Field Size` property value that can store the values you will be entering. Limiting the `Field Size` property of Number fields saves disk space.

Second, to get help with a field property, you click the property line in the Field Properties pane and press F1.

 **LET ME TRY IT**

The `Format` Property: Determining How Access Displays Data

The `Format` property enables you to customize the way Access displays and prints numbers, dates, times, and text. You can select a predefined format or create a custom format.

Here's a tip to save you a lot of time: You can move between the two panes of the Design view window by pressing F6.

To select a predefined display format (from Design view), follow these steps:

1. Select the desired field.
2. Click the `Format` property text box in the Field Properties pane.
3. Click the drop-down arrow that appears after you click in the `Format` property.
4. Select the desired format based on the type of field you are formatting.

You create a custom format by using a combination of the special characters, called *placeholders*, listed in Table 5.2.

Table 5.2   Placeholders That Allow You to Build a Custom Format

Placeholder	Function
0	Displays a digit if one exists in the position; otherwise, displays a zero. You can use the 0 placeholder to display leading zeros for whole numbers and trailing zeros for decimals.
#	Displays a digit if one exists in the position; otherwise, displays a blank space.

Table 5.2   Placeholders That Allow You to Build a Custom Format

Placeholder	Function
$	Displays a dollar sign in the position.
. % ,	Displays a decimal point, percent sign, or comma at the indicated position.
/	Separates the day, month, and year to format date values.
M	Used as a month placeholder: m displays 1, mm displays 01, mmm displays Jan, mmmm displays January.
D	Used as a day placeholder: d displays 1, dd displays 01, ddd displays Mon, dddd displays Monday.
Y	Used as a year placeholder: yy displays 95, yyyy displays 1995.
:	Separates hours and minutes.
h, n, s	Used as time placeholders for h hours, n minutes, and s seconds.
AM/PM	Displays time in 12-hour format, with AM or PM appended.
@	Indicates that a character is required in the position in a text or memo field.
&	Indicates that a character is optional.
>	Changes all the text characters to uppercase.
<	Changes all the text characters to lowercase.

 LET ME TRY IT

Create a Custom Display Format

To create a custom display format, follow these steps while in Design view of a form:

1. Select the desired field.

2. Click the Format text box in the Field Properties pane.

3. Type the desired format, using the placeholders listed in Table 5.2.

Field names, as a general rule, should be short and should not contain spaces. You can, however, assign to the field a Caption property that is descriptive of the field's contents. Access displays the Caption property as the field label on forms and reports. For example, you can assign "Fax Number" to the Caption property for a field named FaxNum.

The `Caption` Property: Providing Alternatives to the Field Name

The text you place in the `Caption` property becomes the caption for fields in Datasheet view. Access also uses the contents of the `Caption` property as the caption for the attached label it adds to data-bound controls when you add them to forms and reports. The `Caption` property becomes important whenever you name fields without spaces. Whatever is in the `Caption` property overrides the field name for use in Datasheet view, on forms, and on reports.

A *data-bound control* is a control that is bound to a field in a table or query. The term *attached label* refers to the label that is attached to a data-bound control.

 LET ME TRY IT

Set the `Caption` Property from Design View

To set the `Caption` property (from Design view), follow these steps:

1. Select the desired field name from the top pane of the Design view window.

2. Click the Caption text box in the Field Properties pane.

3. Type the desired caption.

The `Default Value` Property: Saving Data-Entry Time

Assigning a `Default Value` property to a field causes a specified value to be filled in for the field in new records. Setting a commonly used value as the `Default Value` property facilitates the data entry process. When adding data, you can accept the default entry or replace it with another value. For example, if most of your customers are in California, you can assign a default value of `"CA"`. When doing data entry, if the customer is in California you will not need to change the value for the state. If the customer is in another state, you just replace the `"CA"` with the appropriate state value.

 **LET ME TRY IT**

Set the Default Value **Property from Design View**

To set a Default Value property (from Design view), follow these steps:

1. Select the desired field from the top pane of the Design view window.

2. Click the Default Value property text box in the Field Properties pane.

3. Type the desired value.

A Default Value property can be constant, such as CA for California, or a function that returns a value, such as Date(), which displays the current date.

The data users enter in tables must be accurate if the database is to be valuable to you or your organization. You can use the Validation Rule property to add data entry rules to the fields in tables.

Date() is a built-in Visual Basic for Applications (VBA) function that returns the current date and time. When it is used as a default value for a field, Access enters the current date into the field when the user adds a new row to the table.

The Validation Rule **and** Validation Text **Properties: Controlling What the User Enters in a Field**

The Default Value property suggests a value to the user, but the Validation Rule property actually limits what the user can place in the field. Validation rules cannot be violated; the database engine strictly enforces them. As with the Default Value property, this property can contain either text or a valid Access expression, but you cannot include user-defined functions in the Validation Rule property. You also cannot include references to forms, queries, or tables in the Validation Rule property.

You can use operators to compare two values; the less than (<) and greater than (>) symbols are examples of comparison operators. And, Or, Is, Not, Between, and Like are called *logical operators*. Table 5.3 provides a few examples of validation rules.

Whereas the validation rule limits what the user can enter into the table, the validation text provides the error message that appears when the user violates the validation rule.

Table 5.3   Examples of Validation Rules

Validation Rule	Validation Text Examples
>0	Please enter a valid Employee ID Number.
"H" or "S" or "Q"	Only H or S or Q codes will be accepted.
Between Date()-365 and Date()+365	Date cannot be later than one year ago today or more than one year from today.
>0 or is Null	Enter a valid ID number or leave blank if not approved.
Between 0 and 9 or is Null	Rating range is 0 through 9 or is blank.
>Date()	Date must be after today.

If you set the `Validation Rule` property but do not set the `Validation Text` property, Access automatically displays a standard error message whenever the user violates the validation rule. To display a custom message, you must enter message text in the `Validation Text` property.

 LET ME TRY IT

Set the `Validation Rule` **Property from Design View**

To establish a field-level validation rule (from Design view), follow these steps:

1. Select the desired field name from the top pane of the Design view window.

2. Click the Validation Rule text box in the Field Properties pane.

3. Type the desired validation rule (for example, **Between 0 and 120**).

 LET ME TRY IT

Set the `Validation Text` **Property from Design View**

To add validation text, follow these steps:

1. Click the Validation Text text box in the Field Properties pane.

2. Type the desired text (for example, **Age Must be Between 0 and 120**).

You can require users of a database to enter a valid value in selected fields when editing or adding records. For example, you can require a user to enter a date for each record in an Invoice table.

The `Required` **Property: Making the User Enter a Value**

The `Required` property is very important: It determines whether you require a user to enter a value in a field. This property is useful for foreign key fields, when you want to make sure the user enters data into the field. It's also useful for any field containing information that's needed for business reasons (company name, for example).

A *foreign key field* is a field that is looked up in another table. For example, in the case of a Customers table and an Orders table, both might contain a CustomerID field. In the Customers table, the CustomerID field is the primary key field. In the Orders table, the CustomerID field is the foreign key field because its value is looked up in the Customers table.

 LET ME TRY IT

Set the `Required` **Property from Design View**

To designate a field as required (from Design view), follow these steps:

1. Select the desired field.

2. Click the Required text box in the Field Properties pane.

3. Type **Yes**.

The `Allow Zero Length` **Property: Accommodating for Situations with Nonexistent Data**

You can use the `Allow Zero Length` property to allow a string of no characters. You enter a zero-length string by typing a pair of quotation marks with no space between them (`""`). You use the `Allow Zero Length` property to indicate that you know there is no value for a field.

 LET ME TRY IT

Set the `Allow Zero Length` **Property from Design View**

To allow a zero-length field (from Design view), follow these steps:

1. Select the desired field.

2. Click the Allow Zero Length text box in the Field Properties pane.

3. Select Yes from the drop-down list box.

The `Input Mask` Property: Determining What Data Goes into a Field

An input mask controls data the user enters into a field. For instance, a short date input mask appears as - - / - - / - - - - when the field is active. You can then simply type **07042005** to display or print 7/4/2005. Based on the input mask, you can ensure that the user enters only valid characters into the field.

Table 5.4 lists some of the placeholders that you can use in character strings for input masks in fields of the Text data type.

Table 5.4   Placeholders That Can Be Included in an Input Mask

Placeholder	Description
0	A number (0–9) is required.
9	A number (0–9) is optional.
#	A number (0–9), a space, or a plus or minus sign is optional; a space is used if no number is entered.
L	A letter (A–Z) is required.
?	A letter (A–Z) is not required; a space is used if no letter is entered.
A	A letter (A–Z) or number (0–9) is required.
A	A letter (A–Z) or number (0–9) is optional.
&	Any character or space is required.
C	Any character or space is optional.
>	Any characters to the right are converted to uppercase.
<	All the text characters to the right are changed to lowercase.

 **LET ME TRY IT**

Set the `Input Mask` Property from Design View

To create an input mask (from Design view), follow these steps:

1. Select the desired field.

2. Click the Input Mask text box.

3. Type the desired format, using the placeholders listed in Table 5.4.

Access includes an Input Mask Wizard that appears when you place the cursor in the Input Mask text box and click the build button to the right of the text box. The wizard, shown in Figure 5.11, provides common input mask formats from which to choose. To start the Input Mask Wizard, you click the button to the right of the Input Mask property.

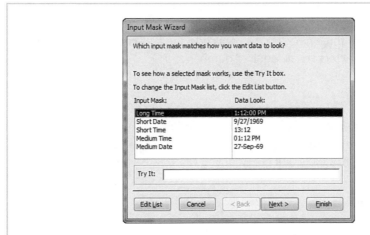

Figure 5.11   *Entering an input mask with the Input Mask Wizard.*

The Input Mask Wizard is available only if you selected the Additional Wizards component during Access setup. If you did not select this component and then you try to open the Input Mask Wizard, Access prompts you to install the option on-the-fly the first time you use it.

For example, the input mask 000-00-0000;;_ (converted to 000\-00\-0000;;_ as soon as you tab away from the property) forces the entry of a valid social security number. Everything that precedes the first semicolon designates the actual mask. The zeros force the entry of the digits 0 through 9. The dashes are literals that appear within the control as the user enters data. The character you enter between the first and second semicolon determines whether literal characters (the dashes, in this case) are stored in the field. If you enter a 0 in this position, literal characters are stored in the field; if you enter 1 or leave this position blank, the literal characters aren't stored. The final position (after the second semicolon) indicates what character is displayed to denote the space where the user types the next character (in this case, the underscore).

Here's a more detailed example: In the mask \(999") "000\-0000;;_, the first back-slash causes the character that follows it (the open parenthesis) to be displayed as a literal. The three nines allow the user to enter optional numbers or spaces. Access displays the close parenthesis and space within the quotation marks as literals. The first three zeros require values 0 through 9. The dash that follows the next back-slash is displayed as a literal. Four additional numbers are then required. The two semicolons have nothing between them, so the literal characters aren't stored in the field. The second semicolon is followed by an underscore, so an underscore is displayed to indicate the space where the user types the next character. This sounds pretty complicated, but here's how it works. The user types **8054857632**. What appears is (805)485-7632. What is actually stored is 8054857632. Because the input mask contains three nines for the area code, the area code is not required. The remaining characters are all required numbers.

The Lookup Wizard

You can select Lookup Wizard as a field's data type. The Lookup Wizard guides you through the steps to create a list of values from which you can choose. You can select the values from a table or a query, or you can create a list of your own values.

 LET ME TRY IT

Use the Lookup Wizard

To use the Lookup Wizard (from Design view), follow these steps:

1. Select the desired field.

2. Choose Lookup Wizard as the data type (see Figure 5.12).

3. Select the desired source of the values, and then click Next.

4. Select the table or query to provide the values, and then click Next.

5. Double-click the fields that contain the desired values, and then click Next.

6. Drag the Lookup column to the desired width, and then click Next.

7. Type a name for the Lookup column, and then click Finish.

When working with the Lookup Wizard, you should be aware of a few things. When you create a form based on a table with a Lookup field, the form automat-ically displays a combo box (or another designated control) for that field. As you add records to the table that is the source for the lookup values, the new infor-mation appears in the list.

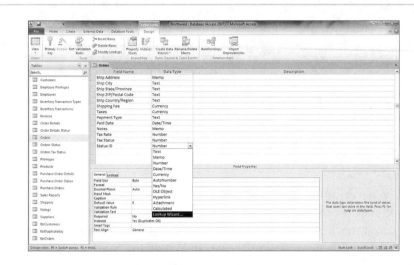

Figure 5.12   *Activating the Lookup Wizard.*

 SHOW ME   Media 5.5—Working with Field Properties
Access this video file through your registered Web Edition at
my.safaribooksonline.com/9780132117128/media.

 TELL ME MORE   Media 5.6—The All-Important Primary Key
Access this audio recording through your registered Web Edition at
my.safaribooksonline.com/9780132117128/media.

Using Access 2010 you can relate the tables in your database.

6

Relating the Information in Your Database

A *relationship* exists between two tables when one or more key fields from one table are matched to one or more key fields in another table. The fields in both tables usually have the same name, data type, and size. This chapter first introduces you to relational database design. You will then learn the types of relationships available in Access, and how to establish those relationships. Finally, you'll learn how to establish referential integrity between the tables in your database.

Introduction to Relational Database Design

Many people believe Access is such a simple product to use that database design is something they don't need to worry about. I couldn't disagree more! Just as a poorly planned vacation will generally not be very fun, a database with poorly designed tables and relationships will fail to meet the needs of its users.

The History of Relational Database Design

Dr. E. F. Codd first introduced formal relational database design in 1969 while he was at IBM. *Relational theory*, which is based on set theory and predicate logic, applies to both databases and database applications. Codd developed 12 rules that determine how well an application and its data adhere to the relational model. Since Codd first conceived these 12 rules, the number of rules has expanded into the hundreds.

You should be happy to learn that, although Microsoft Access is not a perfect application development environment, it measures up quite well as a relational database system.

Goals of Relational Database Design

The number one goal of relational database design is to, as closely as possible, develop a database that models some real-world system. This involves breaking the real-world system into tables and fields and determining how the tables relate to each other. Although on the surface this might appear to be a trivial task, it can be an extremely cumbersome process to translate a real-world system into tables and fields.

A properly designed database has many benefits. The processes of adding, editing, deleting, and retrieving table data are greatly facilitated in a properly designed database. In addition, reports are easy to build. Most important, the database is easy to modify and maintain.

Rules of Relational Database Design

To adhere to the relational model, you must follow certain rules. These rules determine what you store in a table and how you relate the tables. The rules are as follows

- The rules of tables
- The rules of uniqueness and keys
- The rules of foreign keys and domains

The Rules of Tables

Each table in a system must store data about a single entity. An *entity* usually represents a real-life object or event. Examples of objects are customers, employees, and inventory items. Examples of events include orders, appointments, and doctor visits.

The Rules of Uniqueness and Keys

Tables are composed of rows and columns. To adhere to the relational model, each table must contain a unique identifier. Without a unique identifier, it is programmatically impossible to uniquely address a row. You guarantee uniqueness in a table by designating a *primary key*, which is a single column or a set of columns that uniquely identifies a row in a table.

Each column or set of columns in a table that contains unique values is considered a *candidate key*. One candidate key becomes the *primary key*. The remaining candidate keys become *alternate keys*. A primary key made up of one column is considered a *simple key*. A primary key composed of multiple columns is considered a *composite key*.

It is generally a good idea to choose a primary key that is

- Minimal (has as few columns as possible)
- Stable (rarely changes)
- Simple (is familiar to the user)

Following these rules greatly improves the performance and maintainability of a database application, particularly if it deals with large volumes of data.

Consider the example of an employee table. An employee table is generally composed of employee-related fields such as social security number, first name, last name, hire date, salary, and so on. The combination of the first name and the last name fields could be considered a primary key. This might work until the company hires two employees who have the same name. Although the first and last names could be combined with additional fields (for example, hire date) to constitute uniqueness, that would violate the rule of keeping the primary key minimal. Furthermore, an employee might get married, and her last name might change. This violates the rule of keeping a primary key stable. Therefore, using a name as the primary key violates the principle of stability. The social security number might be a valid choice for primary key, but a foreign employee might not have a social security number. This is a case in which a derived, rather than a natural, primary key is appropriate. A *derived key* is an artificial key that you create. A *natural key* is one that is already part of the database.

In examples such as this, I suggest adding EmployeeID as an AutoNumber field. Although the field would violate the rule of simplicity (because an employee number is meaningless to the user), it is both small and stable. Because it is numeric, it is also efficient to process. In fact, I use `AutoNumber` fields as primary keys for most of the tables that I build.

The Rules of Foreign Keys and Domains

A *foreign key* in one table is the field that relates to the primary key in a second table. For example, the CustomerID field may be the primary key in a Customers table and the foreign key in an Orders table.

A domain is a pool of values from which columns are drawn. A simple example of a domain is the specific data range of employee hire dates. In the case of the Orders table, the domain of the CustomerID column is the range of values for the CustomerID in the Customers table.

Normalization and Normal Forms

Some of the most difficult decisions that you face as a developer are what tables to create and what fields to place in each table, and how to relate the tables that you create. *Normalization* is the process of applying a series of rules to ensure that a database achieves optimal structure. *Normal forms* are a progression of these rules. Each successive normal form achieves a better database design than the previous form. Although there are several levels of normal forms, it is generally sufficient to apply only the first three levels of normal forms. The following sections describe the first three levels of normal forms.

First Normal Form

To achieve first normal form, all columns in a table must be *atomic*. This means, for example, that you cannot store first name and last name in the same field. The reason for this rule is that data becomes very difficult to manipulate and retrieve if you store multiple values in a single field. Let's use the full name as an example. It would be impossible to sort by first name or last name independently if you stored both values in the same field. Furthermore, you or the user would have to perform extra work to extract just the first name or just the last name from the field.

Another requirement for first normal form is that the table must not contain repeating values. An example of repeating values is a scenario in which Item1, Quantity1, Item2, Quantity2, Item3, and Quantity3 fields are all found within the Orders table (see Figure 6.1). This design introduces several problems. What if the user wants to add a fourth item to the order? Furthermore, finding the total ordered for a product requires searching several columns. In fact, all numeric and statistical calculations on the table are extremely cumbersome. Repeating groups make it difficult to summarize and manipulate table data. The alternative, shown in Figure 6.2, achieves first normal form. Notice that each item ordered is located in a separate row. All fields are atomic, and the table contains no repeating groups.

Order#	CustInfo	OrderTotal	OrderDate	Item1Name	Item1Suppli	Item1Quant	Item1Price
1	12 Any Street Anywhere, CA	$350.00	5/1/2001	Widget	Good Supplier	5	$1.50
2	12 Any Street Anywhere, CA	$0.00		Gadget	Bad Supplier	2	$2.25
3	12 Any Street Anywhere, CA	$0.00		Nut	Okay Supplier	7	$7.70
4	12 Any Street Anywhere, CA	$0.00		Bolt	Another Supplier	9	$3.00
5	45 Any Street Somewhere,	$0.00		Pencil	Good Supplier	2	$1.50
6	45 Any Street Somewhere,	$0.00		Eraser	Someone	4	$2.20
*	(New)	$0.00				0	$0.00

Figure 6.1   *A table that contains repeating groups.*

Second Normal Form

For a table to achieve second normal form, all nonkey columns must be fully dependent on all the fields that make up the primary key. This rule only applies to

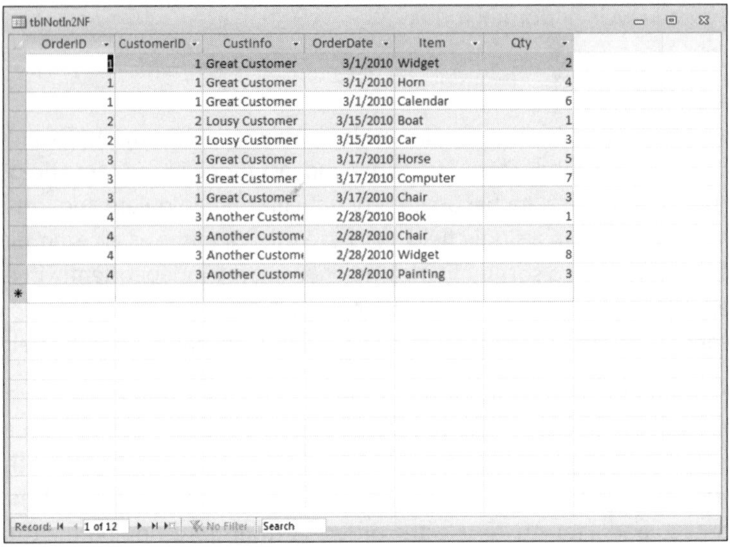

tblNotIn2NF

OrderID	CustomerID	CustInfo	OrderDate	Item	Qty
1	1	Great Customer	3/1/2010	Widget	2
1	1	Great Customer	3/1/2010	Horn	4
1	1	Great Customer	3/1/2010	Calendar	6
2	2	Lousy Customer	3/15/2010	Boat	1
2	2	Lousy Customer	3/15/2010	Car	3
3	1	Great Customer	3/17/2010	Horse	5
3	1	Great Customer	3/17/2010	Computer	7
3	1	Great Customer	3/17/2010	Chair	3
4	3	Another Custom	2/28/2010	Book	1
4	3	Another Custom	2/28/2010	Chair	2
4	3	Another Custom	2/28/2010	Widget	8
4	3	Another Custom	2/28/2010	Painting	3

Record: 1 of 12 No Filter Search

Figure 6.2 *A table achieves first normal form.*

tables that have a composite key: a key made up of two or more fields. For example, the table shown in Figure 6.2 has a primary key made up of the OrderID and CustomerID. The combination of those two keys ensures that the primary key is unique for every row in the table, which is the purpose of the primary key.

However, this table is not in second normal form because some of the information in the table depends only on part of the primary key. For instance, the CustInfo field depends only on the CustomerId field: If you were to change the CustomerId field you'd also have to change the CustInfo field. In real life, of course, there is every possibility that the CustomerId field would be changed and the CustInfo would not, leading to problems in the application.

To achieve second normal form, you must break this data into two tables—an order table and a customer table. The customer table would contain the CustomerId field from the primary key and the fields that depend on it (the CustInfo field, in this case); the order table would consist of the OrderId field and the fields that depend upon it. The order table would still have the CustomerId field (so you'd know which customer to ship the order to) but wouldn't have any other customer information (all other customer information would be in the customer table). If you assign the order to another customer, you'd only have to change the CustomerId field.

The process of breaking the data into two tables is called *decomposition*. Decomposition is considered to be *nonloss* decomposition because no data is lost during the decomposition process. After you separate the data into two tables, you can easily bring the data back together by joining the two tables via a query. Figure 6.3 shows the data separated into two tables. These two tables achieve second normal form for two reasons. First, neither table has a composite key—their primary keys now have only a single field (second normal form only applies to tables with a composite primary key). Second, the fields in each table depend on the whole of the primary key rather than on just part of the key.

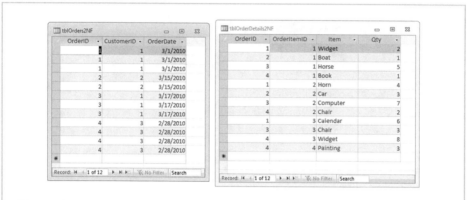

Figure 6.3   *Tables that achieve second normal form.*

Third Normal Form

To attain third normal form, a table must meet all the requirements for first and second normal forms, and all nonkey columns dependent only on the primary key field and not dependent on each other—all the fields are independent of each other. This means that you must eliminate any calculations, and you must break out the data into lookup tables. Lookup tables include tables such as Inventory tables, Course tables, State tables, and any other table where we look up a set of values from which we select the entry that we store in the foreign key field. For example, from our Customer table, we look up within the set of states in the state table to select the state associated with the customer.

An example of a calculation stored in a table is the product of price multiplied by quantity; the extended price is dependent on two other fields in the table—the price and the quantity. If either of those fields is changed, then the extended price would also have to be changed. As with the example in second normal form, there is every possibility of changing one or two of these fields without changing the third one, leading to problems in the application. Instead of storing the result of this calculation in the table, you would generate the calculation in a query or in the control source of a control on a form or a report.

The example in Figure 6.3 does not achieve third normal form because the description of the inventory items is stored in the Order Details table. If the description changes, all rows with that inventory item need to be modified. The Order Details table, shown in Figure 6.4, shows the item descriptions broken into an Inventory table. This design achieves third normal form. We have moved the description of the inventory items to an Inventory table, and ItemID is stored in the Order Details table. All fields are mutually independent. You can modify the description of an inventory item in one place.

Figure 6.4   *A table (on the right) that achieves third normal form.*

Denormalization: Purposely Violating the Rules

Although a developer's goal is normalization, sometimes it makes sense to deviate from normal forms. This process is called *denormalization*. The primary reason for applying denormalization is to enhance performance.

An example of when denormalization might be the preferred tact could involve an open invoices table and a summarized accounting table. It might be impractical to calculate summarized accounting information for a customer when you need it. Instead, you can maintain the summary calculations in a summarized accounting table so that you can easily retrieve them as needed. Although the upside of this scenario is improved performance, the downside is that you must update the summary table whenever you make changes to the open invoices. This imposes a definite trade-off between performance and maintainability. You must decide whether the trade-off is worth it.

If you decide to denormalize, you should document your decision. You should make sure that you make the necessary application adjustments to ensure that you properly maintain the denormalized fields. Finally, you need to test to ensure that the denormalization process actually improves performance.

Integrity Rules

Although integrity rules are not part of normal forms, they are definitely part of the database design process. Integrity rules are broken into two categories: overall integrity rules and database-specific integrity rules.

Overall Integrity Rules

The two types of overall integrity rules are referential integrity rules and entity integrity rules. *Referential integrity rules* dictate that a database does not contain any orphan foreign key values. This means that

- Child rows cannot be added for parent rows that do not exist. In other words, an order cannot be added for a nonexistent customer.

- A primary key value cannot be modified if the value is used as a foreign key in a child table. This means that a CustomerID in the customers table cannot be changed if the Orders table contains rows with that CustomerID.

- A parent row cannot be deleted if child rows have that foreign key value. For example, a customer cannot be deleted if the customer has orders in the Orders table.

Entity integrity dictates that the primary key value cannot be `Null`. This rule applies not only to single-column primary keys, but also to multicolumn primary keys. In fact, in a multicolumn primary key, no field in the primary key can be `Null`. This makes sense because if any part of the primary key can be `Null`, the primary key can no longer act as a unique identifier for the row. Fortunately, the Jet Engine does not allow a field in a primary key to be `Null`.

Database-Specific Integrity Rules

Database-specific integrity rules are not applicable to all databases, but are, instead, dictated by business rules that apply to a specific application. Database-specific rules are as important as overall integrity rules. They ensure that the user enters only valid data into a database. An example of a database-specific integrity rule is requiring the delivery date for an order to fall after the order date.

The Types of Relationships

Three types of relationships can exist between tables in a database: one to many, one to one, and many to many. Setting up the proper type of relationship between two tables in a database is imperative. The right type of relationship between two tables ensures

- Data integrity
- Optimal performance
- Ease of use in designing system objects

The reasons behind these benefits are covered throughout this hour. Before you can understand the benefits of relationships, though, you must understand the types of relationships available.

One-to-Many Relationships

A one-to-many relationship is by far the most common type of relationship. In a *one-to-many relationship*, a record in one table can have many related records in another table. A common example is a relationship set up between a Customers table and an Orders table. For each customer in the Customers table, you want to have more than one order in the Orders table. On the other hand, each order in the Orders table can belong to only one customer. The Customers table is on the "one" side of the relationship, and the Orders table is on the "many" side. For you to implement this relationship, the field joining the two tables on the "one" side of the relationship must be unique.

In the Customers and Orders tables example, the CustomerID field that joins the two tables must be unique within the Customers table. If more than one customer in the Customers table has the same customer ID, it is not clear which customer belongs to an order in the Orders table. For this reason, the field that joins the two tables on the "one" side of the one-to-many relationship must be a primary key or have a unique index. In almost all cases, the field relating the two tables is the primary key of the table on the "one" side of the relationship. The field relating the two tables on the "many" side of the relationship is the foreign key.

One-to-One Relationships

In a one-to-one relationship, each record in the table on the "one" side of the relationship can have only one matching record in the table on the "many" side of the relationship. This relationship is not common and is used only in special circumstances. Usually, if you have set up a one-to-one relationship, you should have combined the fields from both tables into one table. The following are the most common reasons to create a one-to-one relationship:

- The number of fields required for a table exceeds the number of fields allowed in an Access table.
- Several fields in a table are required for only a subset of records in the table.

The maximum number of fields allowed in an Access table is 255. There are very few reasons a table should ever have more than 255 fields. In fact, before you even get close to 255 fields, you should take a close look at the design of the system. On the rare occasion when having more than 255 fields is appropriate, you can simulate a single table by moving some of the fields to a second table and creating a one-to-one relationship between the two tables.

The second situation in which you would want to define one-to-one relationships is when you will use certain fields in a table for only a relatively small subset of records. An example is an Employees table and a Vesting table. Certain fields are required only for employees who are vested. If only a small percentage of a company's employees are vested, it is not efficient, in terms of performance or disk space, to place all the fields containing information about vesting in the Employees table. This is especially true if the vesting information requires a large number of fields. By breaking the information into two tables and creating a one-to-one relationship between the tables, you can reduce disk-space requirements and improve performance. This improvement is particularly pronounced if the Employees table is large.

Many-to-Many Relationships

In a *many-to-many relationship*, records in two tables have matching records. You cannot directly define a many-to-many relationship in Access; you must develop this type of relationship by adding a table called a *junction table*. You relate the junction table to each of the two tables in one-to-many relationships. For example, with an Orders table and a Products table, each order will probably contain multiple products, and each product is likely to be found on many different orders. The solution is to create a third table, called OrderDetails. You relate the OrderDetails table to the Orders table in a one-to-many relationship based on the OrderID field. You relate it to the Products table in a one-to-many relationship based on the ProductID field.

Establishing Relationships in Access

You use the Relationships window to establish relationships between Access tables, as shown in Figure 6.5. To open the Relationships window, you must select Relationships from the Relationships group on the Database Tools tab of the Ribbon. If you have not established any relationships, the Show Table dialog box appears. The Show Table dialog box allows you to add tables to the Relationships window.

By looking at the Relationships window, you can see the types of relationships for each table. All the one-to-many and one-to-one relationships defined in a database are represented with join lines. If you enforce referential integrity between the tables involved in a one-to-many relationship, the join line between the tables

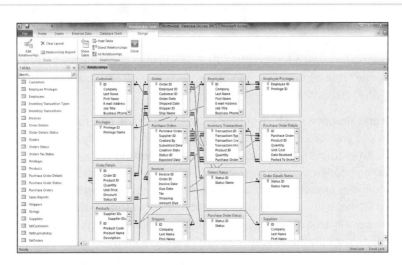

Figure 6.5 *The Relationships window, which enables you to view, add, modify, and remove relationships between tables*

appears with the number 1 on the "one" side of the relationship and with an infinity symbol on the "many" side of the relationship. A one-to-one relationship appears with a 1 on each end of the join line.

LET ME TRY IT

Establish a Relationship Between Two Tables

To establish a relationship between two tables, you follow these steps:

1. Open the Relationships window.

2. If this is the first time that you've opened the Relationships window of a particular database, the Show Table dialog box appears. Select each table you want to relate and click Add.

3. If you have already established relationships in the current database, the Relationships window appears. If the tables you want to include in the relationship do not appear, click the Show Table button in the Relationships group of the Design tab of the Ribbon. To add the desired tables to the Relationships window, select a table and then click Add. Repeat this process for each table you want to add. To select multiple tables at once, press Shift while clicking to select contiguous tables or press Ctrl while clicking to select noncontiguous tables; then click Add. Click Close when you are finished.

4. Click and drag the field from one table to the matching field in the other table. The Edit Relationships dialog box appears.

5. Determine whether you want to establish referential integrity and whether you want to cascade update related fields or cascade delete related records by enabling the appropriate check boxes (see Figure 6.6). These topics are covered later in this chapter, in the section "Establishing Referential Integrity."

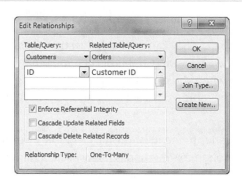

Figure 6.6 *The Edit Relationships dialog box, which enables you to view and modify the relationships between the tables in a database.*

6. Click OK. The dialog closes and you return to the Relationships window.

 SHOW ME Media 6.1—Establishing a Relationship **Between Two Tables**
Access this video file through your registered Web Edition at
my.safaribooksonline.com/9780132117128/media.

Following Guidelines for Establishing Relationships

You must remember a few important things when establishing relationships. If you are not aware of these important gotchas, you could find yourself in some pretty hairy situations:

- It is important to understand the correlation between the Relationships window and the actual relationships established within a database. The Relationships window lets you view and modify the existing relationships. When you establish relationships, Access creates the relationship the moment you click OK. You can delete the tables from the Relationships window (by selecting them and pressing Delete), but the relationships still exist. (The "Modifying an Existing Relationship" section of this chapter covers the process of permanently removing relationships.) The Relationships window provides a visual blueprint of the relationships that are established. If you modify the layout of the window by moving around tables, adding tables to the window, or removing tables from the window, Access prompts you to save the layout after you close the Relationships window. Access is not asking whether you want to save the relationships you have established; it is simply asking whether you want to save the visual layout of the window.

- When you're adding tables to the Relationships window by using the Show Tables dialog box, it is easy to accidentally add a table to the window many times. This is because the tables you are adding can hide behind the Show Tables dialog box, or they can appear below the portion of the Relationships window that you are viewing. If this occurs, you see multiple occurrences of the same table when you close the Show Tables dialog box. Access gives each occurrence of the table a different alias, and you must remove the extra occurrences.

- You can add queries to the Relationships window by using the Show Tables dialog box. Although this method is rarely used, it might be useful if you regularly include the same queries within other queries and want to permanently establish relationships between them.

- If you remove tables from the Relationships window (remember that this does not delete the relationships) and you want to once again show all relationships that exist in the database, you can click All Relationships in the Relationships group on the Design tab of the Ribbon. All existing relationships are then shown.

- To delete a relationship, you can click the join line and press Delete.

Modifying an Existing Relationship

Modifying an existing relationship is easy. Access gives you the capability to delete an existing relationship or to simply modify the nature of the relationship.

 LET ME TRY IT

Delete a Relationship Between Tables

To permanently remove a relationship between two tables, you follow these steps:

1. Click the Relationships button in the Relationships group on the Database Tools tab of the Ribbon.

2. Click the line joining the two tables whose relationship you want to delete.

3. Press Delete. Access prompts you to verify your actions. Click Yes.

 LET ME TRY IT

Modify a Relationship Between Tables

You often need to modify the nature of a relationship rather than remove it. To modify a relationship, you follow these steps:

1. Click the Relationships button in the Relationships group on the Database Tools tab of the Ribbon.

2. Double-click the line joining the two tables whose relationship you want to modify.

3. Make the required changes.

4. Click OK. All the normal rules regarding the establishment of relationships apply.

 SHOW ME   Media 6.2—Modifying Existing Relationships
Access this video file through your registered Web Edition at
my.safaribooksonline.com/9780132117128/media.

Establishing Referential Integrity

As you can see, establishing a relationship is quite easy. Establishing the right kind of relationship is a little more difficult. When you attempt to establish a relationship between two tables, Access makes some decisions based on a few predefined factors:

- Access establishes a one-to-many relationship if one of the related fields is a primary key or has a unique index.

- Access establishes a one-to-one relationship if both of the related fields are primary keys or have unique indexes.

- Access creates an indeterminate relationship if neither of the related fields is a primary key and neither has a unique index. You cannot establish referential integrity in this case.

As discussed earlier in this chapter, *referential integrity* consists of a series of rules that Access applies to ensure that it properly maintains the relationships between tables. At the most basic level, referential integrity rules prevent the creation of orphan records in the table on the "many" side of the one-to-many relationship. After you establish a relationship between a Customers table and an Orders table, for example, all orders in the Orders table must be related to a particular customer in the Customers table. Before you can establish referential integrity between two tables, the following conditions must be met:

- The matching field on the "one" side of the relationship must be a primary key field or must have a unique index.

- The matching fields must have the same data types. (For linking purposes, AutoNumber fields match Long Integer fields.) With the exception of Text fields, the matching fields also must have the same size. Number fields on both sides of the relationship must have the same size (for example, Long Integer).

- Both tables must be part of the same Access database.

- Both tables must be stored in one of the proprietary Access file (MDB or ACCDB) formats. (They cannot be external tables from other sources.)

- The database that contains the two tables must be open.

- Existing data within the two tables cannot violate any referential integrity rules. All orders in the Orders table must relate to existing customers in the Customers table, for example.

Although Text fields involved in a relationship do not have to be the same size, it is prudent to make them the same size. Otherwise, you degrade performance and risk the chance of unpredictable results when you create queries based on the two tables.

After you establish referential integrity between two tables, Access applies the following rules:

- You cannot enter in the foreign key of the related table a value that does not exist in the primary key of the primary table. For example, you cannot enter in the CustomerID field of the Orders table a value that does not exist in the CustomerID field of the Customers table.

- You cannot delete a record from the primary table if corresponding records exist in the related table. For example, you cannot delete a customer from the

Customers table if related records (for example, records with the same value in the CustomerID field) exist in the Orders table.

- You cannot change the value of a primary key on the "one" side of a relationship if corresponding records exist in the related table. For example, you cannot change the value in the CustomerID field of the Customers table if corresponding orders exist in the Orders table.

If you attempt to violate any of these three rules and you have enforced referential integrity between the tables, Access displays an appropriate error message, as shown in Figure 6.7.

Figure 6.7 *An error message that appears when you attempt to delete a customer who has orders.*

When you establish referential integrity in Access, its default behavior is to prohibit the deletion of parent records that have associated child records and to prohibit the change of a primary key value of a parent record when that parent has associated child records. You can override these restrictions by using the Cascade Update Related Fields and Cascade Delete Related Records check boxes that are available in the Relationships dialog box when you establish or modify a relationship.

The Cascade Update Related Fields Option

The Cascade Update Related Fields option is available only if you have established referential integrity between tables. When this option is selected, the user can change the primary key value of the record on the "one" side of the relationship. When the user attempts to modify the field joining the two tables on the "one" side of the relationship, Access cascades the change down to the foreign key field on the "many" side of the relationship. This is useful if the primary key field is modifiable. For example, a purchase number on a purchase order master record might be updateable. If the user modifies the purchase order number of the parent record, you would want to cascade the change to the associated detail records in the purchase order detail table.

It is easy to accidentally introduce a loophole into a system. If you create a one-to-many relationship between two tables but forget to set the `Required` property of the foreign key field to `Yes`, you allow the addition of orphan records. Figure 6.8 illustrates this point. In this example, I added an order to tblOrders without entering a customer ID. This record is an orphan record because no records in `tblCustomers` have `CustomerID` set to `Null`. To eliminate the problem, you set the `Required` property of the foreign key field to `Yes`.

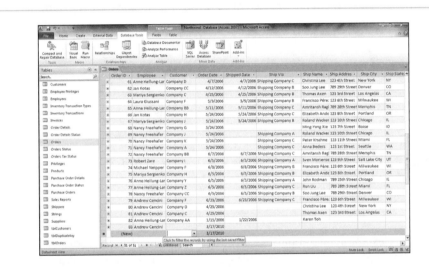

Figure 6.8   *An orphan record with* `Null` *in the foreign key field.*

There is no need to select the Cascade Update Related Fields option when the related field on the "one" side of the relationship is an AutoNumber field. You can never modify an AutoNumber field. The Cascade Update Related Fields option has no effect on AutoNumber fields. In fact, this is why, in the preceding Task, you make the CustomerID a Text field. It provides an example that you can later use with a cascade update.

The Cascade Delete Related Records Option

The Cascade Delete Related Records option is available only if you have established referential integrity between tables. When this option is selected, the user can delete a record on the "one" side of a one-to-many relationship, even if related records exist in the table on the "many" side of the relationship. A user can delete a customer even if the customer has existing orders, for example. The Jet Engine maintains referential integrity between the tables because it automatically deletes all related records in the child table.

If you attempt to delete a record from the table on the "one" side of a one-to-many relationship and no related records exist in the table on the "many" side of the relationship, you get the usual warning message, as shown in Figure 6.9. On the other hand, if you attempt to delete a record from the table on the "one" side of a one-to-many relationship and related records exist in the child table, Access warns you that you are about to delete the record from the parent table and any related records in the child table (see Figure 6.10).

Figure 6.9   *A message that appears after the user attempts to delete a parent record that does not have related child records.*

Figure 6.10   *A message that appears after the user attempts to delete a parent record that has related child records.*

The Cascade Delete Related Records option is not always appropriate. It is an excellent feature, but you should use it prudently. Although it is usually appropriate to cascade delete from an Orders table to an Order Details table, for example, it generally is not appropriate to cascade delete from a Customers table to an Orders table. This is because you generally do not want to delete all your order history from the Orders table if for some reason you want to delete a customer. Deleting the order history causes important information, such as the profit and loss history, to change. It is therefore appropriate to prohibit this type of deletion and handle the customer in some other way, such as marking him or her as inactive or archiving his or her data. On the other hand, if you delete an order because the customer cancelled it, you probably want to remove the corresponding order detail information, too. In this case, the Cascade Delete Related Records option is appropriate. You need to make the most prudent decision in each situation, based on business needs. You need to carefully consider the implications of each option before you make a decision.

SHOW ME   Media 6.3—Working with Cascade Update and Cascade Delete

Access this video file through your registered Web Edition at ***my.safaribooksonline.com/9780132117128/media***.

TELL ME MORE   Media 6.4—The Importance of Relationships

Access this audio recording through your registered Web Edition at ***my.safaribooksonline.com/9780132117128/media***.

Using Access 2010, you can build queries that allow you to view just the data that you need.

7

Enhancing the Queries That You Build

Although tables act as the ultimate foundation for any application you build, queries are very important, too. Most of the forms and reports that act as the user interface for an application are based on queries. Having an understanding of queries—what they are and when and how to use them—is imperative for your success as an Access application developer. In this chapter, you will learn all the basics of working with a query. The chapter covers many topics, including how to add tables to a query, how to add and remove fields, and how to sort on multiple fields. You'll learn how to add formulas to the queries you build, and how to use a tool called the Expression Builder. You'll learn how to build a powerful type of query called a Parameter query. You'll also learn how to run action queries: queries that update data. Finally, you'll learn two important techniques: how to work with aggregate functions, and how to create outer joins.

Everything You Need to Know About Query Basics

Creating a basic query is easy because Microsoft has provided a user-friendly, drag-and-drop interface. To start a new query, select Query Design from the Other group of the Create tab of the Ribbon; the Show Table dialog appears (see Figure 7.1). If you prefer, you can select Query Wizard from the Other group of the Create tab of the Ribbon. In that case the New Query dialog appears, allowing you to select from four predefined query wizards (see Figure 7.2). The Simple Query Wizard walks you through the steps of creating a basic query. The other wizards help you create three specific types of queries: Crosstab, Find Duplicates, and Find Unmatched queries.

Adding Tables to Queries

If you choose to use Design view rather than one of the wizards, the Show Table dialog box appears (refer to Figure 7.1). In this dialog box, you can select the tables or queries that supply data to a query. Access doesn't care whether you select tables or queries as the foundation for queries. You can select a table or query by

double-clicking the name of the table or query you want to add or by single-click-
ing the table and then selecting the Add command button. You can select multiple
tables or queries by holding down the Shift key while you select a contiguous
range of tables or the Ctrl key while you select noncontiguous tables. After you
have selected the tables or queries you want, you click Add and then click Close.
This brings you to the Query Design window, shown in Figure 7.3.

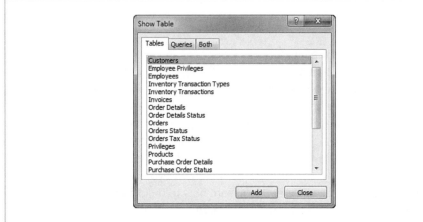

Figure 7.1   *The Show Table dialog box.*

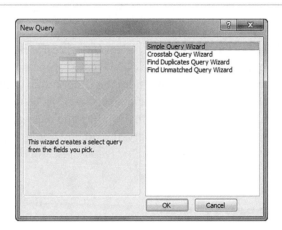

Figure 7.2   *The New Query dialog box.*

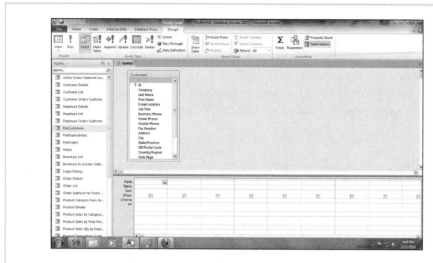

Figure 7.3 *The Query Design window.*

Adding Fields to Queries

After you add tables to a query, you can select the fields you want to include in the query. The query shown in Figure 7.3 is based on the Customers table from the Northwind database that ships with Microsoft Access. Notice that the query window is divided into two sections: The top half of the window shows the tables or queries that underlie the query you're designing, and the bottom half shows any fields that you will include in the query output. You can add a field to the query design grid on the bottom half of the query window in several ways:

- You can double-click the name of the field you want to add.

- You can click and drag a single field from the table in the top half of the query window to the query design grid below.

- You can select multiple fields at the same time by using the Shift key (for a contiguous range of fields) or the Ctrl key (for a noncontiguous range). You can double-click the title bar of the field list to select all fields and then click and drag any one of the selected fields to the query design grid.

SHOW ME Media 7.1—Adding Fields to Queries
Access this video file through your registered Web Edition at
my.safaribooksonline.com/9780132117128/media.

You can double-click the asterisk in the field list to include all fields within the table in the query result. Although this is very handy in that changes to the table structure magically affect the query's output, this "trick" is dangerous. When you select the asterisk, you include all table fields in the query result, whether you need them or not. This can cause major performance problems in a local area network (LAN), wide area network (WAN), or client/server application.

The easiest way to run a query is to click the Run button on the toolbar. (It looks like an exclamation point.) You can click the Query View button to run a query, but this method works only for Select queries, not for Action queries. The Query View button has a special meaning for Action queries (explained in the Action Queries section of this chapter). Clicking Run is preferable because when you do that, you don't have to worry about what type of query you're running. After you run a Select query, you should see what looks like a datasheet that contains only the fields you selected. To return to the query's design, you click the Query View button.

Access 2002 introduced shortcut keys that allow you to easily toggle between the various query views: Ctrl+>, Ctrl+period, Ctrl+<, and Ctrl+comma. Ctrl+> and Ctrl+period take you to the next view; Ctrl+< and Ctrl+comma take you to the previous view.

 **LET ME TRY IT**

Removing a Field from the Query Design Grid

To remove a field from the query design grid, follow these steps:

1. Find the field you want to remove.

2. Click the column selector (that is, the small horizontal gray button) immediately above the name of the field. The entire column of the query design grid should become black (see Figure 7.4).

3. Press the Delete key or select Delete from the Edit menu. Access removes the field from the query.

Figure 7.4 *Removing a field from the query design grid.*

Inserting a Field After a Query Is Built

The process for inserting a field after you have built a query depends on where you want to insert the new field. If you want to insert it after the existing fields, it's easiest to double-click the name of the field you want to add. If you prefer to insert the new field between two existing fields, it's best to click and drag the field you want to add and drop it onto the field you want to appear to the right of the inserted field.

LET ME TRY IT

Moving a Field to a Different Location on the Query Design Grid

Although the user can move a column while in a query's Datasheet view, sometimes you want to permanently alter the position of a field in the query output. You can do this as a convenience to the user or, more importantly, to use the query as a foundation for forms and reports. The order of the fields in the query becomes the default order of the fields on any forms and reports you build by using any of the wizards. You can save yourself quite a bit of time by ordering queries effectively.

To move a single column, follow these steps:

1. Select a column while in the query's Design view by clicking its column selector.

2. Click the selected column a second time, and then drag it to a new location on the query design grid.

LET ME TRY IT

Move More Than One Column

Follow these steps to move more than one column at a time:

1. Drag across the column selectors of the columns you want to move.

2. Click any of the selected columns a second time, and then drag them to a new location on the query design grid.

Moving a column in Datasheet view doesn't modify the query's underlying design. If you move a column in Datasheet view, subsequent reordering in Design view isn't reflected in Datasheet view. In other words, Design view and Datasheet view are no longer synchronized, and you must reorder both manually. This actually serves as an advantage in most cases. As you will learn later in this chapter, if you want to sort by the Country field and then by the CompanyName field, the Country field must appear to the left of the CompanyName field in the design of the query. If you want the CompanyName field to appear to the left of the Country field in the query's result, you must make that change in Datasheet view. The fact that Access maintains the order of the columns separately in both views allows you to easily accomplish both objectives.

SHOW ME   Media 7.2—Moving Fields on the Query Grid
Access this video file through your registered Web Edition at
my.safaribooksonline.com/9780132117128/media.

Saving and Naming Queries

To save a query at any time, you can click the Save button on the toolbar. If the query is a new one, Access prompts you to name the query.

Access supplies default names for the queries that you create (for example, Query1, Query2). I suggest that you supply a more descriptive name. A query name should begin with *qry* so that you can easily recognize and identify it as a query.

It's important to understand that when you save a query, you're saving only the query's definition, not the actual query result.

Ordering Query Results

When you run a new query, the query output appears in no particular order. Generally, however, you want to order query output. You can do this by using the Sort row of the query design grid.

 **LET ME TRY IT**

Order Results of a Query

To order the results of a query, follow these steps:

1. In Design view, click within the query design grid in the Sort cell of the column you want to sort by (see Figure 7.5).

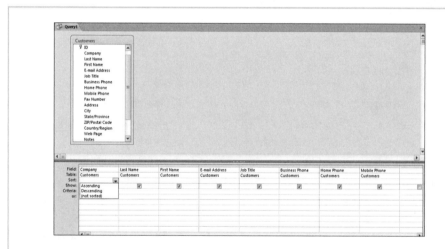

Figure 7.5 *Changing the order of query results.*

2. Use the drop-down combo box to select an ascending or descending sort. Ascending or Descending appears in the sort cell for the field, as appropriate.

Sorting by More Than One Field

You might often want to sort query output by more than one field. The columns you want to sort must be placed in order, from left to right, on the query design grid, with the column you want to act as the primary sort on the far left and the secondary, tertiary, and any additional sorts following to the right. If you want the columns to appear in a different order in the query output, you must move them manually in Datasheet view after you run the query.

SHOW ME   **Media 7.3—Ordering Query Results**
Access this video file through your registered Web Edition at
my.safaribooksonline.com/9780132117128/media.

Refining a Query by Using Criteria

So far in this chapter, you have learned how to select the fields you want and how to indicate the sort order for query output. One of the important features of queries is the ability to limit output by using selection criteria. Access allows you to combine criteria by using several operators to specify the criteria for multiple fields. Table 7.1 covers the operators and their meanings.

Table 7.1   Access Operators

Operator	Meaning	Example	Result of Example
=	Equal to.	=`"Sales"`	Finds only records with `"Sales"` as the field value.
<	Less than.	`<100`	Finds all records with values less than 100 in that field.
<=	Less than or equal to.	`<=100`	Finds all records with values less than or equal to 100 in that field.
>	Greater than.	`>100`	Finds all records with values greater than 100 in that field.
>=	Greater than or equal to.	`>=100`	Finds all records with values greater than or equal to 100 in that field.
<>	Not equal to.	`<>"Sales"`	Finds all records with values other than Sales in the field.
And	Both conditions must be true.	Created by adding criteria on the same line of the query design grid to more than one field	Finds all records where the conditions in both fields are true.
Or	Either condition can be true.	`"CA" or "NY" or "UT"`	Finds all records with the value `"CA"`, `"NY"`, or `"UT"` in the field.

Like	Compares a string expression to a pattern.	Like"Sales*"	Finds all records with the value "Sales" at the beginning of the field. (The asterisk is a wildcard character.)
Between	Finds a range of values.	Between 5 and 10	Finds all records with the values 5-10 (inclusive) in the field.
In	Same as Or.	In("CA","NY","UT")	Finds all records with the value "CA", "NY", or "UT" in the field.
Not	Same as <>.	Not "Sales"	Finds all records with values other than Sales in the field.
Is Null	Finds nulls	Is Null	Finds all records where no data has been entered in the field.
Is Not Null	Finds all records that are not null	Is Not Null	Finds all records where data has been entered into the field.

Criteria entered for two fields on a single line of the query design grid are considered an And condition, which means that both conditions need to be true for the record to appear in the query output. Entries made on separate lines of the query design grid are considered an Or condition, which means that either condition can be true for Access to include the record in the query output. Take a look at the example in Figure 7.6; this query would output all records in which the Job Title field begins with either Accounting or Purchasing, regardless of the customer ID.

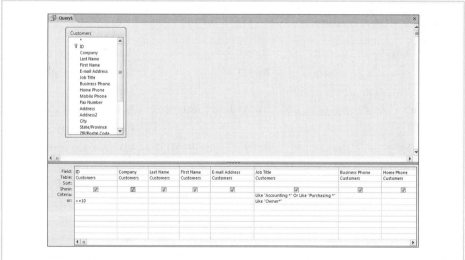

Figure 7.6 *Adding* And *and* Or *conditions to a query.*

It outputs the records in which the Job Title field begins with Owner only for the customers whose IDs are greater than or equal to 10. Notice that the word *Owner* is immediately followed by the asterisk. This means that customer would be included in the output. On the other hand, *Accounting* and *Purchasing* are both followed by spaces. That means that only entries that begin with Marketing or Owner followed by a space are included in the output.

Working with Dates in Criteria

Access gives you significant power for adding date functions and expressions to query criteria. Using these criteria, you can find all records in a certain month, on a specific weekday, or between two dates. Table 7.2 lists the date criteria expressions and examples.

The `Weekday(Date, [FirstDayOfWeek])` function works based on your locale and how your system defines the first day of the week. `Weekday()` used without the optional `FirstDayOfWeek` argument defaults to `vbSunday` as the first day. A value of `0` defaults `FirstDayOfWeek` to the system definition. Other values can be set, too.

Figure 7.7 illustrates the use of a date function. Notice that `DatePart("q",[Order Date])` is entered as the expression, and the value `2` is entered for the criterion. `Year([Order Date])]` is entered as another expression, with the number `2006` as the criterion. Therefore, this query outputs all records in which the order date is in the second quarter of 2006.

Table 7.2 Date Criteria Expressions

Expression	Meaning	Example	Result
`Date()`	Current date	`Date()`	Records the current date within a field.
`Day(Date)`	The day of a date	`Day ([OrderDate])=1`	Records the order date on the first day of the month.
`Month(Date)`	The month of a date	`Month ([OrderDate])=1`	Records the order date in January.
`Year(Date)`	The year of a date	`Year ([OrderDate])=1991`	Records the order date in 1991.
`Weekday(Date)`	The weekday of a date	`Weekday ([OrderDate])=2`	Records the order date on a Monday.
`Between Date And Date`	A range of dates	`Between #1/1/95# and #12/31/95#`	Finds all records in 1995.
`DatePart(Interval, Date)`	A specific part of a date	`DatePart ("q",[OrderDate])=2`	Finds all records in the second quarter.

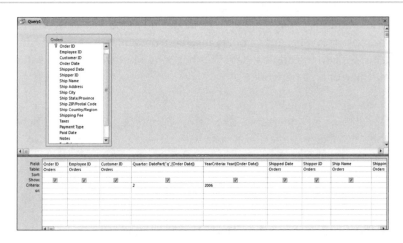

Figure 7.7   *Using the* `DatePart()` *and* `Year()` *functions in a query.*

 SHOW ME   Media 7.4—Refining a Query with Criteria
Access this video file through your registered Web Edition at
my.safaribooksonline.com/9780132117128/media.

Updating Query Results

If you haven't realized it yet, you can usually update the results of a query. This means that if you modify the data in the query output, Access permanently modifies the data in the tables underlying the query.

 LET ME TRY IT

Update Results of a Query

To see how this works, follow these steps:

1. Build a query based on the Customers table.

2. Add the ID, Company, Address, City, and State/Province fields to the query design grid and then run the query.

3. Change the address of a particular customer and make a note of the ID of the customer whose address you changed. Make sure you move off the record so that Access writes the change to disk.

4. Close the query, open the actual table in Datasheet view, and find the record whose address you modified. The change you made was written to the original table; this is because a query result is a dynamic set of records that maintains a link to the original data. This happens whether you're on a standalone machine or on a network.

It's essential that you understand how Access updates query results; otherwise, you might mistakenly update table data without realizing you've done so. Updating multitable queries is covered later in this chapter, in the section "Pitfalls of Multitable Queries."

SHOW ME   Media 7.5—Updating Query Results

Access this video file through your registered Web Edition at **my.safaribooksonline.com/9780132117128/media.**

Building Queries Based on Multiple Tables

If you have properly normalized your table data, you probably want to bring the data from your tables back together by using queries. Fortunately, you can do this quite easily by using Access queries.

The query in Figure 7.8 joins the Customers, Orders, and Order Details tables, pulling fields from each. Notice in the figure that I have selected the ID and Company fields from the Customers table, the Order ID and Order Date fields from the Orders table, and the Unit Price and Quantity fields from the Order Details table. After you run this query, you should see the results shown in Figure 7.9. Notice that you get a record in the query's result for every record in the Order Details table. In other words, there are 68 records in the Order Details table, and that's how many records appear in the query output. By creating a multitable query, you can look at data from related tables, along with the data from the Order Details table.

Chapter 6, "Relating the Information in Your Database," discusses how setting up the right type of relationship ensures ease of use in designing system objects. By setting up relationships between tables in a database, Access knows how to properly join them in the queries that you build.

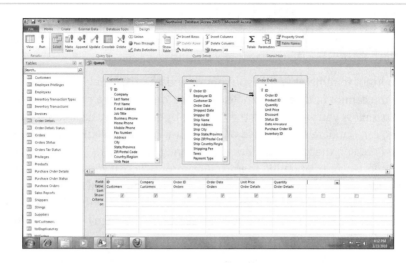

Figure 7.8   *A query joining the Customers, Orders, and Order Details tables.*

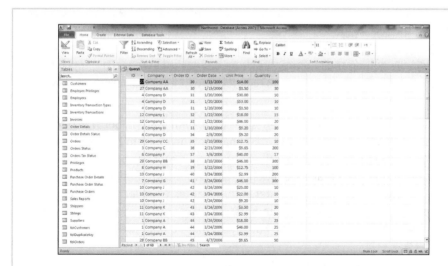

Figure 7.9   *The results of querying multiple tables.*

To remove a table from a query, you click anywhere on the table in the top half of the query design grid and then press the Delete key. You can add tables to the query at any time by clicking the Show Table button on the toolbar. If you prefer, you can select the Database window and then click and drag tables directly from the Database window to the top half of the query design grid.

Pitfalls of Multitable Queries

You should be aware of some pitfalls of multitable queries: They involve updating and which records you see in the query output.

It's important to remember that you cannot update certain fields in a multitable query. You cannot update the join fields on the "one" side of a one-to-many relationship (unless you've activated the Cascade Update Referential Integrity feature). You also can't update the join field on the "many" side of a relationship after you've updated data on the "one" side. More importantly, which fields you *can* update, and the consequences of updating them, might surprise you. If you update the fields on the "one" side of a one-to-many relationship, you must be aware of that change's impact. You're actually updating that record in the original table on the "one" side of the relationship, and several records on the "many" side of the relationship may be affected.

For example, Figure 7.10 shows the result of a query based on the Customers, Orders, and Order Details tables. I have changed Company D to InfoTech Services Group on a specific record of the query output. You might expect this change to affect only that specific order detail item. However, pressing the down-arrow key to move off the record shows that all records associated with Company D are changed (see Figure 7.11). This happens because all the orders for Company D were actually getting their information from one record in the Customers table— the record for ID 12—and that is the record I modified while viewing the query result.

The second pitfall of multitable queries has to do with figuring out which records result from a multitable query. So far, you have learned how to build only inner joins. You need to understand that the query output contains only customers who have orders and orders that have order details. This means that not all the customers or orders might be listed. Later in this chapter, you'll learn how to build queries in which you can list all customers, regardless of whether they have orders. You'll also learn how to list only the customers that do not have orders.

AutoLookup in Multitable Queries

The AutoLookup feature is automatically available in Access. As you fill in key values on the "many" side of a one-to-many relationship in a multitable query, Access automatically looks up the non-key values in the parent table. Most database developers refer to this as *enforced referential integrity*. A foreign key must first exist on the "one" side of the query to be entered successfully on the "many" side. As you can imagine, you don't want to be able to add to a database an order for a nonexistent customer.

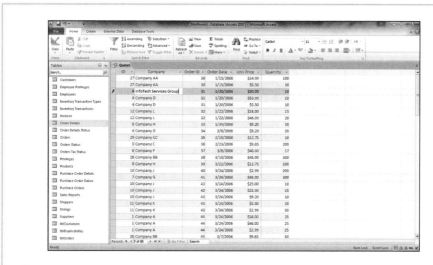

Figure 7.10   *Changing a record on the "one" side of a one-to-many relationship.*

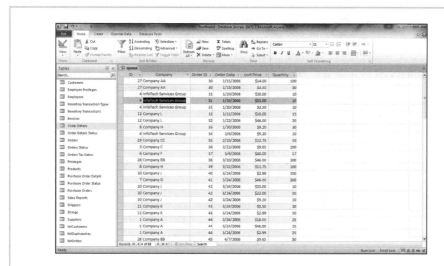

Figure 7.11   *The result of changing a record on the "one" side of a one-to-many relationship.*

For example, I have based the query in Figure 7.12 on the Customers and Orders tables. The fields included in the query are CustomerID from the Orders table; Company, Address, and City from the Customers table; and Order ID and Order Date from the Orders table. If you change the CustomerID field associated with an order, Access looks up the Company, Address, and City fields from the Customers table and immediately displays them in the query result.

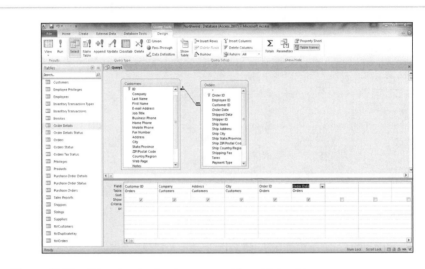

Figure 7.12 *Using AutoLookup in a query with multiple tables.*

Notice in Figure 7.13 how the information for Company F is displayed in the query result. Figure 7.14 shows that the Company and Address fields change automatically when the Customer field is changed to Company C. Don't be confused by the combo box used to select the customer ID. The presence of the combo box within the query is a result of Access's Lookup feature. The customer ID associated with a particular order is actually being modified in the query. If you add a new record to the query, Access fills in the customer information as soon as you select the customer ID associated with the order.

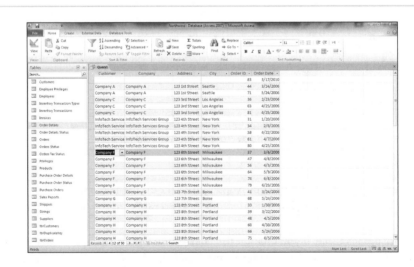

Figure 7.13 *A query result before another customer ID is selected.*

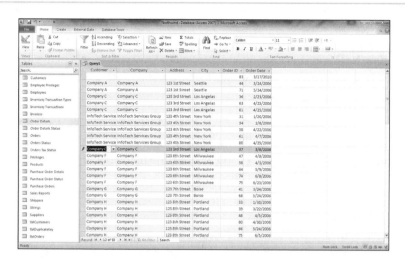

Figure 7.14 *The result of an autolookup after the customer ID is changed.*

SHOW ME   Media 7.6—AutoLookup in Multitable Queries
Access this video file through your registered Web Edition at
my.safaribooksonline.com/9780132117128/media.

Creating Calculated Fields

One of the rules of data normalization is that you shouldn't include the results of calculations in a database. You can output the results of calculations by building those calculations into queries, and you can display the results of the calculations on forms and reports by making the query the foundation for a form or report. You can also add to forms and reports controls that contain the calculations you want. In certain cases, this can improve performance.

The columns of a query result can hold the result of any valid expression. This makes queries extremely powerful. For example, you could enter the following expression:

```
Left([First Name],1) & "." & Left([Last Name],1) & "."
```

This expression would give you the first character of the first name, followed by a period, the first character of the last name, and another period. An even simpler expression would be this one:

```
[Unit Price]*[Quantity]
```

This calculation would simply multiply the Unit Price field by the Quantity field. In both cases, Access would automatically name the resulting expression. For example, Figure 7.15 shows the calculation that results from concatenating the first and last initials. Notice in the figure that Access gives the expression a name (often referred to as an *alias*). To give the expression a name, such as Initials, you must enter it as follows:

```
Initials:Left([First Name],1) & "." & Left([Last Name],1) & "."
```

The text preceding the colon is the name of the expression—in this case, Initials. If you don't explicitly give an expression a name, the name defaults to Expr1.

You can enter any valid expression in the Field row of the query design grid. Notice that Access automatically surrounds field names that are included in an expression with square brackets, unless the field name has spaces. If the field name includes any spaces, you must enclose the field name in brackets; otherwise, the query won't run properly. This is just one of the many reasons field and table names shouldn't contain spaces.

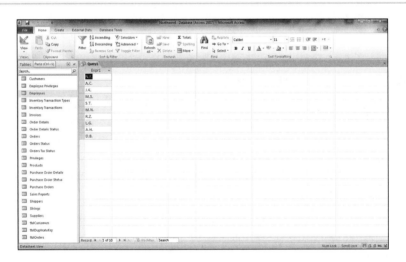

Figure 7.15   *The result of using the expression* `Left([First Name],1) & "." & Left([Last Name],1) & "."` *in a query.*

Getting Help from the Expression Builder

The Expression Builder is a helpful tool for building expressions in queries and in many other situations in Access. To invoke the Expression Builder, you click the Field cell of the query design grid and then click Build on the toolbar. The Expression Builder appears (see Figure 7.16). Notice that the Expression Builder is divided into three columns. The left-hand column shows the objects in the database. After you select an element in the left column, select the elements you want to paste from the middle and right columns.

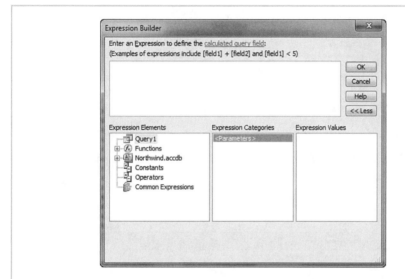

Figure 7.16   *The Expression Builder.*

The example in Figure 7.17 shows Functions selected in the left column. Within Functions, both user-defined and built-in functions are listed. Here, the Functions object is expanded with Built-In Functions selected. In the center column, Date/Time is selected. After you select Date/Time, all the built-in date and time functions appear in the right column. If you double-click a particular function—in this case, the DatePart function—Access places the function and its parameters in the text box at the top of the Expression Builder window. Notice that the DatePart function has four parameters: Interval, Date, FirstWeekday, and FirstWeek. If you know what needs to go into each of these parameters, you can simply replace the parameter placeholders with your own values. If you need more information, you can invoke Help on the selected function to learn more about the required parameters. Figure 7.18 shows two parameters filled in: the interval and the name of the field being evaluated. After you click OK, Access places the expression in the Field cell of the query.

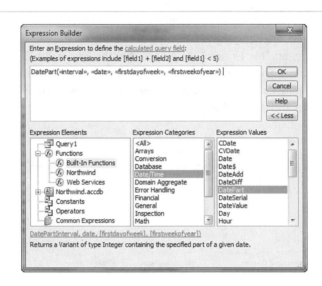

Figure 7.17   *The Expression Builder with the* DatePart *function selected and pasted in the expression box.*

Figure 7.18   *A function pasted by the Expression Builder, with the parameters updated with appropriate values.*

SHOW ME Media 7.7—Creating Calculated Fields within the
Expression Builder
Access this video file through your registered Web Edition at
my.safaribooksonline.com/9780132117128/media.

Creating and Running Parameter Queries

You might not always know the parameters for the query output when you're
designing a query—and your application's users also might not know the parameters. *Parameter queries* let you specify specific criteria at runtime so that you don't
have to modify the query each time you want to change the criteria.

For example, imagine you have a query, like the one shown in Figure 7.19, for
which you want users to specify the date range they want to view each time they
run the query. You have entered the following clause as the criterion for the Order
Date field:

```
Between [Enter Starting Date] And [Enter Ending Date]
```

This criterion causes two dialog boxes to appear when the user runs the query. The
first one, shown in Figure 7.20, prompts the user with the text in the first set of
brackets. Access substitutes the text the user types for the bracketed text. A second
dialog box appears, prompting the user for whatever is in the second set of brackets. Access uses the user's responses as criteria for the query.

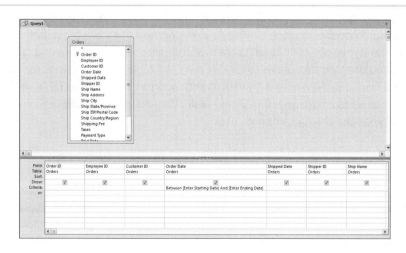

Figure 7.19 *A Parameter query that prompts for a starting date and an ending date.*

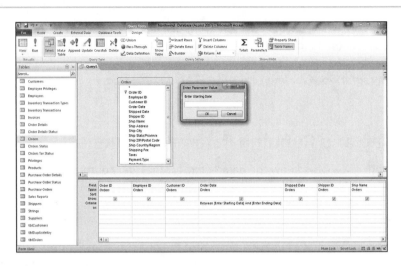

Figure 7.20   *A dialog box that appears when a Parameter query is run.*

SHOW ME   Media 7.8—Creating and Running Parameter Queries
Access this video file through your registered Web Edition at
my.safaribooksonline.com/9780132117128/media.

Creating and Running Action Queries

With Action queries, you can easily modify data without writing any code. In fact, using Action queries is often a more efficient method of modifying data than using code. Four types of Action queries are available: Update, Delete, Append, and Make Table. You use Update queries to modify data in a table, Delete queries to remove records from a table, Append queries to add records to an existing table, and Make Table queries to create an entirely new table. The sections that follow explain these query types and their appropriate uses.

Creating and Running Update Queries

You use Update queries to modify all records or any records that meet specific criteria. You can use an Update query to modify the data in one field or several fields (or even tables) at one time. For example, you could create a query that increases the salary of everyone in California by 10%. As mentioned previously, using Action queries, including Update queries, is usually more efficient than performing the same task with Visual Basic for Applications (VBA) code, so you can consider Update queries a respectable way to modify table data.

LET ME TRY IT

Build an Update Query

To build an Update query, follow these steps:

1. Select Query Design from the Queries group on the Create tab of the Ribbon. The Show Table dialog box appears.

2. In the Show Table dialog box, select the tables or queries that will participate in the Update query and click Add. Click Close when you're ready to continue.

3. To let Access know you're building an Update query, select Update from the Query Type group on the Design tab of the Ribbon.

4. Add to the query fields that either you will use for criteria or Access will update as a result of the query. In Figure 7.21, `Ship State/Province` is included on the query grid because we will use it as a criterion for the update. `Shipping Fee` is included because it's the field that Access will update.

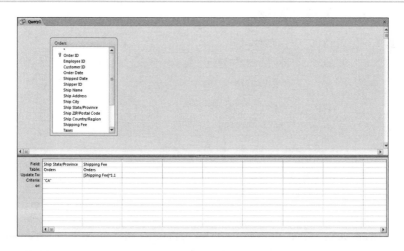

Figure 7.21 *An Update query that increases* `DefaultRate` *for all clients in California.*

5. Add any further criteria, if you want. In Figure 7.21, the criterion for `Ship State/Province` is `CA`.

6. Add the appropriate Update expression. The example illustrated in Figure 7.21 increases `DefaultRate` by 10%.

7. Click Run in the Results group on the Design tab of the Ribbon. The message box shown in Figure 7.22 appears. Click Yes to continue. Access updates all records that meet the selected criteria.

Figure 7.22   *The confirmation message you see when you run an Update query.*

You should name Access Update queries with the prefix *qupd*. In fact, you should give each type of Action query a prefix indicating what type of query it is. This makes your application easier to maintain, and makes your code more readable, and renders your code self-documenting. Table 7.3 lists all the commonly accepted prefixes for Action queries.

Table 7.3   Naming Prefixes for Action Queries

Type of Query	Prefix	Example
Update	*qupd*	`qupdDefaultRate`
Delete	*qdel*	`qdelOldTimeCards`
Append	*qapp*	`qappArchiveTimeCards`
Make Table	*qmak*	`qmakTempSales`

Access displays each type of Action query in the Navigation Pane with a distinctive icon.

Access stores all queries as Structured Query Language (SQL) statements. You can display the SQL for a query by selecting SQL View from the View drop-down list on the toolbar. The SQL behind an Access Update query looks like this:

```
UPDATE tblClients SET tblClients._
    DefaultRate = [DefaultRate]*1.1
    WHERE (((tblClients.StateProvince)="CA"));
```

You cannot reverse the actions taken by an Update query or by any Action queries. You must therefore exercise extreme caution when running any Action query.

Creating and Running Delete Queries

Rather than just modify table data, Delete queries permanently remove from a table any records that meet specific criteria; they're often used to remove old records. You might want to use a Delete query to delete all orders from the previous year, for example.

It's important to remember that if you have turned on the Cascade Update Related Fields Referential Integrity setting and the Update query tries to modify a primary key field, Access updates the foreign key of each corresponding record in related tables. If you have not turned on the Cascade Update Related Fields setting and you have enforced referential integrity, the Update query doesn't allow you to modify the offending records.

 LET ME TRY IT

Build a Delete Query

To build a Delete query, follow these steps:

1. While in a query's Design view, select Delete from the Query Type group on the Design tab of the Ribbon.

2. Add to the query grid the criteria you want. The query shown in Figure 7.23 deletes all orders with a Status ID of 3 (closed).

Figure 7.23 *A Delete query that is used to delete all time cards entered more than a year ago.*

3. Click Run in the Results group on the Design tab of the Ribbon. The message box shown in Figure 7.24 appears.

Figure 7.24   *The Delete query confirmation message box.*

4. Click Yes to permanently remove the records from the table.

The SQL behind a Delete query looks like this:

```
DELETE tblTimeCards.DateEntered
    FROM tblTimeCards
    WHERE (((tblTimeCards.DateEntered)<Date()-365));
```

It's often useful to view the results of an Action query before you actually affect the records included in the criteria. To view the records affected by an Action query, you click the View button in the Results group on the Design tab of the Ribbon before you select Run. All records that will be affected by the Action query appear in Datasheet view. If necessary, you can temporarily add key fields to the query to get more information about the records that are about to be affected.

Remember that if you turn on the Cascade Delete Related Records Referential Integrity setting, Access deletes all corresponding records in related tables. If you do not turn on the Cascade Delete Related Records setting and you do enforce referential integrity, the Delete query doesn't allow you to delete the offending records. If you want to delete the records on the "one" side of the relationship, first you need to delete all the related records on the "many" side.

Creating and Running Append Queries

You can use Append queries to add records to existing tables. You often perform this function during an archive process. First, you append to the history table the records that need to be archived by using an Append query. Next, you remove the records from the master table by using a Delete query.

 LET ME TRY IT

Build an Append Query

To build an Append query, follow these steps:

1. While in Design view of a query, select Append from the Query Type group on the Design tab of the Ribbon. The dialog box shown in Figure 7.25 appears.

Figure 7.25 *The dialog box in which you identify the table to which data will be appended and the database containing that table.*

2. Select the table to which you want Access to append the data.

3. Drag all the fields whose data you want included in the second table to the query grid. If the field names in the two tables match, Access automatically matches the field names in the source table to the corresponding field names in the destination table (see Figure 7.26). If the field names in the two tables don't match, you need to explicitly designate which fields in the source table match which fields in the destination table.

4. Enter any criteria in the query grid. Notice in Figure 7.26 that the example appends to the destination table all records with an order date before 2/1/2006.

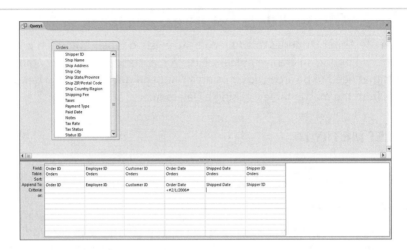

Figure 7.26 *An Append query that appends to another table the Order ID, Employee ID, Customer ID, Order Date, Shipped Date, and Shipper ID of each order with an order date prior to 2/1/2006.*

5. To run the query, click Run in the Results group on the Design tab of the Ribbon. The message box shown in Figure 7.27 appears.

Figure 7.27 *The Append query confirmation message box.*

6. Click Yes to finish the process.

The SQL behind an Append query looks like this:

```
INSERT INTO tblTimeCardsArchive ( TimeCardID, EmployeeID, DateEntered )
    SELECT tblTimeCards.TimeCardID, tblTimeCards.EmployeeID,
    tblTimeCards.DateEntered
    FROM tblTimeCards
    WHERE (((tblTimeCards.DateEntered) Between #1/1/95# And #12/31/95#));
```

Append queries don't allow you to introduce any primary key violations. If you're appending any records that duplicate a primary key value, the message box shown in Figure 7.28 appears. If you go ahead with the append process, Access appends to the destination table only records without primary key violations.

Figure 7.28 *The warning message you see when an Append query and conversion, primary key, lock, or validation rule violation occurs.*

Creating and Running Make Table Queries

Whereas an Append query adds records to an existing table, a Make Table query creates a new table, which is often a temporary table used for intermediary processing. You might want to create a temporary table, for example, to freeze data while you are running a report. By building temporary tables and running a report from those tables, you make sure users can't modify the data underlying the report during the reporting process. Another common use of a Make Table query is to supply a subset of fields or records to another user.

 **LET ME TRY IT**

Build a Make Table Query

To build a Make Table query, follow these steps:

1. While in the query's Design view, select Make Table from the Query Type group on the Design tab of the Ribbon. The dialog box shown in Figure 7.29 appears.

2. Enter the name of the new table and click OK.

3. Move all the fields you want included in the new table to the query grid (see Figure 7.30). You will often include the result of an expression in the new table.

4. Add to the query the criteria you want.

5. Click Run on the toolbar to run the query. The message shown in Figure 7.31 appears.

6. Click Yes to finish the process.

Figure 7.29   *The dialog box in which you enter a name for a new table and selecting which database to place it in.*

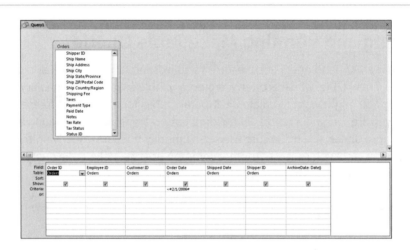

Figure 7.30   *Adding an expression to a Make Table query.*

Figure 7.31   *The Make Table query confirmation message box.*

If you try to run the same Make Table query more than one time, Access permanently deletes the table with the same name as the table you're creating. (See the warning message in Figure 7.32.)

Figure 7.32   *The Make Table query warning message that is displayed when an existing table already has the same name as the table to be created.*

The SQL for a Make Table query looks like this:

```
SELECT tblTimeCards.TimeCardID, tblTimeCards.EmployeeID,
     tblTimeCards.DateEntered, [DateEntered]+365 AS ArchiveDate
     INTO tblOldTimeCards
     FROM tblTimeCards
     WHERE (((tblTimeCards.TimeCardID) Between 1 And 10));
```

 SHOW ME   **Media 7.9—Creating and Running Action Queries**
Access this video file through your registered Web Edition at
my.safaribooksonline.com/9780132117128/media.

Using Aggregate Functions to Summarize Numeric Data

By using aggregate functions, you can easily summarize numeric data. You can use aggregate functions to calculate the sum, average, count, minimum, maximum, and other types of summary calculations for the data in a query result. These queries let you calculate one value for all the records in a query result or group the calculations as desired. For example, you could determine the total sales for every record in the query result, as shown in Figure 7.33, or you could output the total sales by ship country/region and ship city, as shown in Figure 7.34. You could also calculate the total, average, minimum, and maximum sales amounts for all customers in the United States. The possibilities are endless.

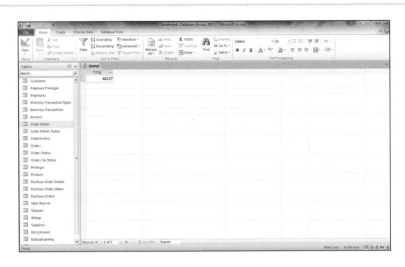

Figure 7.33 *Total sales for every record in a query result.*

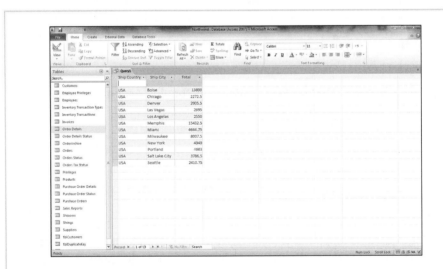

Figure 7.34 *Total sales by* Ship Country/Region *and* Ship City.

LET ME TRY IT

Creating Totals Queries

To create a Totals query, follow these steps:

1. Add to the query grid the fields or expressions you want to summarize. It's important that you add the fields in the order in which you want them grouped. For example, Figure 7.35 shows a query grouped by country and then by city.

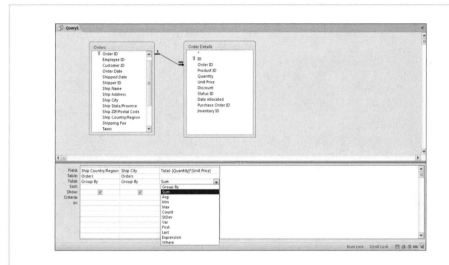

Figure 7.35   *Selecting from a drop-down list the type of calculation for the Total row.*

2. Click Totals in the Show/Hide group on the Design tab of the Ribbon to add a Total row to the query. By default, each field in the query has Group By in the Total row.

3. Click the Total row on the design grid.

4. Open the combo box and choose the calculation you want, as shown in Figure 7.35.

5. Leave Group By in the Total row for any field you want to group by, as shown in Figure 7.35. Remember to place the fields in the order in which you want them grouped. For example, if you want the records grouped by

country and then by sales representative, you must place the Country field to the left of the Sales Representative field on the query grid. On the other hand, if you want records grouped by sales representative and then by country, you must place the Sales Representative field to the left of the Country field on the query grid.

6. Add to the query the criteria you want.

Figure 7.36 shows the design of a query that finds the total, minimum, maximum, and average sales by country and city; Figure 7.37 shows the results of running the query. As you can see, aggregate functions can give you valuable information.

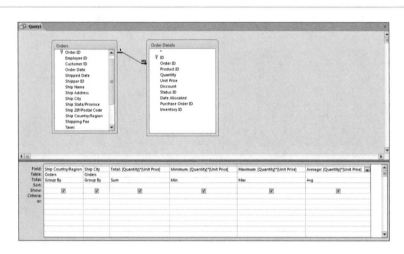

Figure 7.36   *A query that finds the total, minimum, maximum, and average sales by country and city.*

If you save this query and reopen it, you should see that Access has made some changes to its design. Access changes the Total cell for Sum to Expression, and it changes the Field cell to the following:

```
Total: Sum([Unit Price]*[Quantity])
```

If you look at the Total cell for Avg, you should see that Access changes it to Expression. Access changes the Field cell to the following:

```
Average: Avg([Unit Price]*[Quantity])
```

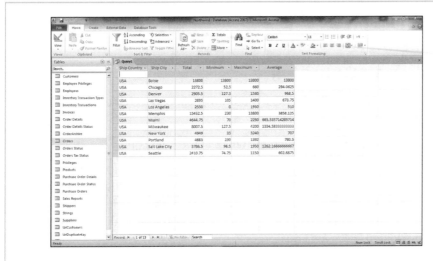

Figure 7.37   *The result of running a query that has many aggregate functions.*

Access modifies the query in this way when it determines that you're using an aggregate function on an expression that has more than one field. You can enter the expression either way. Access stores and resolves the expression as noted.

SHOW ME   Media 7.10—Using Aggregate Functions to Summarize Data

Access this video file through your registered Web Edition at ***my.safaribooksonline.com/9780132117128/media.***

Working with Outer Joins

Outer joins are used when you want the records on the one side of a one-to-many relationship to be included in the query result, regardless of whether there are matching records in the table on the many side. With a Customers table and an Orders table, for example, users often want to include only customers with orders in the query output. An *inner join* (the default join type) does this. In other situations, users want all customers to be included in the query result, regardless of whether they have orders. This is when an outer join is necessary.

LET ME TRY IT

Establish an Outer Join

To establish an outer join, you must modify the join between the tables included in the query:

1. Double-click the line joining the tables in the query grid.

2. The Join Properties window appears (see Figure 7.38). Select the type of join you want to create. To create an outer join between the tables, select Option 2 or Option 3. Notice in Figure 7.38 that the description is Include All Records from Orders and Only Those Records from Order Details Where the Joined Fields Are Equal.

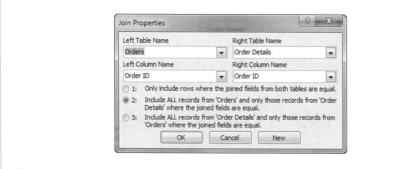

Figure 7.38 *Establishing a left outer join.*

3. Click OK to accept the join. An outer join should be established between the tables. Notice that the line joining the two tables now has an arrow pointing to the many side of the join.

The SQL statement produced when this change is made looks like this:

```
SELECT Customers.CustomerID, Customers.CompanyName
FROM Customers
LEFT JOIN Orders ON Customers.CustomerID = Orders.CustomerID;
```

You can use an outer join to identify all the records on the one side of a join that don't have any corresponding records on the many side. To do this, simply enter

Is Null as the criteria for any required field on the many side of the join. A common solution is to place the criteria on the foreign key field. In the query shown in Figure 7.39, only customers without orders are displayed in the query result.

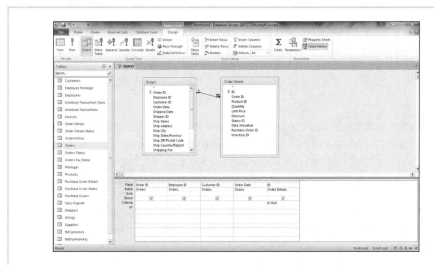

Figure 7.39   *A query showing orders without order details.*

 SHOW ME   Media 7.11—Working with Outer Joins
Access this video file through your registered Web Edition at
my.safaribooksonline.com/9780132117128/media.

 TELL ME MORE   Media 7.12—Building Queries Based on Multiple
Tables
Access this audio recording through your registered Web Edition at
my.safaribooksonline.com/9780132117128/media.

When building forms in Access 2010, you must be familiar with many important techniques.

8

Building Powerful Forms

Forms allow you to display the information stored in your database. In Chapter 3, "Using Forms to Enter and Edit Table Data," you learned the basics of working with forms. Here we expand on your knowledge quite a bit. We begin by working with controls. You then learn about conditional formatting where Access displays data in a control differently depending on the value associated with the control. Next we cover how to customize the behavior of both forms and controls using form and control properties. You learn how to work with combo boxes and how to generate macros with the Command Button Wizard. Finally, you learn how to build forms based on data stored in more than one table.

Power Control Techniques

To work with a form effectively, you must first learn how to manipulate its controls. The sections that follow cover the processes of adding controls to a form, and then selecting, moving, sizing, deleting, and aligning those controls. The text also includes the process of changing control properties and changing the tab order of the controls on a form.

 **LET ME TRY IT**

Add Fields to a Form

You can use the Field List window to easily add controls to a form. The Field List window contains all the fields that are part of the form's record source. The *record source* for a form is the table, query, or embedded SQL (Structured Query Language) statement that produces the data for the form. For example, in Figure 8.1, the form's record source is the Customers table. The fields listed in the Field List window are the fields that make up the Customers table. To add controls to a form, you drag and drop fields from the Field List onto the form. Each field becomes a control on the form with the control type appropriate for that field. For example, whereas a

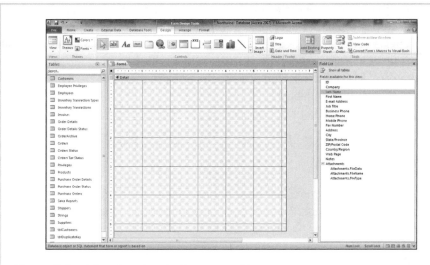

Figure 8.1 *A form based on the Customers table.*

Text field appears as a text box, a Yes/No field appears as a check box. Follow these two steps to add a control to your form:

1. Make sure the Field List window is visible. If it isn't, click the Add Existing Fields button in the Tools group on the Design tab of the Ribbon.

2. Locate the field you want to add to the form; then click and drag the field from the field list to the place on the form where you want it to appear. The location you select becomes the upper-left corner of the text box, and the attached label appears to the left of where you dropped the control.

A *control* is an object that you add to a form or report. Types of controls include text boxes, combo boxes, list boxes, and check boxes.

 LET ME TRY IT

Add Multiple Fields to a Form at the Same Time

To add multiple fields to a form at the same time, complete the following steps:

1. Select several fields from the field list.

2. Hold down the Ctrl key to select noncontiguous (not together) fields or the Shift key to select contiguous (together) fields. For example, if you hold down

the Ctrl key and click three noncontiguous fields, each of these three fields is selected. If you click a field, hold down the Shift key, and click another field, all fields between the two selected fields are selected. If you want to select all the fields in a list, you double-click the field list title bar, and then click and drag any one of the selected fields to the form; all the fields are then added to the form simultaneously.

Selecting, Moving, Aligning, and Sizing Form Objects

You must know several important tricks of the trade for selecting, moving, aligning, and sizing form objects. These tips will save you hours of frustration and wasted time.

Selecting Form Objects

The easiest way to select a single object on a form is to click it. After you have selected the object, you can move it, size it, or change any of its properties. Selecting multiple objects is a bit trickier, but you can accomplish it in several ways. Different methods are more efficient in different situations.

It's important to understand which objects you've actually selected. Figure 8.2 shows a form with four selected objects. The ID text box, the Company label, and the Address label and Address text box are all selected; however, the Customer ID label and CompanyName text box aren't selected. If you look closely at the figure, you can see that the selected objects are completely surrounded by selection handles. The ID label and Company text box each has just a single selection handle because each is attached to an object that is selected. If you changed any properties of the selected objects, the ID label and Company text box would be unaffected.

One way to select multiple objects is to hold down the Shift key and click each object you want to select. Access surrounds each selected object with selection handles, indicating that you have selected it.

You can also select objects by lassoing them. Objects to be lassoed must be adjacent to one another on the form. To lasso objects, you place the mouse pointer on a blank area of the form (that is, not over any objects) and then click and drag the mouse pointer around the objects you want to select. You can see a thin line around the objects the mouse pointer is encircling. When you let go of the mouse button, any objects that were within the lasso, including those only partially surrounded, are selected. If you want to deselect any of the selected objects to exclude them, you hold down the Shift key and click the objects you want to deselect.

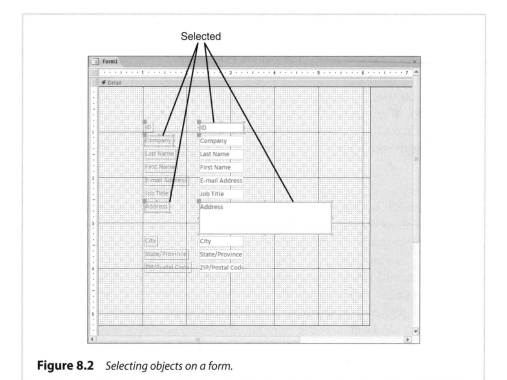

Figure 8.2   *Selecting objects on a form.*

One of my favorite ways to select multiple objects is to use the horizontal and vertical rulers that appear at the edges of the Form Design window. You click and drag within the ruler, and as you do this, two horizontal lines appear, indicating which objects are selected. As you click and drag across the horizontal ruler, two vertical lines appear, indicating the selection area. When you let go of the mouse button, any objects within the lines are selected. As with the process of lassoing, to remove any objects from the selection, you hold down the Shift key and click the objects you want to deselect.

You can use the Ctrl+A keystroke combination to select all controls on a form. After you have selected them, you can move them, size them, or change any of their other properties as a unit.

Moving Things Around

To move a single control with its attached label, you don't need to select it first. You place the mouse over the object and click and drag. An outline appears, indicating the object's new location. When the object reaches the position you want, you release the mouse. The attached label automatically moves with its corresponding control.

To move more than one object at a time, you must first select the objects you want to move. You select the objects by using one of the methods outlined in the previous section. When you place the mouse over any of the selected objects and click and drag, an outline appears, indicating the proposed new position for the objects. You release the mouse when you have reached the position you want for the objects.

Sometimes you want to move a control independently of its attached label, and this requires a special technique. If you click a control, such as a text box, as you move the mouse over the border of the control, a hand icon with five fingers pointing upward appears. If you click and drag, both the control and the attached label move as a unit, and the relationship between them is maintained. Figure 8.3 shows the label and text box before they've been moved as a unit. Figure 8.4 shows them after they've been moved as a unit. If you place the mouse pointer over the larger handle in the upper-left corner of the object, the mouse pointer appears as a hand with only the index finger pointing upward. If you click and drag here, the control moves independently of its attached label, and the relationship between the objects changes. Figure 8.5 depicts objects after they've been moved independently.

Aligning Objects to One Another

Access makes it easy to align objects. Figure 8.6 shows several objects that aren't aligned. Notice that the attached labels of three of the objects are selected. If you align the attached labels, the controls (in this case, text boxes) remain in their original positions. If you also select the text boxes, the text boxes try to align with the attached labels. Because Access doesn't allow the objects to overlap, the text boxes end up immediately next to their attached labels. To left-align any objects (even objects of different types), you select the objects you want to align and then choose Left from the Align drop-down in the Sizing & Ordering group on the Arrange tab of the Ribbon. Access aligns the selected objects (see Figure 8.7). You can align the left, right, top, or bottom edges of any objects on a form.

You shouldn't confuse the Align feature on the Arrange tab of the Ribbon with the Align tools (that is, Align Left, Center, and Align Right) on the Home tab of the Ribbon. Whereas the Align feature on the Arrange tab of the Ribbon aligns objects one to the other, the Align tools on the Home tab of the Ribbon justify the text inside an object.

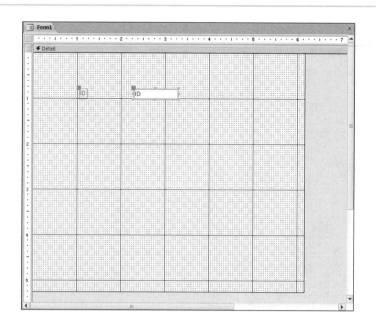

Figure 8.3   *Objects before moving.*

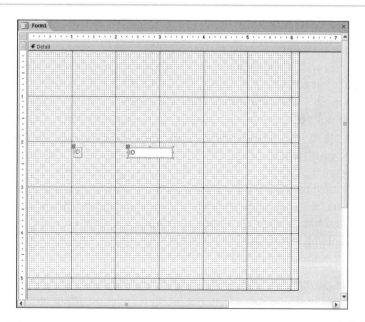

Figure 8.4   *Objects after moving as a unit.*

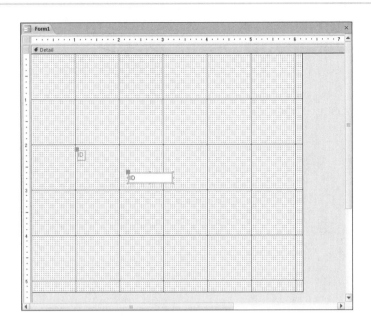

Figure 8.5 *Objects after moving independently.*

Sizing Your Controls

Just as there are several ways to move objects, you have several options for sizing objects. When you select an object, you can use each handle, except for the handle in the upper-left corner of the object, to size the object. The handles at the top and bottom of the object enable you to change the object's height, and the handles at the left and right of the object let you change the object's width. You can use the handles in the upper-right, lower-right, and lower-left corners of the object to change the width and height of the object simultaneously. To size an object, you place the mouse pointer over a sizing handle, click, and drag. You can select several objects and size them all simultaneously. Each of the selected objects increases or decreases in size by the same percentage; their relative sizes stay intact. You use the upper-left handle to move an object independent of its attached label. This means, for example, that you can place the label associated with a text box above the text box, rather than to its left.

Access offers several powerful methods of sizing multiple objects, which you access by selecting Size/Space from the Sizing & Ordering group on the Arrange tab of the Ribbon:

- **To Fit**—Sizes the selected objects to fit the text within them
- **To Grid**—Sizes the selected objects to the nearest gridlines

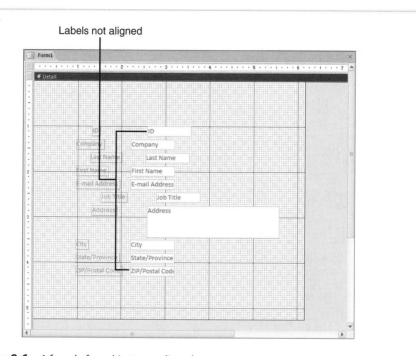

Figure 8.6   *A form before objects are aligned.*

- **To Tallest**—Sizes the selected objects to the height of the tallest object in the selection
- **To Shortest**—Sizes the selected objects to the height of the shortest object in the selection
- **To Widest**—Sizes the selected objects to the width of the widest object in the selection
- **To Narrowest**—Sizes the selected objects to the width of the narrowest object in the selection

Probably the most confusing of the options is To Fit. This option is somewhat deceiving because it doesn't perfectly size text boxes to the text within them. In today's world of proportional fonts, it isn't possible to perfectly size a text box to the largest possible entry it contains. Generally, however, you can visually size text boxes to a sensible height and width. You use a field's Size property to limit what's typed in the text box. If the entry is too large to fit in the allocated space, the user can scroll to view the additional text. As the following tip indicates, the To Fit option is much more appropriate for labels than it is for text boxes.

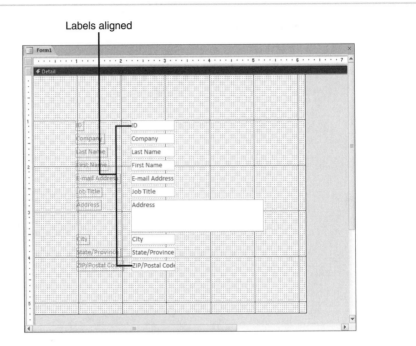

Figure 8.7   *A form after objects are aligned.*

To quickly size a label to fit the text within it, you can select the label and then double-click any of its sizing handles, except the sizing handle in the upper-left corner of the label.

Controlling Object Spacing

Access provides excellent tools for spacing the objects on a form an equal distance from one another. Notice in Figure 8.8 that the ID, Company, Address, and City text boxes aren't equally spaced vertically from one another. To make the vertical distance between selected objects equal, you choose Equal Vertical from the Size/Space drop-down in the Arrange tab of the Ribbon. In Figure 8.9, you can see the result of using this command on the selected objects.

You can make the horizontal distance between objects equal by choosing Equal Horizontal from the Size/Space drop-down. Other related commands on the same drop-down are Increase Vertical (or Decrease) and Increase Horizontal (or Decrease). These commands maintain the relationships between objects while proportionally increasing or decreasing the distances between them.

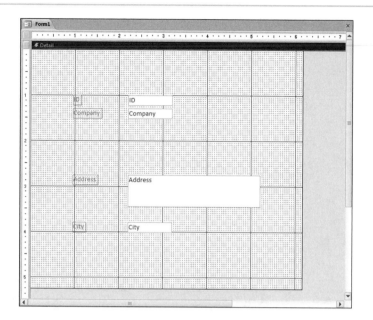

Figure 8.8 *A form before vertical spacing is modified.*

Modifying Object Tab Order

Access bases the tab order for the objects on a form on the order in which you add the objects to the form. However, this order isn't necessarily appropriate for the user. You might need to modify the tab order of the objects on a form yourself. To do so, you select Tab Order from the Tools group on the Design tab of the Ribbon. The Tab Order dialog box, shown in Figure 8.10, appears. This dialog box offers two options. First, you can click the Auto Order button to tell Access to set the tab order based on each object's location in a section on the form. Second, if you want to customize the order of the objects, you click and drag the gray buttons to the left of the object names listed under the Custom Order heading to specify the objects' tab order.

SHOW ME   Media 8.1—Working with Controls
Access this video file through your registered Web Edition at
my.safaribooksonline.com/9780132117128/media.

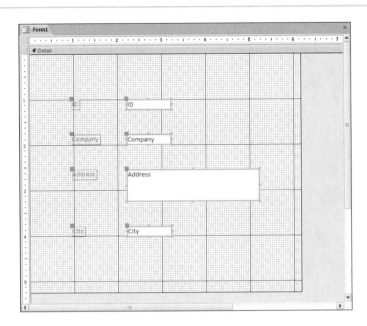

Figure 8.9 *A form after vertical spacing is modified.*

Figure 8.10 *The Tab Order dialog box, where you select the tab order of the objects in each section of a form.*

Conditional Formatting

With conditional formatting, data meeting specified criteria displays differently than does data meeting other criteria. For example, you can use conditional formatting to display sales higher than a certain amount in one color and sales lower than that amount in another color.

 LET ME TRY IT

Conditionally Format Data

To conditionally format data displayed within a control, follow these steps:

1. Select the control you want to conditionally format.

2. Select Conditional Formatting from the Control Formatting group on the Format tab of the Ribbon. The Conditional Formatting Rules Manager dialog box appears (see Figure 8.11).

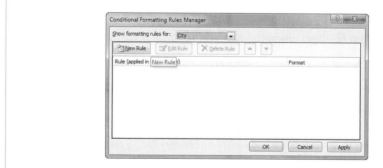

Figure 8.11 *The Conditional Formatting dialog enables you to display data in a control differently based on a specific condition.*

3. Click New Rule. The New Formatting Rule dialog appears (see Figure 8.12).

4. Select Check Values in the Current Record or Use Expression.

5. Select Field Value Is, Expression Is, or Field Has Focus from the first combo box in the Formatting dialog box. Select Field Value Is when you want to select from a predefined set of operators such as between, not between, equal to, etc. Select Expression when you want to build your own conditional expression that Access will evaluate at runtime. Finally, select Field Has Focus if you want Access to apply the conditional format only when that field has the focus.

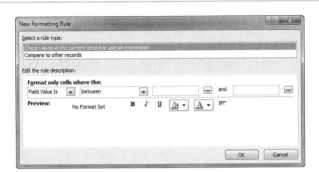

Figure 8.12   *The New Formatting Rule dialog enables you to designate the specifics for a formatting rule.*

6. Select the appropriate operator from the second combo box in the dialog box.

7. Enter the values you are testing for in the text boxes that appear on the right of the dialog box.

8. Select the special formatting (bold, italic, background color, and so on) that you want to apply when the conditional criteria are met.

9. Click OK to return to the Conditional Formatting Rules Manager.

 SHOW ME   Media 8.2—Conditional Formatting
Access this video file through your registered Web Edition at
my.safaribooksonline.com/9780132117128/media*.*

Form Properties and Why Should You Use Them

Forms have many properties that you can use to affect their look and behavior. The properties are broken down into categories: Format, Data, Event, and Other.

To view a form's properties, you must first select the form. To do that, click the form selector (the small gray button at the intersection of the horizontal and vertical rulers).

It is important that you understand how to work with form properties. The sections that follow begin by focusing on the Properties window. They then hone in on a discussion of some of the important form properties.

Working with the Properties Window

After you have selected a form, you can click the Properties button on the toolbar to view its properties. The Properties window, shown in Figure 8.13, consists of five tabs: Format, Data, Event, Other, and All. Many developers prefer to view all properties at once on the All tab, but a form can have a total of 119 properties! Instead of viewing all 119 properties at once, you should try viewing the properties by category. The Format category includes all the physical attributes of the form—the ones that affect the form's appearance, such as background color. The Data category includes all the properties of the data that the form is bound to, such as the form's underlying record source. The Event category contains all the Windows events to which a form can respond. For example, you can write code that executes in response to the form being loaded, becoming active, displaying a different record, and so on. The Other category holds a few properties that don't fit into the other three categories.

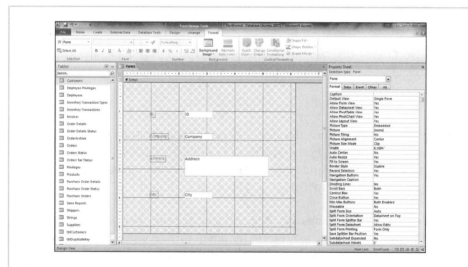

Figure 8.13   *Viewing the Format properties of a form.*

Working with the Important Form Properties

As mentioned in the preceding section, a form has 119 properties. Of those 119 properties, 52 are Event properties, and they are covered in most books focused on Access programming. The following sections cover the Format, Data, and Other properties of forms.

The Format Properties of a Form

The Format properties of a form affect its physical appearance. A form has 39 Format properties. The most important ones are described in the following sections.

The Caption Property   The Caption property sets the text that appears on the form's title bar.

The Default View Property   The Default View property allows you to select from five available options:

- **Single Form**—Allows only one record to be viewed at a time
- **Continuous Forms**—Displays as many records as will fit within the form window at one time, presenting each as the detail section of a single form
- **Datasheet**—Displays the records in a spreadsheet-like format, with the rows representing records and the columns representing fields
- **PivotTable**—Displays the records in a Microsoft Excel-type pivot table format
- **PivotChart**—Displays the records in a Microsoft Excel-type pivot chart format

The selected option becomes the default view for the form.

The Scroll Bars Property   The Scroll Bars property determines whether scrollbars appear if the controls on a form don't fit within the form's display area. You can select from both vertical and horizontal scrollbars, neither vertical nor horizontal scrollbars, just vertical scrollbars, or just horizontal scrollbars.

The Record Selectors Property   A record selector is the gray bar to the left of a record in Form view, or the gray box to the left of each record in Datasheet view. It's used to select a record to be copied or deleted. The Record Selectors property determines whether the record selectors appear. If you give the user a custom menu, you can opt to remove the record selector to make sure the user copies or deletes records using only the features specifically built into the application.

The Navigation Buttons Property   Navigation buttons are the controls that appear at the bottom of a form; they allow the user to move from record to record within a form. The Navigation Buttons property determines whether the navigation buttons are visible. You should set it to No for any dialog box forms, and you might want to set it to No for data-entry forms, too, and add your own toolbar or command buttons to enhance or limit the functionality of the standard buttons.

For example, in a client/server environment, you might not want to give users the ability to move to the first or last record because that type of record movement can be inefficient in a client/server architecture.

The Dividing Lines Property   The Dividing Lines property indicates whether you want a line to appear between records when the default view of the form is set to Continuous Forms. It also determines whether Access places dividing lines between the form's sections (that is, header, detail, and footer).

The Auto Resize Property   The Auto Resize property determines whether Access automatically sizes a form to display a complete record.

The Auto Center Property   The Auto Center property specifies whether a form should automatically be centered within the Application window whenever it's opened.

The Border Style Property   The Border Style property is far more powerful than its name implies. The options for the Border Style property are None, Thin, Sizable, and Dialog. The Border Style property is often set to None for splash screens, in which case the form has no border. When the Border Style property is set to Thin, the border is not resizable and the Size command isn't available in the Control menu. This setting is a good choice for pop-up forms, which remain on top even when other forms are given the focus. The Sizable setting is standard for most forms; it includes all the standard options in the Control menu. The Dialog setting creates a border that looks like the border created by the Thin setting. A form with the Border Style property set to Dialog can't be maximized, minimized, or resized; when the border style of a form is set to Dialog, the Maximize, Minimize, and Resize options aren't available in the form's Control menu. The Dialog setting is often used along with the Pop Up and Modal properties to create custom dialog boxes.

The Close Button Property   The Close Button property determines whether the user can close the form by using the Control menu or double-clicking the Control icon. If you set the value of this property to No, you must give the user another way to close the form; otherwise, the user might have to reboot his or her computer to close the application.

The SubdatasheetHeight Property   The SubdatasheetHeight property is used to designate the maximum height for a sub-datasheet.

The SubdatasheetExpanded Property   The SubdatasheetExpanded property allows you to designate whether a sub-datasheet is initially displayed in an expanded format. When this property is set to False, the sub-datasheet appears collapsed. When it is set to True, the sub-datasheet appears in expanded format.

The `Moveable` Property   The `Moveable` property determines whether the user can move the form window around the screen by clicking and dragging the form by its title bar.

The Data Properties of a Form

You use the Data properties of a form to control the source for the form's data, what sort of actions the user can take on the data in the form, and how the data in the form is locked in a multiuser environment. A form has 14 Data properties (several of which we cover here).

The `Record Source` Property   The `Record Source` property indicates the table, stored query, or SQL statement on which the form's records are based. After you have selected a record source for a form, the controls on the form can be bound to the fields in the record source.

The Field List window is unavailable until you have set the `Record Source` property of the form.

The `Filter` Property   You use the `Filter` property to automatically load a stored filter along with the form. I prefer to base a form on a query that limits the data displayed on the form. You can pass the query parameters at runtime to customize exactly what data Access displays.

The `Order By` Property   The `Order By` property specifies in what order the records on a form appear. You can modify this property at runtime.

The `Allow Filters` Property   The `Allow Filters` property controls whether you can filter records at runtime. When this option is set to No, all filtering options become disabled to the user.

The `Allow Edits`, `Allow Deletions`, and `Allow Additions` Properties   The `Allow Edits`, `Allow Deletions`, and `Allow Additions` properties let you specify whether the user can edit data, delete records, or add records from within a form. These options can't override any permissions that you have set for the form's underlying table or queries

The `Data Entry` Property   The `Data Entry` property determines whether users can only add records within a form. You should set this property to Yes if you don't want users to view or modify existing records but want them to be able to add new records.

The Other Properties of a Form

Format properties affect the appearance of a form. Data properties affect the data underlying a form. This section focuses on the Other properties of a form. As you'll see, although these properties don't fit neatly into the Format and Data categories, they are extremely robust and powerful properties. The most commonly used properties are covered here.

- **Pop Up**—The Pop Up property indicates whether a form always remains on top of other windows. You will often set this property, along with the Modal property (discussed next), to Yes when creating custom dialog boxes.

- **Modal**—The Modal property indicates whether the user can remove focus from a form while it's open. When the Modal property is set to Yes, the user must close the form before he or she can continue working with the application. As mentioned earlier, this property is used with the Pop Up property to create custom dialog boxes.

- **Cycle**—The Cycle property controls the behavior of the Tab key in a form. The settings are All Records, Current Record, and Current Page. When you set the Cycle property to All Records, the user moves to the next record on a form when he or she presses Tab from the last control on the previous record. When the property is set to Current Record, the user is moved from the last control on a form to the first control on the same record. The Current Page option refers only to multipage forms; when you set the Cycle property to Current Page, the user tabs from the last control on the page to the first control on the same page. All three options are affected by the tab order of the objects on the form.

- **Tag**—The Tag property is used to store miscellaneous information about a form. This property is often set and monitored at runtime to store necessary information about a form. You could use the Tag property to add a tag to each of several forms that should be unloaded as a group.

- **Allow Design Changes**—The Allow Design Changes property determines whether changes can be made to the design of a form while you're viewing form data. If this property is set to All Views, the Properties window is available in Form view, and changes made to form properties while you're in Form view are permanent if the form is saved.

 SHOW ME Media 8.3—Working with Form Properties
Access this video file through your registered Web Edition at
my.safaribooksonline.com/9780132117128/media.

Control Properties and Why to Use Them

Available control properties vary quite a bit, depending on the type of control. The following sections cover the most common properties. To view the properties of a control, select the control, and then open the Properties window.

The Format Properties of a Control

The Format properties of a control affect the appearance of the control. You use these properties to change the color, size, font, and other physical attributes of the control. To view the Format properties of a control, with the control already selected, and the Properties window open, click the Format tab (see Figure 8.14). The text that follows discusses many of these properties and their uses.

- **Format**—The Format property of a control determines how Access displays the data in the control. A control's format is automatically inherited from its underlying data source. Access lets you use this property in three situations: when the Format property is not set for the underlying field, when you want to override the existing Format setting for the field, and when you want to apply a format to an unbound control. You can select from a multitude of predefined values for a control's format, or you can create a custom format. I often modify the Format property at runtime to vary the format of a control, depending on a certain condition. For example, the format for a Visa card number is different from the format for an ATM card number.

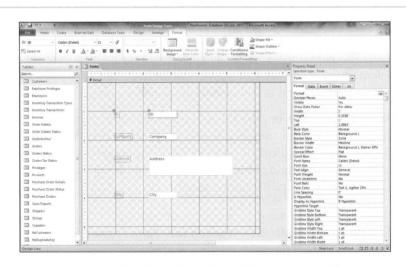

Figure 8.14   *The Format properties of a control.*

- **Decimal Places**—The Decimal Places property specifies how many decimal places you want to appear in the control. This property is used with the Format property to determine the control's appearance.

- **Caption**—You use the Caption property to specify information that is helpful to the user. It's available for labels, command buttons, and toggle buttons.

- **Visible**—The Visible property indicates whether a control is visible. This property can be toggled at runtime, depending on specific circumstances. For example, a question on the form might apply only to records in which the gender is set to Female; if the gender is set to Male, the question isn't visible.

- **Display When**—The Display When property is used when you want certain controls on a form to be sent only to the screen or only to the printer. The three settings for this property are Always, Print Only, and Screen Only. An example of the use of the Display When property is for a label containing instructions. You can use the Display When property to have the instructions appear onscreen but not on the printout.

- **Scroll Bars**—The Scroll Bars property determines whether scrollbars appear when the data in a control doesn't fit within the control's size. The options are None and Vertical. I often set the Scroll Bars property to Vertical when the control is used to display data from a memo field. The scrollbar makes it easier for the user to work with a potentially large volume of data in the memo field.

- **Back Style** and **Back Color**—You can set the Back Style property to Normal or Transparent. When this property is set to Transparent, the form's background color shows through the control. This is often the preferred setting for an option group. The control's Back Color property specifies the background color (as opposed to text color) for the control.

If the Back Style property of a control is set to Transparent, the control's Back Color property is ignored.

- **Special Effect**—The Special Effect property adds 3D effects to a control. The settings for this property are Flat, Raised, Sunken, Etched, Shadowed, and Chiseled. Each of these effects gives a control a different look.

- **Border Style, Border Color**, and **Border Width**—The Border Style, Border Color, and Border Width properties affect the look, color, and thickness of a control's border. The settings for the Border Style property are Transparent, Solid, Dashes, Short Dashes, Dots, Sparse Dots, Dash Dot, and Dash Dot Dot. The Border Color property specifies the color of the border; you can select from a variety of colors. The `Border Width` property can be set to one of several point sizes.

If the `Border Style` property of a control is set to Transparent, Access ignores the control's `Border Color` and `Border Width` properties.

- **`Fore Color`, `Font Name`, `Font Size`, `Font Weight`, `Font Italic`,** and **`Font Underline`**—The `Fore Color`, `Font Name`, `Font Size`, `Font Weight`, `Font Italic`, and `Font Underline` properties control the appearance of the text in a control. As their names imply, they let you select a color, font, size, and thickness of the text and determine whether the text is italicized or underlined. You can modify these properties in response to a runtime event. For example, you can modify a control's text color if the value in that control exceeds a certain amount. The `Font Weight` property settings generally exceed what is actually available for a particular font and printer—normally, you have a choice of only Regular and Bold in whatever value you select for this property.

- **`Text Align`**—The `Text Align` property is often confused with the ability to align controls, but the `Text Align` property affects how the data is aligned *within* a control.

- **`Left Margin`, `Top Margin`, `Right Margin`,** and **`Bottom Margin`**—The `Left Margin`, `Top Margin`, `Right Margin`, and `Bottom Margin` properties determine how far the text appears from the left, top, right, and bottom of the control. They are particularly useful with controls such as text boxes based on memo fields, which are generally large controls.

- **`Line Spacing`**—The `Line Spacing` property is used to determine the spacing between lines of text in a multiline control. This property is most commonly used with text boxes based on memo fields.

Notice Figure 8.15. This TextBox control uses many of the Format properties that we just learned about. I set the `Scroll Bars` property to Vertical so that the control appears with a vertical scroll bar. I modified the `Back Color` property. I then set the `Border Style` to Solid, modified its color, and made it *very* wide. I modified and enlarged the font, made it extra bold and italic. Finally, I aligned the text so that it is centered within the control. Notice that you can see all of these changes graphically, as well as the properties that affect the control.

The Data Properties of a Control

Whereas Format properties affect the appearance of the control, Data properties affect the data that displays in the control. In this section, we explore the various

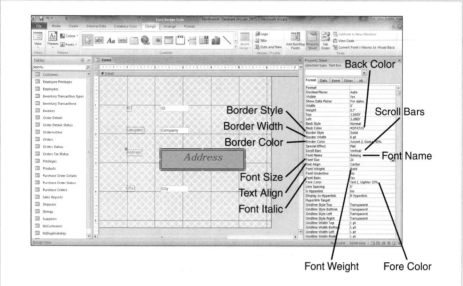

Figure 8.15   *A TextBox control using many of the Format properties.*

Data properties. We cover everything from the `Control Source` property that determines what data displays in the control, to the `Input Mask` property that determines what data the user can enter into each character of the control. As you'll see, there's a very rich list of Data properties for a control. They appear in Figure 8.16, and many are described in the text that follows. To access the data properties of a control, select the control, open the Property Sheet, and click to select the Data tab.

- `Control Source`—The `Control Source` property specifies the field from the record source that's associated with a particular control. The `Control Source` property can also be set to any valid Access expression.

- `Input Mask`—Whereas the `Format` and `Decimal Places` properties affect the appearance of a control, the `Input Mask` property affects what data the user can enter into the control. The input mask of the field underlying the control is automatically inherited into the control. If no input mask is entered as a field property, the input mask can be entered directly in the form. If you entered the input mask for the field, you can use the input mask of the associated control on a form to further restrict what the user enters into that field via the form. If you select the `Input Mask` property and click the Build button, the Input Mask Wizard appears (see Figure 8.17).

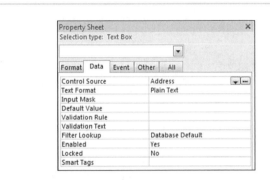

Figure 8.16   *The Data properties of a control.*

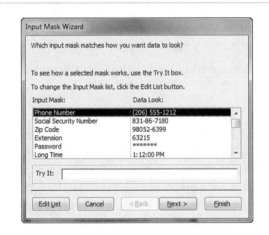

Figure 8.17   *The Input Mask Wizard.*

If a control's Format property and Input Mask property are set to different values, the Format property affects the display of the data in the control until the control gets the focus. When the control gets the focus, the Input Mask property prevails.

- **Default Value**—The Default Value property of a control determines the value assigned to new records entered in a form. You can set this property within the field properties of the underlying table. A default value set at the field level of the table is automatically inherited into the form. The default value set for the control overrides the default value set at the field level of the table.

- **Validation Rule** and **Validation Text**—The Validation Rule and Validation Text properties of a control perform the same functions as they do for a field. This means that the Validation Rule enables you to validate the data that users enter into the control, and the Validation Text enables you to supply users with the error message that appears when they enter a value that violates the validation rule.

Because a validation rule is enforced at the database engine level, the validation rule set for a control can't be in conflict with the validation rule set for the field to which the control is bound. If the two rules conflict, the user can't enter data into the control.

- **Enabled**—The Enabled property determines whether you allow a control to get the focus. If this property is set to No, the control appears dimmed.

- **Locked**—The Locked property determines whether the user can modify the data in a control. When the Locked property is set to Yes, the control can get the focus but can't be edited. The Enabled and Locked properties of a control interact with one another. Table 8.1 summarizes their interactions. Where you see the Enabled column equal to Yes in the table, that means that the Enabled property is set to Yes. Where you see Locked property equal to Yes in the table, that means that the Locked property is set to Yes. The third column shows the effect of the combination of those two property settings. For example, if you set Enabled to Yes and Locked to Yes, the control can get the focus and its data can be copied but not modified.

Table 8.1 How Enabled and Locked Properties Interact

Enabled	Locked	Effect
Yes	Yes	The control can get the focus; its data can be copied but not modified.
Yes	No	The control can get the focus, and its data can be edited.
No	Yes	The control can't get the focus.
No	No	The control can't get the focus; its data appears dimmed.

- **Filter Lookup**—The Filter Lookup property indicates whether you want the values associated with a bound text box to appear in the Filter by Form window.

Take a look at the example in Figure 8.18. Notice that the text box control has its Control Source property set to State/Province, indicating that it is bound to the

Region field in the underlying data source. Its `Default Value` property is CA. This means that when the user adds a new record, the Region field defaults to CA. The `Validation Rule` property connotes that the Region must be CA, UT, AZ, NJ, or NY. The `Validation Text` property provides the error message the user will receive if the user violates the validation rule.

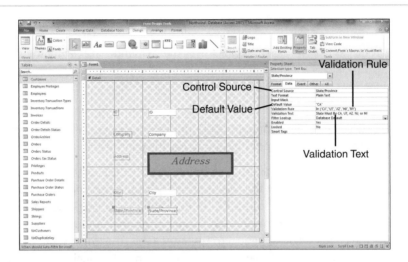

Figure 8.18   *The* `Display Control` *property, on the Lookup tab of the Table Design window.*

The Other Properties of a Control

The Other properties of a control are properties that did not fit neatly into any other category. This does not mean that they are unimportant. In fact, you can find some of the most important and useful control properties under the Other properties of a control. To access these properties, select the control, invoke the Properties window, and then click the Other tab of the Properties window (see Figure 8.19). Let's take a look.

- **Name**—The `Name` property allows you to name a control. You use the name that is set in this property when you refer to the control in code, and this name is also displayed in various drop-down lists that show all the controls on a form. It's important to name controls because named controls improve the readability of code and make working with Access forms and other objects easier.

- **Status Bar Text**—The `Status Bar Text` property specifies the text that appears in the status bar when a control gets focus. The setting of this property overrides the `Description` property that you can set in a table's design.

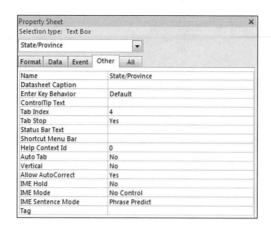

Figure 8.19   *The Other properties of a control.*

- **Enter Key Behavior**—The Enter Key Behavior property determines whether the Enter key causes the cursor to move to the next control or to add a new line in the current control. You will often change the setting of this property for text boxes that you use to display the contents of memo fields.

- **Allow AutoCorrect**—The Allow AutoCorrect property specifies whether the AutoCorrect feature is available in a control. The AutoCorrect feature automatically corrects common spelling errors and typos.

- **Vertical**—The Vertical property is used to control whether the text in a control is displayed horizontally or vertically. The default setting is No, or horizontal. When you select Yes (vertical display), Access rotates the text in the control 90 degrees (see Figure 8.20).

- **Auto Tab**—When the Auto Tab property is set to Yes, the cursor automatically advances to the next control when the user enters the last character of an input mask. Some users like this option, and others find it annoying, especially if they must tab out of some fields but not others.

- **Default**—The Default property applies to a command button or to an ActiveX control and specifies whether the control is the default button on a form.

- **Cancel**—The Cancel property applies to a command button or to an ActiveX control. It indicates that you want the control's code to execute when the user presses the Esc key while the form is active.

- **Status Bar Text**—The Status Bar Text property specifies the message that appears in the status bar when a control has the focus.

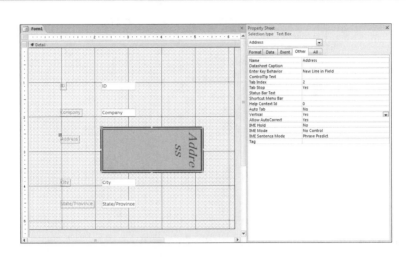

Figure 8.20   *The Address text box with the Vertical property set to Yes.*

- **Tab Stop**—The Tab Stop property determines whether the user can use the Tab key to enter a control. It's appropriate to set this property to No for controls whose values rarely get modified. The user can opt to click in the control when necessary.

- **Tab Index**—The Tab Index property sets the tab order for a control. I generally set the Tab Index property by using the Tab Order button found in the Tools group on the Design tab of the Ribbon rather than by setting the value directly in the control's Tab Index property. This allows me to set the tab order graphically, which is more intuitive, easier, and saves me a lot of time.

- **ControlTip Text**—The ControlTip Text property specifies the ToolTip associated with a control. The ToolTip automatically appears when the user places the mouse pointer over the control and leaves it there for a moment.

- **Tag**—The Tag property is used to store information about a control. Your imagination determines how you use this property. The Tag property can be read and modified at runtime.

 SHOW ME   Media 8.4—Working with Control Properties
Access this video file through your registered Web Edition at
my.safaribooksonline.com/9780132117128/media.

Working with Combo Boxes

Combo boxes allow users to select from a list of appropriate choices. Access offers several easy ways to add a combo box to a form. If you have set a field's Display Control property to Combo Box, Access adds a combo box to a form when you add the field to the form. The combo box automatically knows the source of its data as well as all its other important properties.

If a field's Display Control property hasn't been set to Combo Box, the easiest way to add a combo box to a form is to use the Control Wizards tool. The Control Wizards tool helps you add combo boxes, list boxes, option groups, and subforms to forms. Although you can manually set all the properties set by the Combo Box Wizard, using the wizard saves both time and energy.

If you want Access to launch the Combo Box Wizard when you add a combo box to the form, you need to make sure you click the Control Wizards tool in the toolbox before you add the combo box. Then you select the Combo Box tool in the toolbox and then click and drag to place the combo box on the form. Doing so launches the Combo Box Wizard. As shown in Figure 8.21, the first step of the Combo Box Wizard gives you three choices for the source of the combo box's data. You use the first option if the combo box will select the data that's stored in a field, such as the state associated with a particular customer. I rarely, if ever, use the second option, which requires that you type the values for the combo box. Populating a combo box this way makes it difficult to maintain. Every time you want to add an entry to the combo box, you must modify the application. You use the third option when you want to use the combo box as a tool to search for a specific record. For example, a combo box can be placed in a form's header to display a list of valid customers. After you select a customer, the user is moved to the appropriate record. This option is available only when the form is bound to a record source.

If you select to have the combo box look up the values in a table or query, in the second step of the Combo Box Wizard (shown in Figure 8.22), you select a table or query to populate the combo box and then click Next. In the third step of the wizard (shown in Figure 8.23), you select the fields that appear in the combo box. We'll use the combo box being built in the example to select the customer associated with the current order. Although the Company field will be the only field visible in the combo box, I have selected both ID and Company because ID is a necessary element of the combo box. After the user has selected a company name from the combo box, Access stores the ID associated with the company name in the Customer ID field of the Orders table.

The fourth step of the wizard allows you to designate the sort order for the data in the combo box (see Figure 8.24). You can opt to sort on as many as four fields.

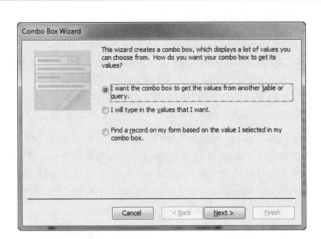

Figure 8.21   *The first step of the Combo Box Wizard: selecting the source of the data.*

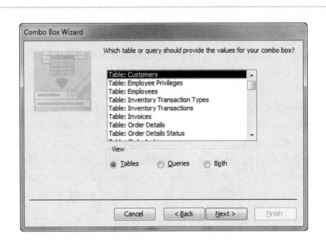

Figure 8.22   *The second step of the Combo Box Wizard: selecting a table or query.*

The fifth step of the wizard lets you specify the width of each field in the combo box. Notice in Figure 8.25 that Access recommends that you hide the key column, ID. The idea is that the user will see the meaningful English description, while Access worries about storing the appropriate key value in the record.

In the wizard's sixth step, you specify whether you want Access to just remember the selected value or store it in a particular field in a table. In the example shown in Figure 8.26, I have told Access to store the selected combo box value in the Customer ID field of the Orders table.

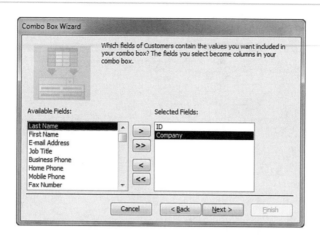

Figure 8.23 *The third step of the Combo Box Wizard: selecting fields.*

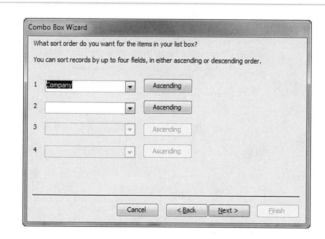

Figure 8.24 *The fourth step of the Combo Box Wizard: selecting the sort order.*

The seventh and final step of the Combo Box Wizard prompts for the text that will become the attached label for the combo box. After you click the Finish button, Access completes the process, building the combo box and filling in all its properties with the appropriate values.

Although the Combo Box Wizard is a helpful tool, it's important that you understand the properties it sets. Figure 8.27 shows the Properties window for a combo box. We're going to take a moment to go over the properties set by the Combo Box Wizard in this example.

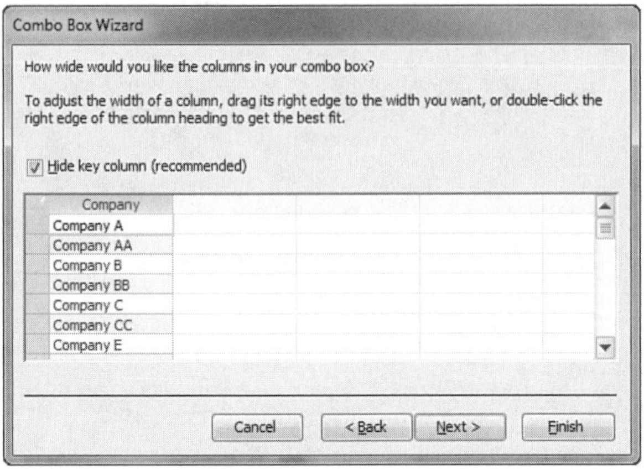

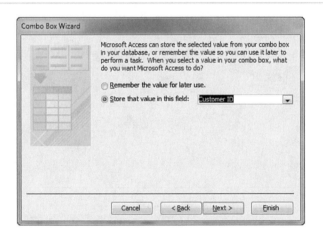

Figure 8.25   *The fifth step of the Combo Box Wizard: setting column widths.*

Figure 8.26   *The sixth step of the Combo Box Wizard: indicating where the selected value will be stored.*

The Control Source property indicates the field in which the selected entry is stored. In Figure 8.27, you can see that the selected entry will be stored in the Customer ID field of the Orders table. The Row Source Type property specifies whether the source used to populate the combo box is a table/query, value list, or field list. In the example, the Row Source Type property is set to Table/Query. The Row Source property is the name of the actual table or query used to populate the combo box. In the example, the Row Source property is a SQL SELECT statement that selects the

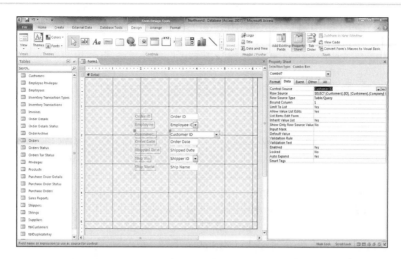

Figure 8.27   *Properties of a combo box, showing that the Customer ID field has been selected as the control source for the Combo7 combo box.*

CustomerID and CompanyName from the Customers table. The Column Count property designates how many columns are in the combo box, and the Column Widths property indicates the width of each column. In the example, the width of the first column is zero, which renders the column invisible. Finally, the Bound Column property is used to specify which column in the combo box is being used to store data in the control source. In the example, this is column 1.

 SHOW ME   Media 8.5—Working with Combo Boxes
Access this video file through your registered Web Edition at
my.safaribooksonline.com/9780132117128/media.

List Boxes

List boxes are similar to combo boxes, but they differ from them in three major ways:

- They consume more screen space.

- They allow the user to select only from the list that's displayed. This means the user can't type new values into a list box (as you can with a combo box).

- They can be configured to let the user select multiple items.

If you set the Display Control property of a field to List Box, Access adds a list box to the form when the field is clicked and dragged from the field list to the form.

The List Box Wizard is almost identical to the Combo Box Wizard. After you run the List Box Wizard, the list box properties affected by the wizard are the same as the combo box properties.

The Command Button Wizard: Programming Without Typing

With the Command Button Wizard, you can quickly and easily add functionality to forms. The wizard writes the code to perform more than 30 commonly required tasks that are separated into record navigation, record operations, form operations, report operations, application operations, and other miscellaneous tasks. The Command Button Wizard is automatically invoked when you add a command button with the Control Wizards tool selected. The first step of the Command Button Wizard is shown in Figure 8.28. In this dialog box, you specify the category of activity and specific action you want the command button to perform. The subsequent wizard steps vary, depending on the category and action you select.

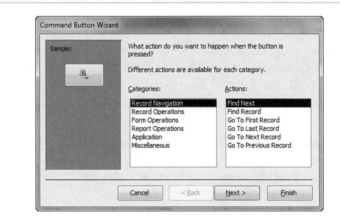

Figure 8.28   *The first step of the Command Button Wizard.*

Figure 8.29 shows the second step of the Command Button Wizard when you select the Form Operations category and the Open Form action in the first step. This step asks which form you want to open. After you select a form and click Next, you're asked whether you want Access to open the form and find specific data to display or whether you want Access to open the form and display all the records. If you indicate that you want to display only specific records, the dialog box shown in Figure 8.30 appears. This dialog box asks you to select fields related to the two forms. You must select the related fields and then click the <> button to notify Access of the relationship. In the next step of the wizard, you select text or a picture for the button. The final step of the wizard asks you to name the button. When you're done, you click Finish.

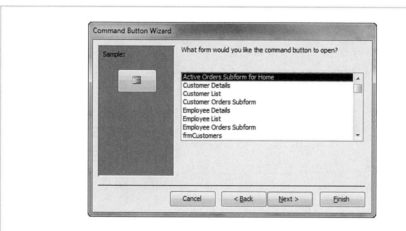

Figure 8.29 *The Command Button Wizard, requesting the name of a form to open.*

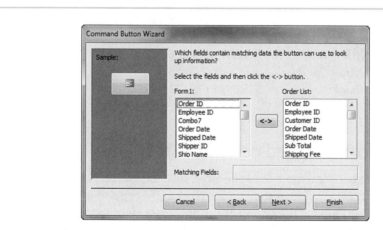

Figure 8.30 *The Command Button Wizard, asking for the fields that relate to each form.*

What's surprising about the Command Button Wizard is how much it varies depending on the features you select. It enables you to add somewhat sophisticated functionality to an application without writing a single line of code. Figure 8.31 shows the embedded macro created by the example just outlined. This code will make a lot more sense to you after you've read Chapter 10, "Automating Your Database with Macros." After you have the Command Button Wizard generate a macro for you, you can modify it; this means that you can have Access do some of the dirty work for you and then customize the work to your liking.

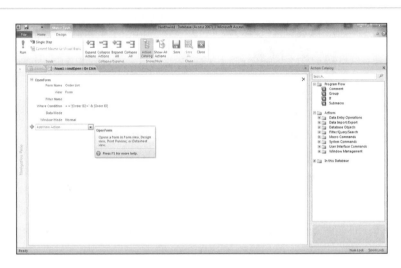

Figure 8.31   *Macro created by the Command Button Wizard.*

 SHOW ME   **Media 8.6—The Command Button Wizard**
Access this video file through your registered Web Edition at
my.safaribooksonline.com/9780132117128/media.

Building Forms Based on More Than One Table

Many forms are based on more than one table; such forms are called *one-to-many forms*. For example, a form that shows a customer at the top and the orders associated with that customer at the bottom is considered a one-to-many form. Forms can also be based on a query that joins more than one table. Rather than see a one-to-many relationship in such a form, you see the two tables displayed as one, with each record on the "many" side of the relationship appearing with its parent's data.

Creating One-to-Many Forms

There are several ways to create one-to-many forms. As with many other types of forms, you can use a wizard to help you or you can build the form from scratch.

Because all the methods for creating a form are helpful to users and developers alike, the available options are covered in the following sections.

 LET ME TRY IT

Build a One-to-Many Form by Using the Form Wizard

Building a one-to-many form by using the Form Wizard is a simple 10-step process:

1. Select Form Wizard in the Forms group on the Create tab of the Ribbon. The Form Wizard launches.

2. From the Tables/Queries drop-down list, select the table or query that will appear on the "one" side of the relationship.

3. Select the fields you want to include from the "one" side of the relationship.

4. Use the Tables/Queries drop-down list to select the table or query that will appear on the "many" side of the relationship.

5. Select the fields you want to include from the "many" side of the relationship.

6. Click Next.

7. Select whether you want the parent form to appear with subforms or the child forms to appear as linked forms. In this example, I want the parent form to appear with subforms, so I clicked the Form with Subforms option (see Figure 8.32). Click Next.

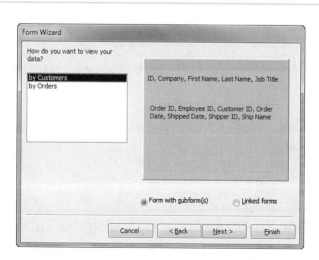

Figure 8.32 *The Form Wizard, creating a parent form with subforms.*

8. Indicate whether you want the subform to appear in a tabular format, as a datasheet, as a pivot table, or as a pivot chart. (This option is not available if you selected Linked Forms in step 7.) Click Next.

9. Select a style for the form and then click Next.

10. Name both the form and the subform, and then click Finish.

The result of this process is a main form that contains a subform. Figure 8.33 shows an example.

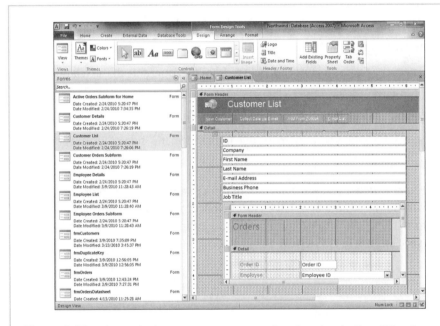

Figure 8.33   *The result of creating a one-to-many form by using the Form Wizard.*

SHOW ME   Media 8.7—Building a One-to-Many Form by Using the Form Wizard

Access this video file through your registered Web Edition at
my.safaribooksonline.com/9780132117128/media.

Building a One-to-Many Form by Using the Subform Wizard

You can create a one-to-many form by building the parent form and then adding a Subform/Subreport control from the toolbox. If you want to use the Subform/Subreport Wizard, you need to make sure that you select the Control

Wizards tool before you add the Subform/Subreport control to the main form. Then you follow these steps:

1. Click to select the Subform/Subreport control.

2. Click and drag to place the Subform/Subreport control on the main form. The Subform/Subreport Wizard appears.

3. Indicate whether you want to use an existing form as the subform or build a new subform from an existing table or query.

4. If you select Use Existing Tables and Queries, the next step of the Sub-form/Subreport Wizard prompts you to select a table or query and which fields you want to include (see Figure 8.34). Select the fields, and then click Next.

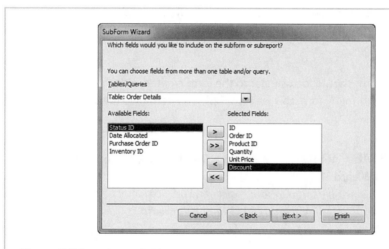

Figure 8.34 *Selecting fields to include in a subform.*

5. The next step of the Subform/Subreport Wizard allows you to define which fields in the main form link to which fields in the subform. You can select from the suggested relationships or define your own (see Figure 8.35). Select the appropriate relationship and click Next.

6. Name the subform and click Finish.

Another way to add a subform to a main form is to click and drag a form from the Database window onto the main form. Access then tries to identify the rela-tionship between the two forms.

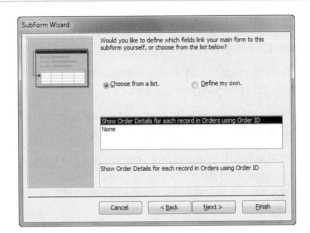

Figure 8.35 *Defining the relationship between the main form and the subform.*

The resulting form should look similar to the form created with the Form Wizard. Creating a one-to-many form this way is simply an alternative to using the Form Wizard.

 SHOW ME   **Media 8.8—Building a One-to-Many Form by Using the Subform Wizard**
Access this video file through your registered Web Edition at
my.safaribooksonline.com/9780132117128/media.

Another way to add a subform to a main form is to click and drag a form from the Database window onto the main form. Access then tries to identify the relationship between the two forms.

Working with Subforms

After you have added a subform to a form, you need to understand how to work with it. To begin, you need to familiarize yourself with a few properties of a Subform control:

- **Source Object**—Specifies the name of the form that's being displayed in the control

- **Link Child Fields**—Specifies the fields from the child form that link the child form to the master form

- **Link Master Fields**—Specifies the fields from the master form that link the child form to the master form

You should also understand how to make changes to a subform. One option is to open a subform in a separate window (as you would open any other form). After you close and save the form, all the changes automatically appear in the parent form. The other choice is to modify a subform from within the main form. With the main form open, the subform is visible. Any changes made to the design of the subform from within the main form are permanent.

When the subform is displayed in Datasheet view, the order of the fields in the subform has no bearing on the datasheet that appears in the main form. The order of the columns in the datasheet depends on the tab order of the fields in the subform. You must therefore modify the tab order of the fields in the subform to change the order of the fields in the resulting datasheet.

The default view of the subform is Datasheet or Continuous Forms, depending on how you added the subform and what options you selected. If you want to modify the default view, you simply change the subform's Default View property.

It is easy to work with subforms and subreports in Design view. You can now open a subform in its own separate Design view window by right-clicking the subform and selecting Subform in New Window.

SHOW ME   Media 8.9—Working with Subforms
Access this video file through your registered Web Edition at
my.safaribooksonline.com/9780132117128/media.

TELL ME MORE   Media 8.10—The Command Button Wizard:
Programming Without Typing
Access this audio recording through your registered Web Edition at
my.safaribooksonline.com/9780132117128/media.

When building reports in Access 2010, you want to be familiar with many important techniques.

9

Building Powerful Reports

Reports allow you to preview and print the information stored in your database. In Chapter 4, "Using Reports to Print Information," you learned the basics of working with reports. Here we take your knowledge to the next level. We begin by discussing report bands and how you use them. We then explore report controls and how you can control their behavior by using control properties. Next you learn how to add sorting and grouping to the reports that you build. You also learn how you can create one-to-many reports, and how to work with subreports. Finally, the chapter covers report properties and the advantages and disadvantages of storing a report's record source as a stored query.

The Anatomy of a Report

Reports can have many parts, referred to as *sections* of the report. A new report is automatically made up of the following three sections, as shown in Figure 9.1:

- Page Header section
- Detail section
- Page Footer section

The Detail section is the main section of the report; it's used to display the detailed data of the table or query underlying the report. Certain reports, such as Summary reports, have nothing in the Detail section. Instead, Summary reports contain data in group headers and footers.

The Page Header section automatically prints at the top of every page of the report. It often includes information such as the report's title. The Page Footer section automatically prints at the bottom of every page of the report and usually contains information such as the page number and date. Each report can have only one page header and one page footer.

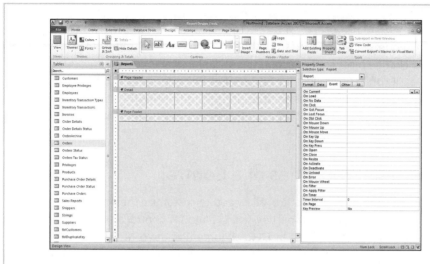

Figure 9.1 *Sections of a report.*

In addition to the three sections that Access automatically adds to every report, a report can have the following sections:

- Report Header section
- Report Footer section
- Group Headers section
- Group Footers section

A report header prints once, at the beginning of the report; the report footer prints once, at the end of the report. Each Access report can have only one report header and one report footer. The report header is often used to create a cover sheet for a report. It can include graphics or other fancy effects to add a professional look to a report. The most common use of the report footer is for grand totals, but it can also include any other summary information for a report.

In addition to report and page headers and footers, an Access report can have up to 10 group headers and footers. Report groupings separate data logically and physically. The group header prints before the detail for the group, and the group footer prints after the detail for the group. For example, you can group customer sales by country and city, printing the name of the country or city for each related group of records. If you total the sales for each country and city, you can place the country and city names in the country and city group headers and the totals in the country and city group footers.

Control Properties and Why to Use Them

Control properties enable you to change the behavior and appearance of a control. You can change most control properties at design time or at runtime; this allows you to easily build flexibility in to reports. For example, certain controls are visible only when specific conditions are true. This section begins by discussing the Format properties of a control. It then continues by covering the Data and Other properties of a control.

The Format Properties of a Control

The Format properties of a control allow you to customize the appearance of the control. Using the Format properties, you can modify control attributes such as the back color, font, special effect, and text alignment of the control. You can modify many of the Format properties of selected objects by using the Format tab of the Ribbon (see Figure 9.2). If you prefer, you can set the Format properties in the Properties window (see Figure 9.3). The remainder of this section discusses the Format properties available to you.

Figure 9.2 *The Format toolbar.*

- **Format**—The Format property determines how Access displays the data in a control. This property is automatically inherited from the underlying field. If you want the control's format on the report to differ from the underlying field's format, you must set the Format property of the control. It's important to note that the format options available vary based on the field type of the underlying field. In other words, the formatting options vary if the underlying field is a Text field versus a Number field.

- **Caption**—The Caption property specifies the text displayed for labels and command buttons. A caption is a string that contains up to 2,048 characters.

- **Decimal Places**—The Decimal Places property defines the number of decimal places displayed for numeric values.

- **Visible**—The Visible property determines whether a control is visible. You can use this property to toggle the visibility of a control in response to different situations.

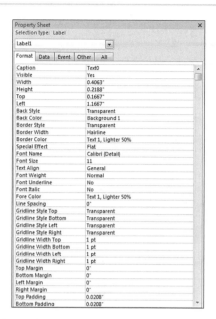

Figure 9.3   *The Format properties of a control.*

- **Hide Duplicates**—The `Hide Duplicates` property hides duplicate data values in a report's Detail section. Duplicate data values occur when one or more consecutive records in a report contain the same value in one or more fields. Figure 9.4 shows a report with the `Hide Duplicates` property set to its default value, False. Notice the duplicate `Order Date` values. Figure 9.5 shows the same report with the `Hide Duplicates` property of the `Order Date` control set to True. Notice that the duplicate order date values no longer appear.

- **Can Grow** and **Can Shrink**—When the `Can Grow` property is set to Yes in a control, the control can expand vertically to accommodate all the data in it. The `Can Shrink` property eliminates blank lines when no data exists in a field for a particular record. For example, if you have a second address line on a mailing label, but there's no data in the Address2 field, you don't want a blank line to appear on the mailing label (see Figure 9.6). You must therefore set the `Can Shrink` property for the Address2 control to Yes (see results in Figure 9.7). Likewise, if you have a memo that sometimes has only one line of data but at other times has multiple lines of data, you might want to set the `Can Grow` property to Yes so that the control grows as necessary.

- **Back Style** and **Back Color**—You can set the `Back Style` property to Normal or Transparent. When this property is set to Transparent, the color of the

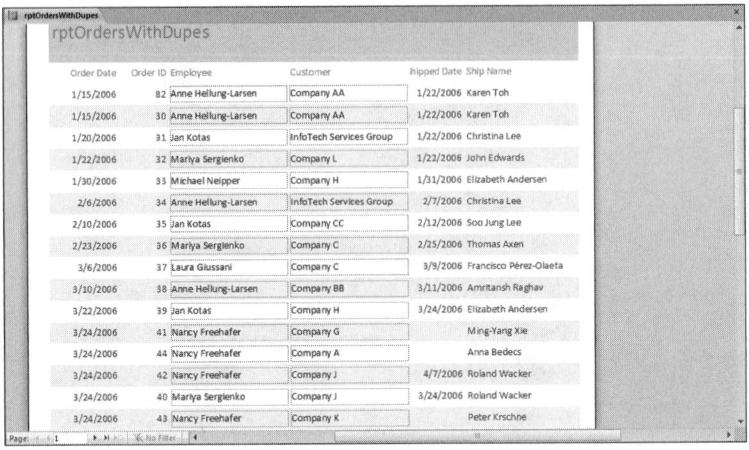

Figure 9.4 *The* Hide Duplicates *property set to False.*

Figure 9.5 *The* Hide Duplicates *property set to True.*

report shows through to the control. When it is set to Normal, the control's Back Color property determines the object's color.

- **Special Effect**—The Special Effect property adds 3D effects to a control.

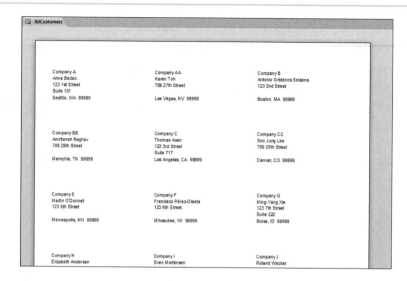

Figure 9.6   *The* Can Shrink *property set to No.*

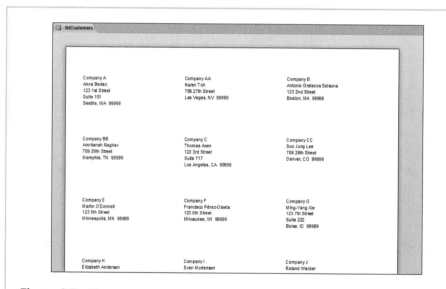

Figure 9.7   *The* Can Shrink *property set to Yes.*

- **Border Style**, **Border Color**, and **Border Width**—These properties set the physical attributes of a control's border.

- **Fore Color**—The Fore Color property sets the color of the text within a control.

- **Font Color, Font Name, Font Size, Font Weight, Font Italic,** and **Font Underline**—These properties affect the appearance of the text within a control.

- **Text Align**—The Text Align property sets the alignment of the text within a control. You can set this property to Left, Center, Right, or Distribute. When it is set to Distribute, text is justified. (See the Ship Name column in Figure 9.8.)

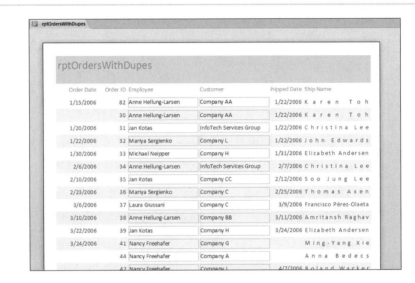

Figure 9.8   *The* Text Align *property of a Control.*

- **Line Spacing**—The Line Spacing property is used to control the spacing between lines of text within a control. The Line Spacing property is designated in inches.

The Data Properties of a Control

The Data properties of a control (see Figure 9.9), described in the following list, specify information about the data underlying a particular report control. Using the Data properties, you can designate everything from what data displays in a control, to whether the data sums as it displays:

- **Control Source**—The Control Source property specifies the field in the report's record source that's used to populate the control. An example is FirstName. A control source can also be a valid expression.

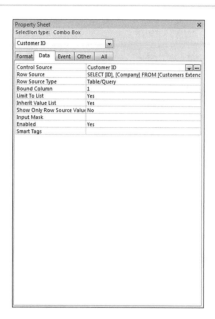

Figure 9.9   *The data properties specify information about the data underlying a report control.*

- **Running Sum**—The Running Sum property (which is unique to reports) is powerful. You can use it to calculate a record-by-record or group-by-group total. You can set it to No, Over Group, or Over All. When set to No, no running sum is calculated. When it is set to Over Group, the value of the text box accumulates from record to record within the group but is reset each time the group value changes. An example is a report that shows deposit amounts for each state, with a running sum for the amount deposited within the state. Each time the state changes, the amount deposited is set to zero. When this property is set to Over All, the sum continues to accumulate over the entire report.

The Other Properties of a Control

The Other properties of a control include properties, such as the following, that don't fit into any other category (see Figure 9.10):

A common mistake many Access developers and users make is to give controls names that conflict with Access names. This type of error is difficult to track

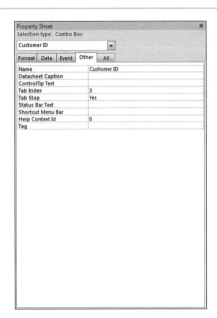

Figure 9.10   *The Other properties of a control.*

down. You need to make sure you use distinctive names for both fields and controls. Furthermore, you should not give a control the same name as a field
within its expression. For example, the expression =ContactName & ContactTitle
shouldn't have the name "ContactName"; that would cause an #error# message
when you run the report. Finally, you shouldn't give a control the same name as
its control source. Access gives a bound control the same name as its field, and
you need to change this name to avoid problems. Following these simple warnings will spare you a lot of grief!

- **Name**—The Name property provides an easy and self-documenting way to refer
  to a control in Visual Basic for Applications (VBA) code and in many other situations. You should name every control so that you can easily identify them
  in queries, macros, and so on.

- **Vertical**—The Vertical property is used to determine whether the text
  within a control is displayed vertically. The default value for this property
  is No.

- **Tag**—Like the Tag property of a report, the Tag property of a control provides
  a user-defined slot for the control. You can place extra information in the Tag
  property.

SHOW ME   Media 9.1—Working with Controls
Access this video file through your registered Web Edition at
my.safaribooksonline.com/9780132117128/media.

Building Reports Based on More Than One Table

The majority of reports you create will probably be based on data from more than one table. This is because a properly normalized database usually requires that you bring table data back together to give users valuable information. For example, a report that combines data from a Customers table, an Orders table, an Order Details table, and a Product table can supply the following information:

- Customer information, such as company name and address

- Order information, such as order date and shipping method

- Order detail information, such as quantity ordered and price

- A product table, including a product description

You can base a multitable report directly on the tables whose data it displays, or you can base it on a query that has already joined the tables, providing a flat table structure.

Creating One-to-Many Reports

You can create a one-to-many report by using the Report Wizard, or you can build a report from scratch. Different situations require different techniques, some of which are covered in the following sections.

LET ME TRY IT

Build a One-to-Many Report by Using the Report Wizard

Building a one-to-many report with the Report Wizard is quite easy. You just follow these steps:

1. Select Report Wizard from the Reports group on the Create tab of the Ribbon.

2. From the Tables/Queries drop-down list box, select the first table or query whose data will appear on the report.

3. Select the fields you want to include from that table.

4. Select each additional table or query you want to include on the report, selecting the fields you need from each (see Figure 9.11). Click Next.

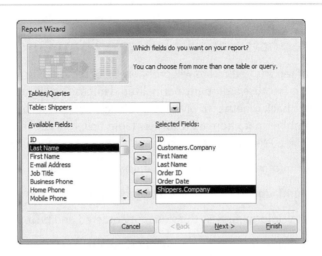

Figure 9.11 *The first step of the Report Wizard: selecting the fields you want on a report.*

5. The next step of the Report Wizard asks you how you want to view the data (see Figure 9.12). You can accept Access's suggestion (by Customers), or you can choose from any of the available options (by Customers, by Orders, or by Shippers). Click Next.

6. The next step of the Report Wizard asks whether you want to add any grouping levels. You can use grouping levels to visually separate data and to provide subtotals. In the example in Figure 9.13, the report is grouped by Shippers Company. After you select grouping levels, click Next.

7. The next step of the Report Wizard lets you select how you want the records in the report's Detail section to be sorted (see Figure 9.14). This step of the wizard also allows you to specify any summary calculations you want to perform on the data (see Figure 9.15). Click the Summary Options button to specify the summary calculations. By clicking the Summary Options button, you can even opt to include the percentage of total calculations. Click OK when you have finished adding the summary options.

8. In the next step of the Report Wizard, you select the layout and orientation of the report. Layout options include Stepped, Blocked, Outline 1, Outline

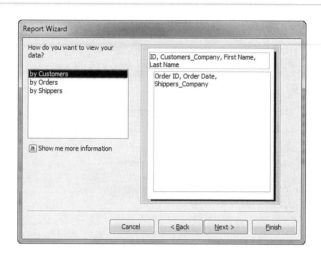

Figure 9.12   *The second step of the Report Wizard: designating how you want to view the data.*

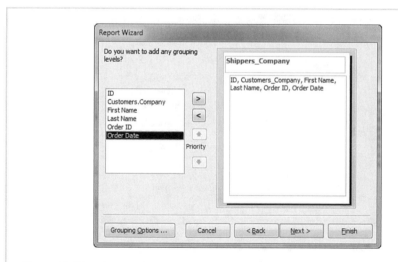

Figure 9.13   *The third step of the Report Wizard: selecting groupings.*

2, Align Left 1, and Align Left 2. You can click the different option buttons to preview how each of the reports will look.

9. In the next step of the Report Wizard, you select a title for the report. The title also becomes the name of the report. I like to select an appropriate name and change the title after the wizard is finished. The final step also allows you

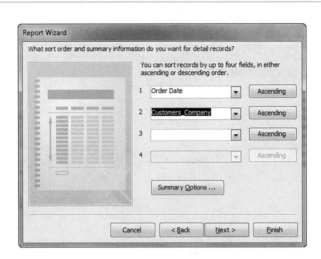

Figure 9.14   *The fourth step of the Report Wizard: selecting a sort order.*

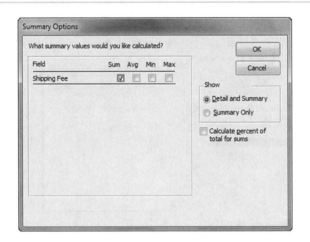

Figure 9.15   *Adding summary calculations.*

to determine whether you want to immediately preview the report or see the report's design first. Click Finish when you are ready to complete the process.

The report created in this example is shown in Figure 9.16. Notice that the report is sorted and grouped by Shippers Company, OrderDate, and Customers Company.

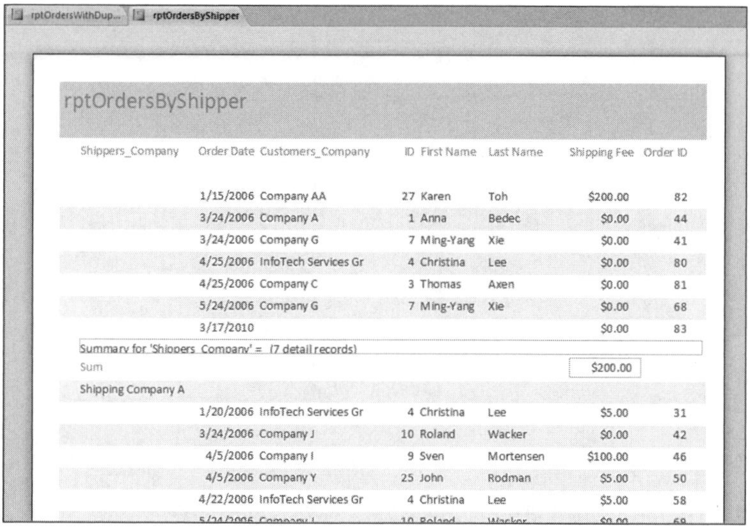

Figure 9.16   *A completed one-to-many report.*

The report's data is in order by OrderDate and Customers Company within a Shippers Company grouping.

This method of creating a one-to-many report is by far the easiest. In fact, the "background join" technology that the wizards use when they allow you to pick fields from multiple tables—figuring out how to build the complex queries needed for the report or form—is one of the major benefits of Access as a database tool. It's a huge timesaver and helps hide unnecessary complexity from you as you build a report. Although you should take advantage of this feature, it's important that you know what's happening under the covers. The following two sections give you this necessary knowledge.

Building a Report Based on a One-to-Many Query

A popular method of building a one-to-many report is from a one-to-many query. A one-to-many report built in this way is constructed as though it were based on the data within a single table. First, you build the query that will underlie the report (see Figure 9.17).

When you have finished the query, you can select it rather than select each individual table (as done in the previous section). After you select the query, you follow the same process to create the report as described in the preceding section.

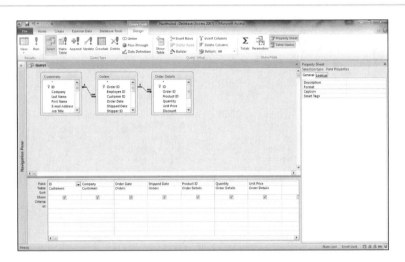

Figure 9.17   *An example of a query underlying a one-to-many report.*

 **LET ME TRY IT**

Build a One-to-Many Report with the SubReport Wizard

You can build a one-to-many report by building the parent report and then adding a SubReport control. This is often the method used to create reports such as invoices that show the report's data in a one-to-many relationship rather than in a denormalized format. If you want to use the SubReport Wizard, you must make sure that you select the Control Wizards tool before you add the SubReport control to the main report. Here is the process:

1. Click to select the SubForm/SubReport control tool.

2. Click and drag to place the SubForm/SubReport control on the main report. You usually place the SubForm/SubReport control in the report's Detail section. When you place the SubForm/SubReport control on the report, the SubReport Wizard is invoked (see Figure 9.18).

3. Indicate whether you want to base the subreport on an existing form or report or whether you want to build a new subreport based on a query or table. Click Next.

4. If you select Table or Query, you have to select the table or query on which you will base the subreport. You can then select the fields you want to include on the subreport. You can even select fields from more than one table or query. When you have finished making selections, click Next.

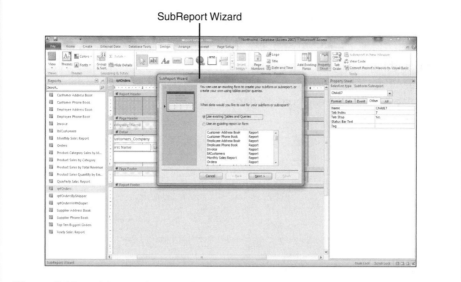

Figure 9.18   *Adding a SubForm/SubReport control invokes the SubReport Wizard.*

5. The next step of the SubReport Wizard suggests a relationship between the main report and the subreport (see Figure 9.19). You can accept the selected relationship, or you can define your own. When you have finished, click Next.

6. The final step of the SubReport Wizard asks you to name the subreport. Click Finish when you're done.

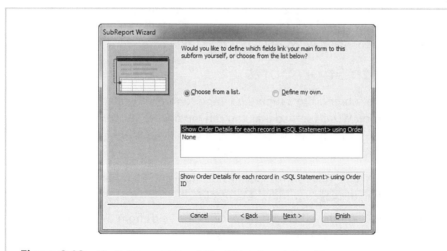

Figure 9.19   *The SubReport Wizard: identifying the relationship.*

To follow standards, the name should begin with the prefix *rsub*.

As you can see in Figure 9.19, the one-to-many relationship between two tables is clearly highlighted by this type of report. In the example in Figure 9.20, each order is listed. All the detail records reflecting the order details for each order are listed immediately following each order's data.

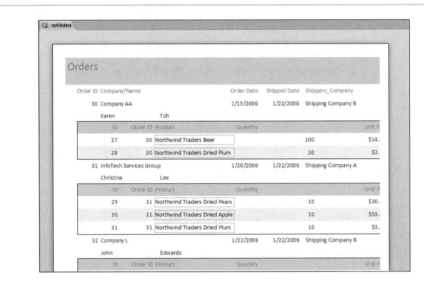

Figure 9.20   *A one-to-many report created with the Subreport Wizard.*

 SHOW ME   **Media 9.2—Basing Reports on Multiple Tables**
Access this video file through your registered Web Edition at
my.safaribooksonline.com/9780132117128/media.

Working with Subreports

When you add a subreport to a report, it's important to understand what properties the SubReport Wizard sets so that you can modify the SubForm/SubReport control, if needed. You should become familiar with the following properties of a SubForm/SubReport control (see Figure 9.21).

- `Source Object`—This control specifies the name of the report or other object that's being displayed within the control.

- `Link Child Fields`—This control specifies the fields from the child report that link the child report to the master report.

- `Link Master Fields`—This control specifies the fields from the master report that link the master report to the child report.

- **Can Grow**—This control determines whether the control can expand vertically to accommodate data in the subreport.

Figure 9.21   *Properties of the SubForm/SubReport control.*

- **Can Shrink**—This control determines whether the control can shrink to eliminate blank lines when no data is found in the subreport.

Not only should you know how to work with the properties of a SubForm/SubReport object, but you should also be able to easily modify the subreport from within the main report. You can always modify the subreport by selecting it from the list of reports in the Database window. To do this, you select the report you want to modify and then click Design. You can also modify a subreport by selecting its objects directly within the parent report.

You can open a subreport in its own separate Design view window by right-clicking the subreport and selecting Subreport in New Window.

SHOW ME   Media 9.3—Working with Subreports

Access this video file through your registered Web Edition at
my.safaribooksonline.com/9780132117128/media.

Working with Sorting and Grouping

Unlike sorting data within a form, sorting data within a report isn't determined by the underlying query. In fact, the underlying query affects the report's sort order only when you have not specified a sort order for the report. Any sort order specified in the query is completely overwritten by the report's sort order, which is determined in the report's Group, Sort, and Total window (see Figure 9.22). The sorting and grouping of a report is affected by what options you select when you run the Report Wizard. You can use the Group, Sort, and Total window to add, remove, or modify sorting and grouping options for a report. Sorting simply affects the order of the records in the report. Grouping adds group headers and footers to the report.

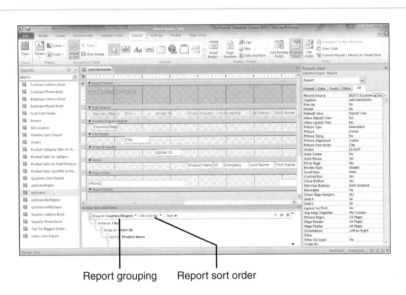

Report grouping   Report sort order

Figure 9.22   *The Sorting and Grouping window, showing grouping by Country, City, and OrderID and sorting by product name.*

 **LET ME TRY IT**

Add Sorting and Grouping to a Report

Often, you want to add sorting or grouping to a report. Grouping enables you to add group headers and group footers to a report, and sorting allows you to designate the sort order within your groups. To add grouping and sorting, follow these five steps:

1. Click Group & Sort in the Grouping & Totals group on the Design tab of the Ribbon to open the Group, Sort, & Total window.

2. Select Add a Group to add a grouping to the report, or select Add a Sort to add an additional sorting level to the report.

3. Select the field on which you want to sort or group (see Figure 9.23).

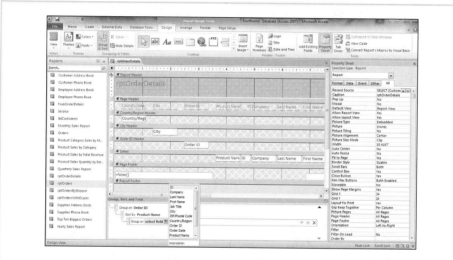

Figure 9.23   *Inserting a sorting or grouping level.*

4. Click and drag the group or sort level until it appears in the appropriate position in the Group, Sort, and Total window.

5. Set the properties to determine the nature of the sorting or grouping (see the next section, "Sorting and Grouping Settings"). Close the Group, Sort, and Total window, if desired.

To remove a sorting or grouping that you have added, you click the X for the appropriate field in the Group, Sort, and Total window that you want to delete. Access warns you that any controls in the group header or footer will be lost.

Sorting and Grouping Settings

Each grouping in a report has settings that define the group's attributes. The settings determine things such as whether the field or expression is used for sorting, grouping, or both. They are also used to specify details about the grouping options. To view the sorting and grouping settings, click More on one of the fields available in the Group, Sort, and Total window. The band expands to appear as in Figure 9.24. You can set the following attributes.

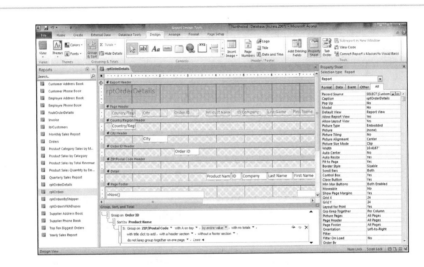

Figure 9.24 *The Group, Sort, and Total window, showing the expanded list of sorting and grouping settings.*

- **Sort Direction**—The `Sort Direction` setting specifies whether you want to sort in ascending or descending order.

- **By Entire Value**—The `By Entire Value` setting specifies whether you want to group by an entire value, or by a specific number of starting characters of the value (for example, the first two characters).

- **With No Totals**—The `With No Totals` setting specifies what fields you want to total on. If you opt to total on a field, you can specify the type of calculation you want to perform (sum, average, count, and so on). You can also designate whether you want to show the grand total, show a group subtotal as a percent of the grand total, and whether you want subtotals in the group header and footer (see Figure 9.25).

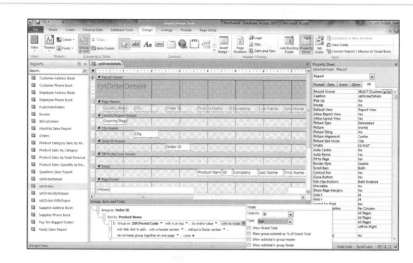

Figure 9.25 *Including totals in a header or footer.*

- **With Title**—You use the `With Title` setting to create a title for the grouping, and to designate a font for that title.

- **With a Header Section**—You use the `With a Header Section` setting to designate whether you want to include a group header.

- **With a Footer Section**—You use the `With a Footer Section` setting to designate whether you want to include a group footer.

- **Do Not Keep Together on One Page**—The `Do Not Keep Together on One Page` setting determines whether Access tries to keep an entire group together on one page, whether it will print the group header on a page only if it can also print the first detail record on the same page, or whether it makes no attempt to keep the header together with the detail section.

If you select `Keep Whole Group Together on One Page`, and the group is too large to fit on a page, Access ignores the property setting. Furthermore, if you select `Keep Header and First Record Together on One Page` and either the group header or the detail record is too large to fit on one page, that setting is ignored, too.

 SHOW ME   Media 9.4—Working with Sorting and Grouping
Access this video file through your registered Web Edition at
my.safaribooksonline.com/9780132117128/media.

Group Header and Footer Properties and Why to Use Them

Each group header and footer has its own properties that determine the behavior of the group header or footer (see Figure 9.26).

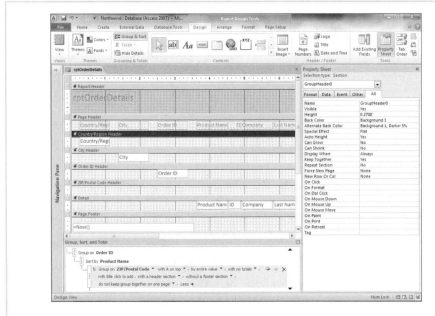

Figure 9.26   *Group header and footer properties.*

- **Force New Page**—You can set the Force New Page property to None, Before Section, After Section, or Before & After. If it is set to None, no page break occurs either before or after the report section. If it is set to Before Section, a page break occurs before the report section prints. If it is set to After Section, a page break occurs after the report section prints. If it is set to Before & After, a page break occurs before the report section prints as well as after it prints.

- **New Row** or **Col**—The New Row or Col property determines whether a column break occurs whenever the report section prints. This property applies only to multicolumn reports. The settings are None, Before Section, After Section, and Before & After. Like the Force New Page property, this property determines whether the column break occurs before the report section prints, after it prints, or before and after, or whether it's affected by the report section break at all.

- **Keep Together**—The Keep Together property specifies whether you want Access to try to keep an entire report section together on one page. If this property is set to Yes, Access starts printing the section at the top of the next page if it can't print the entire section on the current page. When this property is set to No, Access prints as much of the section as possible on the current page, inserting page breaks as necessary. If a section exceeds the page length, Access starts printing the section on a new page and continues printing it on the following page.

- **Visible**—The Visible property indicates whether the section is visible. It's common to hide the visibility of a particular report section at runtime in response to different situations. You can easily accomplish this by changing the value of the report section's Visible property with a macro or VBA code, usually on the Format event.

- **Can Grow** and **Can Shrink**—The Can Grow property determines whether you want the section to stretch vertically to accommodate the data in it. The Can Shrink property specifies whether you want the section to shrink vertically, eliminating blank lines.

- **Repeat Section**—The Repeat Section property is a valuable property that lets you specify whether Access repeats the group header on subsequent pages if a report section needs to print on more than one page.

Report Properties and Why to Use Them

You can modify many different properties on reports to change how the report looks and performs. Like form properties, report properties are divided into categories: Format, Data, Event, and Other. To view a report's properties, you first select the report, rather than a section of the report, in one of two ways:

- Click the report selector (see Figure 9.27), which is the small gray button at the intersection of the horizontal and vertical rulers.

- Select Report from the drop-down list box in the Properties window.

After you have selected a report, you can view and modify its properties.

Working with the Properties Window

To select a report and open the Properties window at the same time, you double-click the report selector. When you select a report, the Properties window appears, showing all the properties associated with the report. A report has 77 properties available on the Property Sheet (there are additional properties available only from code), broken down into the appropriate categories in the Properties window.

Report selector

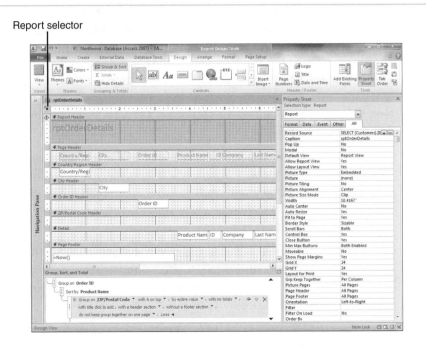

Figure 9.27   *The report selector.*

Fifty of the properties relate to the report's Format, Data, and the properties on the Other tab; the remaining 27 relate to the events that occur when a report is run. The Format, Data, and Other properties are described here.

The Format Properties of a Report

A report has the following 29 Format properties for changing the report's physical appearance. The text that follows explains many of the Format properties:

- **Caption**—The Caption property of a report is the text that appears in the Report window's title bar when the user is previewing the report. You can modify it at runtime to customize it for a particular situation.

- **Default View**—The Default View determines whether a report is opened in Report view or Print Preview.

- **Auto Resize**—The Auto Resize property was introduced with Access 2002. Its setting determines whether a report is resized automatically to display all the data on the report.

- **Auto Center**—You use the Auto Center property, which was introduced with Access 2002, to designate whether you want the Report window to automatically be centered on the screen.

- **Page Header** and **Page Footer**—The Page Header and Page Footer properties determine on what pages the Page Header and Page Footer sections appear. The options are All Pages, Not with Rpt Hdr, Not with Rpt Ftr, and Not with Rpt Hdr/Ftr. You might not want the page header or page footer to print on the report header or report footer pages, and these properties give you control over where those sections print.

- **Grp Keep Together**—In Access, you can keep a group of data together on the same page by using the Grp Keep Together property. The Per Page setting forces the group of data to remain on the same page, and the Per Column setting forces the group of data to remain within a column. A *group of data* refers to all the data within a report grouping (for example, all the customers in a city).

- **Border Style**—The Border Style property was introduced with Access 2002. Like its form counterpart, it is far more powerful than its name implies. The options for the Border Style property are None, Thin, Sizable, and Dialog. If the Border Style property is set to None, the report has no border. If the Border Style property is set to Thin, the border is not resizable; the Size command isn't available in the Control menu. This setting is a good choice for pop-up reports, which remain on top even when other forms or reports are given the focus. Having the Border Style property set to Sizable is standard for most reports. It includes all the standard options in the Control menu. The Dialog setting creates a border that looks like the border created by the Thin setting. The user can't maximize, minimize, or resize a report with the Border Style property set to Dialog. After you set the Border Style property of a report to Dialog, the Maximize, Minimize, and Resize options aren't available in the report's Control menu.

- **Moveable**—The Moveable property determines whether the user can move the Report window around the screen by clicking and dragging the report by its title bar.

The Report's Data Properties

A report has the following six Data properties, which are used to supply information about the data underlying a report:

- **Record Source**—The Record Source property specifies the table or query whose data underlies the report. You can modify the record source of a report at runtime. This feature of the Record Source property makes it easy for you to create generic reports that use different record sources in different situations.

- **Filter**—The `Filter` property allows you to open a report with a specific filter set. I usually prefer to base a report on a query rather than apply a filter to it. At some times, however, it's more appropriate to base the report on a query and then apply and remove a filter as required, based on the report's runtime conditions.

- **Filter On Load**—The `Filter On` property determines whether a report filter is applied. If the `Filter On Load` property is set to No, the `Filter` property of the report is ignored.

- **Order By**—The `Order By` property determines how the records in a report are sorted when the report is opened.

- **Order By On Load**—The `Order By On Load` property determines whether the `Order By` property of the report is used. If the `Order By On Load` property is set to No, the report's `Order By` property is ignored when loading the report.

- **Allow Filters**—The `Allow Filters` property determines whether the report data can be filtered.

Other Properties of a Report

A report has 15 Other properties (see Figure 9.28); these miscellaneous properties, some of which are described in the following text, enable you to control other important aspects of a report:

- **Record Locks**—The `Record Locks` property determines whether Access locks the tables used in producing a report while it runs the report. The two values for this property are No Locks and All Records. No Locks is the default value; it means that no records in the tables underlying the report are locked while the report is being run. Users can modify the underlying data as the report is run; this can be disastrous when running sophisticated reports. If users can change the data in a report as the report is being run, figures for totals and percentages of totals are invalid. Although using the All Records option for this property locks all records in all tables included in the report (thereby preventing data entry while the report is being run), it might be a necessary evil for producing an accurate report.

- **Date Grouping**—The `Date Grouping` property determines how grouping of dates occurs in a report. The US Defaults setting means that Access uses United States defaults for report groupings; therefore, Sunday is the first day of the week, the first week begins January 1, and so on. The Use System Settings setting means that date groupings are based on the locale set in the Control Panel's Regional Settings, rather than on U.S. defaults.

Figure 9.28   *The Other properties of a report.*

- **Pop Up**—The Pop Up property determines whether a report's Print Preview window opens as a pop-up window. In Microsoft Access, pop-up windows always remain on top of other open windows.

- **Modal**—The Modal property instructs Access to open the Report window in a modal or modeless state. The default is No, meaning that the window will not be opened as modal. A modal window retains the application program's focus until the window receives the user input that it requires.

- **Tag**—The Tag property stores information defined by the user at either design time or runtime. It is Microsoft Access's way of giving you an extra property. Access makes no use of this property; if you don't take advantage of it, it will never be used.

A couple of the Has Module property's behaviors deserve special attention. When a report is created, the default value for the Has Module property is No. Access automatically sets the Has Module property to Yes as soon as you try to view a report's module. If you set the `Has Module` property of an existing report to No, Access asks you whether you want to proceed. If you confirm the change, Access deletes the object's class module and all the code it contains.

 SHOW ME   Media 9.5—Taking Advantage of Report Properties
Access this video file through your registered Web Edition at
my.safaribooksonline.com/9780132117128/media.

Basing Reports on Stored Queries or Embedded SQL Statements

Basing Access reports on stored queries offers two major benefits:

- The query underlying the report can be used by other forms and reports.
- Sophisticated calculations need to be built only once—they don't need to be re-created for each report (or form).

In earlier version of Access, reports based on stored queries open faster than reports based on embedded SQL statements. This is because when you build and save a query, Access compiles and creates a query plan. This query plan is a plan of execution that's based on the amount of data in the query's tables as well as all the indexes available in each table. In early versions of Access, if you ran a report based on an embedded SQL statement, the query was compiled, and the query plan was built at runtime, slowing the query's execution. With Access 2010, query plans are built for embedded SQL statements when a form or report is saved. Query plans are stored with the associated form or report.

So what are the benefits of basing a report on a stored query instead of an embedded SQL statement? You may want to build several reports and forms, all based on the same information. An embedded SQL statement can't be shared by multiple database objects. At the very least, you must copy the embedded SQL statement for each form and report you build. Basing reports and forms on stored queries eliminates this problem. You build the query once and then modify it if changes need to be made to it. Many forms and reports can all use the same query (including its criteria, expressions, and so on).

It's easy to save an embedded SQL statement as a query, and doing so allows you to use the Report Wizard to build a report using several tables. You can then save the resulting SQL statement as a query. With the report open in Design view, you bring up the Properties window. After you select the Data tab, click in the Record Source property and click the ellipsis (...). The embedded SQL statement appears as a query. You need to select Save Object As from the File tab, enter a name for the query, and click OK. Then you close the Query window, indicating that you want to update the Record Source property. The query is then based on a stored query instead of an embedded SQL statement.

Reports often contain complex expressions. If a particular expression is used in only one report, nothing is lost by building the expression into an embedded SQL statement. On the other hand, many complex expressions are used in multiple reports and forms. If you build these expressions into queries on which the reports and forms are based, you have to create each expression only one time.

Although basing reports on stored queries offers several benefits, it also has downsides. For example, if a database contains numerous reports, the database container becomes cluttered with a large number of queries that underlie those reports. Furthermore, queries and the expressions within them are often very specific to a particular report. If that is the case, you should opt to use embedded SQL statements rather than stored queries. As a general rule, if several reports are based on the same data and the same complex calculations, you should base them on a stored query. If a report is based on a unique query with a unique set of data and unique calculations, you should base it on an embedded SQL statement.

 TELL ME MORE   Media 9.6—Improving Performance and Reusability by Basing Reports on Stored Queries

Access this audio recording through your registered Web Edition at ***my.safaribooksonline.com/9780132117128/media.***

Access 2010 offers a plethora of macro features that enable you to easily automate the applications that you build.

10

Automating Your Database with Macros

In this chapter, you'll learn the basics of creating a macro. You'll learn how to run an Access macro and how to modify an existing macro. You'll learn many important techniques such as how to create an embedded macro, how to create a data macro, and how to create a drillthrough macro. Finally, you'll learn when macros are appropriate and how to create a special type of macro: an AutoExec macro.

Learning the Basics of Creating and Running a Macro

To create a macro, click to select the Create tab. Then select Macro from the Macros & Code group. The Macro Design window shown in Figure 10.1 appears. In this window, you can build a program by adding macro actions, arguments, and program flow items to the macro.

Macro *actions* are like programming commands or functions. They instruct Access to take a specific action (for example, to open a form). Macro *arguments* are like parameters to a command or function; they give Access specifics on the selected action. For example, if the macro action instructs Access to open a form, the arguments for that action tell Access which form should be opened and how it should be opened (Form, Design, or Datasheet view, or Print Preview). Program flow items allow you to determine when a specific macro action will execute. For example, you might want one form to open in one situation and a second form to open in another situation.

 **LET ME TRY IT**

Working with Macro Actions

As mentioned, macro actions instruct Access to perform a task. You can add a macro action to the Macro Design window in several ways. One way is to click in the macro item and then click to open the drop-down list. A list of all the macro actions appears, as in Figure 10.2. Select the one you want from the list, and it's instantly added to the macro. Use this method of selecting a macro action if you aren't sure of the macro action's name and want to browse the available actions.

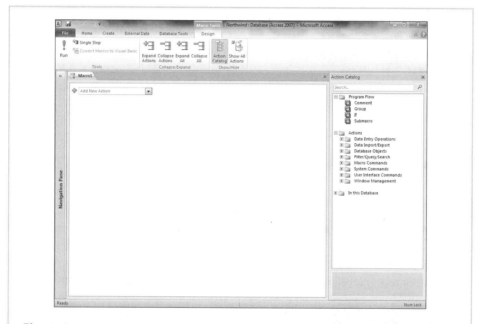

Figure 10.1   *The Macro Design window, showing the Action Catalog and the Macro Tools Design tab of the Ribbon.*

After you have been working with macros for a while, you will know which actions you want to select. Instead of opening the drop-down list and scrolling through the entire list of actions, you can click a cell in the Action column and then start typing the name of the macro action you want to add. Access will find the first macro action beginning with the characters you type.

 **LET ME TRY IT**

Drag and Drop Objects into Macros

The `OpenTable`, `OpenQuery`, `OpenForm`, `OpenReport`, and `OpenModule` actions are used to open a table, query, form, report, or module, respectively. These actions and associ-

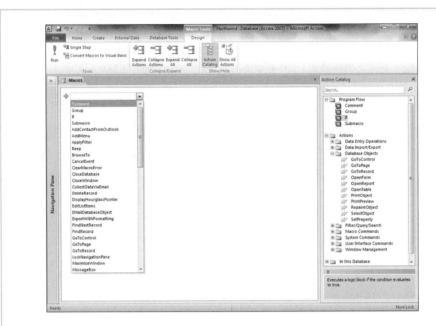

Figure 10.2   *The Macro Action drop-down list, showing all the available macro actions.*

ated arguments can all be filled in quite easily with a drag-and-drop technique:

1. Scroll through the Navigation Pane until you see the object that you want to add to the macro.

2. Click and drag the object you want to open over to the Macro Design window. The appropriate action and arguments are automatically filled in. Figure 10.3 shows the effects of dragging and dropping the Customer List form onto the Macro Design window.

Dragging and dropping a table, query, form, report, or module onto the Macro Design window saves you time because all the macro action arguments are automatically filled in for you. Notice in Figure 10.3 that six action arguments are associated with the OpenForm action: Form Name, View, Filter Name, Where Condition, Data Mode, and Window Mode. Three of the arguments for the OpenForm action have been filled in: the name of the form (Customer List), the view (Form), and the window mode (Normal). Macro action arguments are covered more thoroughly in the next section.

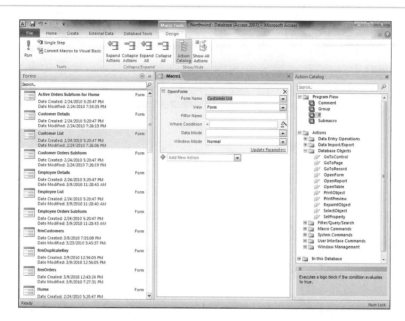

Figure 10.3 *The Macro Design window after the Customer List form was dragged and dropped on it.*

LET ME TRY IT

Working with Action Arguments

As mentioned, macro action arguments are like command or function parameters; they give Access specific instructions on how to execute the selected macro action. The available arguments differ depending on what macro action has been selected. Some macro action arguments force you to select from a drop-down list of appropriate choices; others allow you to enter a valid Access expression. Macro action arguments are automatically filled in when you click and drag a Table, Query, Form, Report, or Module object to the Macro Design window. In all other situations, you must supply Access with the arguments required to properly execute a macro action. To specify a macro action argument, follow these five steps:

1. Select a macro action.

2. If the macro action argument requires selecting from a list of valid choices, click to open the drop-down list of available choices for the first macro action argument associated with the selected macro action. Figure 10.4 shows all the available choices for the Form Name argument associated with

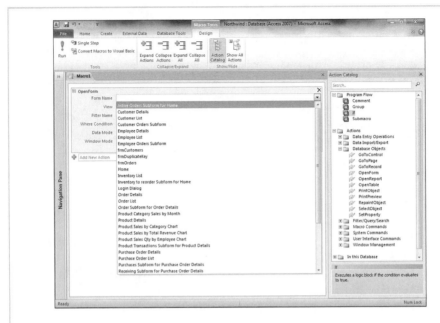

Figure 10.4   *Available choices for* Form Name *argument.*

the OpenForm action. Because the selected argument is Form Name, the names of all the forms included in the database are displayed in the drop-down list.

3. If the macro action argument requires entering a valid expression, you can type the argument into the appropriate text box or get help from the Expression Builder. Take a look at the Where Condition argument of the OpenForm action, for example. After you click in the Where Condition text box, an ellipsis appears. If you click the ellipsis, the Expression Builder dialog box is invoked, as shown in Figure 10.5.

4. To build an appropriate expression, select a database object from the list box on the left, and then select a specific element from the center and right list boxes. Click OK to accept the element into the text box. In Figure 10.5, the currently selected Expression Element is the Customer List form, Expression Category is Job Title, and <value> has been double-clicked to add the expression to the top half of the window. The value of Owner is entered in quotes indicating that the Job Title of each record displayed on the form must be Owner. Click OK to close the Expression Builder. The completed expression appears as shown in Figure 10.6.

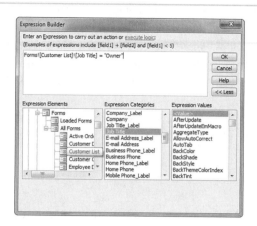

Figure 10.5 *The Expression Builder dialog box enables you to easily add complex expressions to your macros.*

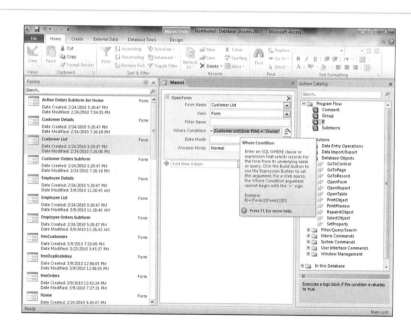

Figure 10.6 *The completed expression for the* Where *argument of the* OpenForm *action.*

Remember that each macro action has different macro action arguments. Some of the arguments associated with a particular macro action are required, and others are optional. If you need help on a particular macro action argument, click in the argument and Access provides a tooltip with a short description of that argument. If you need more help, press F1 to see Help for the macro action and all its arguments.

 LET ME TRY IT

Submacros

Submacros are like subroutines in a programming module; they allow you to place more than one routine in a macro. This means you can create many macro routines without having to create several separate macros. You should include submacros that perform related functions within one particular macro. For example, you might build a macro that contains all the routines required for form handling and another that has all the routines needed for report handling.

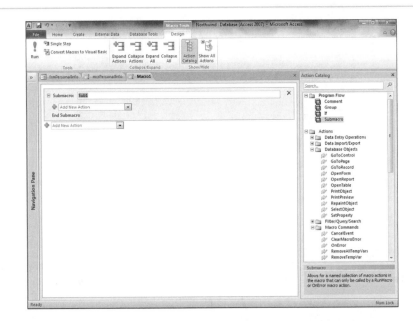

Figure 10.7   *The submacro allows you to create subroutines within a macro.*

Only two steps are needed to add submacros to a macro:

1. Click and drag a submacro from the Action Catalog onto the macro. A submacro appears as in Figure 10.7.

2. Add macro actions to each submacro. Figure 10.8 shows a macro with three submacros: OpenCustomers, OpenOrders, and CloseForm. The OpenCustomers submacro opens the Customer List form, showing all customers. The OpenOrders submacro opens the OrderList form displaying only orders placed in March and April of 2006, and the CloseForm submacro displays a message to the user and then closes the active window.

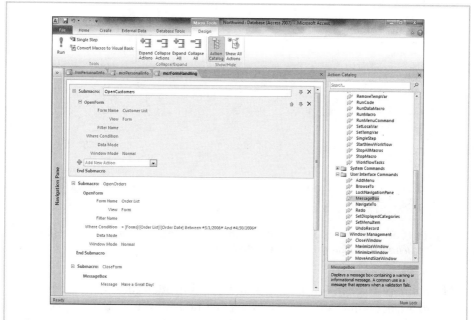

Figure 10.8   *A macro with three submacros.*

 **LET ME TRY IT**

Program Flow

At times, you want a macro action to execute only when a certain condition is true. Fortunately, Access allows you to specify the conditions under which a macro action executes:

1. Make sure that the Action Catalog is visible. (If it isn't, click the Action Catalog tool in the Show/Hide group of the Macro Tools Design tab of the Ribbon.)

2. Click and drag the If statement to the macro. It will appear as in Figure 10.9.

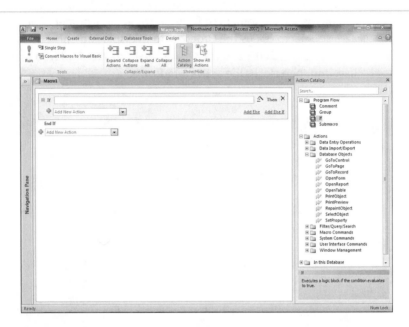

Figure 10.9 *You can designate the condition under which a macro action executes by selecting If from the Program Flow node of the Action Catalog.*

The macro pictured in Figure 10.10 evaluates information entered on a form. The macro evaluates the date entered in the txtBirthDate text box on the frmPersonalInfo form. Here's the expression entered in the first condition:

```
DateDiff("yyyy",[Forms]![frmPersonalInfo]![txtBirthDate],Date()) Between 25
And 49
```

This expression uses the DateDiff function to determine the difference between the date entered in the txtBirthDate text box and the current date. If the difference between the two dates is between 25 and 49 years, a message box is displayed indicating that the person is over a quarter century old.

If the first condition isn't satisfied, the macro continues evaluating each condition. The CheckBirthDate subroutine displays an age-specific message for each person 25 years of age and older. If the person is younger than 25, none of the conditions are met, and no message is displayed.

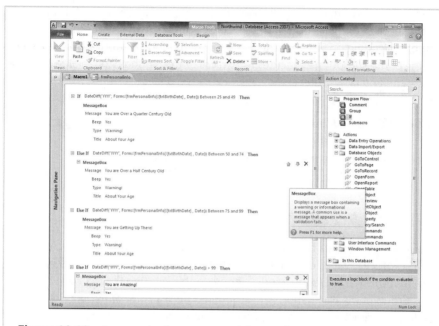

Figure 10.10   *An example of a macro containing conditions.*

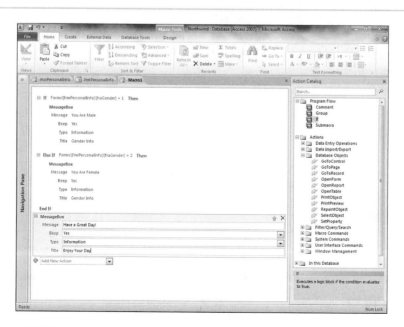

Figure 10.11   *An example of a macro containing conditions.*

The CheckGender macro works a little bit differently (see Figure 10.11). It evaluates the value of the fraGender option group. One of the first two lines of the subroutine execute, depending on whether the first or second option button is selected. The third line of the subroutine executes regardless of the Option Group value because it is after the End If.

SHOW ME   Media 10.1—The Basics of Creating and Running a Macro
Access this video file through your registered Web Edition at
my.safaribooksonline.com/9780132117128/media.

Running an Access Macro

You have learned quite a bit about macros but haven't yet learned how to execute them. This process varies depending on what you're trying to do. You can run a macro from the Macro Design window or by double-clicking the macro in the Macros Group of the Navigation Pane, triggered from a Form or Report event, triggered from a Data Macro, or invoked by selecting a custom Ribbon button.

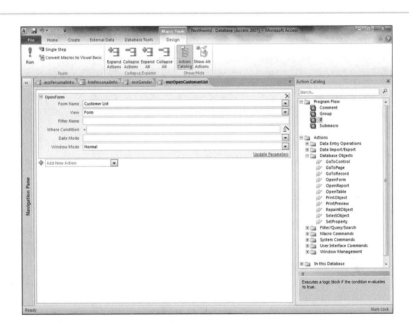

Figure 10.12   *Running a macro from the Macro Design window.*

Running a Macro from the Macro Design Window

A macro can be executed easily from the Macro Design window. Running a macro without groups is simple: Just click Run in the Tools group of the Macro Tools Design tab. Each line of the macro is executed unless conditions have been placed on specific macro actions. After you click the Run button of `mcrOpenCustomerList` (shown in Figure 10.12), the Customer List form is opened.

From Macro Design view, you can run only the first submacro in a macro. To run a macro with submacro, click Run from the Tools group on the Macro Tools Design page to execute the first group in the macro. As soon as the second submacro is encountered, the macro execution terminates. The section "Triggering a Macro from a Form or Report Event," later in this chapter, explains how to execute submacros other than the first one in a macro.

 LET ME TRY IT

Running a Macro from the Macros Group of the Navigation Pane

To run a macro from the Macros group of the Navigation Pane, follow these two steps:

1. Scroll down to the Macros group in the Navigation Pane. If the Macros group does not appear in the Navigation Pane, you will need to select All Access Objects from the Navigation Pane drop-down and then expand the Macros group.

2. Double-click the name of the macro you want to execute, or right-click the macro and select Run.

If the macro you execute contains submacros, only the macro actions within the first group are executed.

 LET ME TRY IT

Triggering a Macro from a Form or Report Event

Sometimes you are going to execute a macro in response to an event on a form or report. Examples are a form opening, someone clicking a command button, or a form closing. Here, you learn how to associate a macro with a command button.

The form in Figure 10.13 illustrates how to associate a macro with the Click event of a form's command button. Four steps are needed to associate a macro with a Form or Report event:

1. Select the object you want to associate the event with. In the example, the cmdCheckGender command button is selected.

2. Open the Property Sheet and click the Event tab.

3. Click the event you want the macro to execute in response to. In the example, the Click event of the command button is selected.

4. Use the drop-down list to select the name of the macro you want to execute. If the macro has submacros, make sure you select the correct submacro subroutine. In the example, the macro mcrPersonalInfo and the macro name GetGender have been selected. Notice the period between the name of the macro and the name of the macro name submacro. The period is used to differentiate the submacro (mcrPersonalInfo, in this case) from the macro name (GetGender, in this example).

SHOW ME   Media 10.2—Ways You Can Launch an Access Macro
Access this video file through your registered Web Edition at
my.safaribooksonline.com/9780132117128/media.

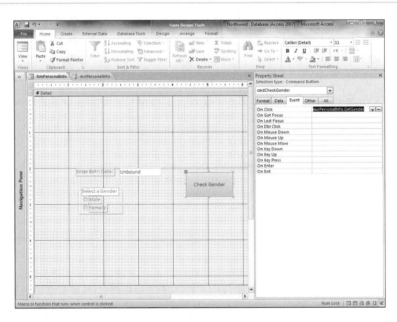

Figure 10.13 *Associating a macro with a Form or Report event.*

Modifying an Existing Macro

You have learned how to create a macro, add macro actions and their associated arguments, create macro subroutines by adding submacros, and conditionally execute the actions in the macro by adding macro conditions. However, after you have created a macro, you might want to modify it. First, you must enter Design view for the macro:

1. Select the Macros group on the Navigation Pane.

2. Select the macro you want to modify.

3. Right-click and select Design View.

When the design of the macro appears, you're then ready to insert new lines, delete existing lines, move the macro actions around, or copy macro actions to the macro you're modifying or to another macro.

 LET ME TRY IT

Inserting New Macro Actions

To insert a macro action, follow these steps:

1. Click the line above where you want the macro action to be inserted. An Add New Action macro line appears.

2. Open the drop-down to select the appropriate macro action, click to Add Else, or click to Add Else If.

 LET ME TRY IT

Deleting Macro Actions

Follow these steps to delete a macro action:

1. Hover your mouse over the macro action, submacro or If statement that you want to delete.

2. Click the *X* that appears on the right side of the macro line.

As an alternative, to delete a line within a macro, just right-click that line and select Delete from the context-sensitive menu.

 **LET ME TRY IT**

Moving Macro Actions

You can move macro actions in a few ways, including dragging and dropping and cutting and pasting. To move macro actions by dragging and dropping, follow these steps:

1. Hover your mouse pointer over the left side of the macro action you want to move until you see a hand.

2. Click and drag to move the macro action to the desired location.

3. Release the mouse button.

You can move multiple macro actions as a group by clicking the first action you want to move. You then hold down your Shift key and click the last action you want to move. When you click and drag the hand of the first action, the actions will move as a group.

If you accidentally drag and drop the selected macro actions to an incorrect place, use the Undo button on the Quick Access toolbar to reverse your action.

 LET ME TRY IT

Copying Macro Actions

Follow these steps to copy macro actions within a macro:

1. Hold down the Ctrl key.

2. Hover your mouse pointer over the macro action you want to copy.

3. When the hand appears, click and drag to copy the macro action to the desired location.

To copy multiple macro actions simultaneously, complete these steps:

1. Click to select the first action you want to copy.

2. While holding down the Shift key, click the last action you want to copy.

3. Hover your mouse pointer over one of the macro actions in the group.

4. When the hand appears, click and drag to copy the macro action to the desired location.

SHOW ME   Media 10.3—Modifying an Existing Macro

Access this video file through your registered Web Edition at **my.safaribooksonline.com/9780132117128/media**.

LET ME TRY IT

Creating an Embedded Macro

Creating an embedded macro is similar to creating a standard macro. The main difference is that the macro is embedded in the object with which it is associated and does not appear in the list of macros in the Navigation Pane. Here's how to create an embedded macro:

1. In Design view, click to select the object to which you want to associate the macro (for example, a command button).

2. Open the Property Sheet, as shown in Figure 10.14.

3. Click the Event tab of the Property Sheet.

4. Click within the event to which you want to associate the embedded macro. In Figure 10.14 the `On Click` event is selected.

5. Click the build button (the ellipse). The Choose Builder dialog box appears (see Figure 10.15).

6. Select Macro Builder and click OK. A Macro Design window appears, as shown in Figure 10.16. Notice in Figure 10.16 that the Macro tab is labeled `cmdSayHello: On Click`, indicating that the macro is associated with the `On Click` event of `cmdSayHello`.

7. Enter the macro commands as you would for any macro, as shown in Figure 10.17.

8. Close the Macro Design window. Access prompts you to save changes to the macro and update the property, as in Figure 10.18.

9. Click Yes to save your changes and close the dialog box. You have now created the embedded macro.

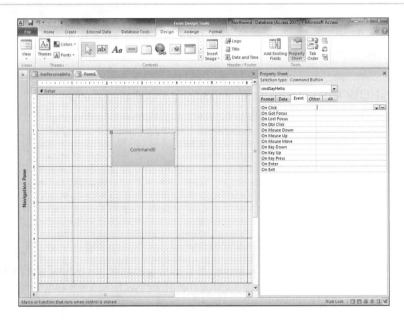

Figure 10.14 *Use the Property Sheet to associate a macro with the event of an object.*

Figure 10.15 *The Choose Builder dialog box enables you to specify that you want to build a macro.*

One advantage of embedded macros is that if you copy the object containing the embedded macro, the macro copies with the object. For example, if you copy a command button from one form to another, the entire embedded macro will be associated with the command button on the second form. If you then change one of the embedded macros, it does not affect the other one.

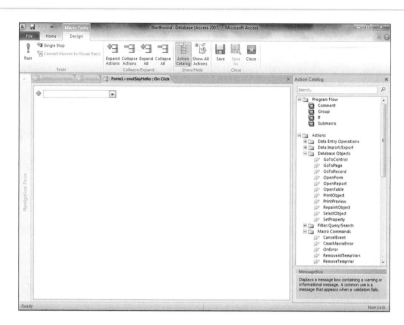

Figure 10.16   *The macro that you create is associated with the appropriate event of the designated object.*

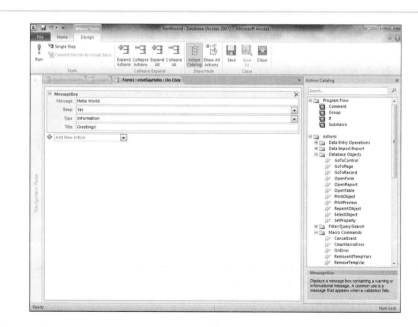

Figure 10.17   *Your macro commands appear just like macros that are not embedded.*

Figure 10.18   *If you save your changes, Access embeds the macro in the object.*

 SHOW ME   Media 10.4—Creating an Embedded Macro
Access this video file through your registered Web Edition at
my.safaribooksonline.com/9780132117128/media*.*

Creating Data Macros

New to Access 2010 are data macros. They are very powerful, and they take Access macros to a whole new level.

A data macro is a macro that executes in response to data changing within a table. The following are the events that you can respond to:

- After data is inserted

- After data is updated

- After data is deleted

- Before data is deleted

- Before data is changed

 LET ME TRY IT

Respond to Events

Here's how it works:

1. Open the table to which you want to add the data macros in Design view.

2. Click the Create Data Macros drop-down in the Field, Record & Table Events drop-down on the Table Tools Design tab of the Ribbon. The drop-down appears as in Figure 10.19.

3. Select the event you wish to respond to. For the example I have selected After Insert (see Figure 10.20).

Figure 10.19   *The Create Data Macros drop-down allows you to select the data event you want to respond to.*

Figure 10.20   *The After Insert event executes after you insert a record into a table.*

4. Open the Action drop-down and select the desired action. In Figure 10.21, I have selected LookUpRecord. Access prompts for the table in which to look up the record, the condition under which to perform the action, and the action to perform. The completed event appears in Figure 10.22. It looks up a record in the Users table where the Order ID in the Orders table matches the Order ID of the current record in the Order Details table. It then increments the value of the field NumberOfDetailItems in the Orders table by 1.

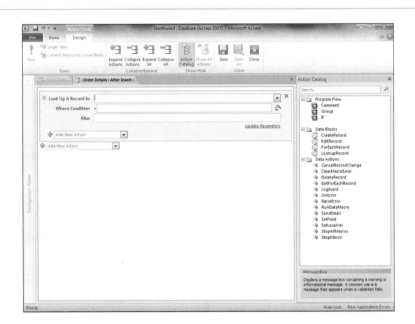

Figure 10.21   *The* LookUpRecord *action looks up a record in another table where the specified condition is true.*

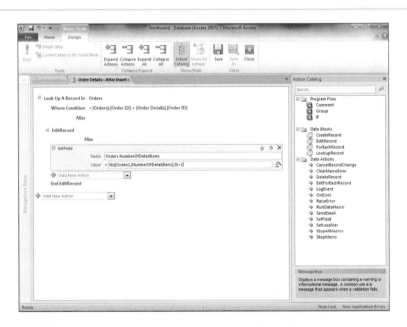

Figure 10.22   *This event increments the value of the NumberOfDetailItems field each time that the user enters an Order Detail record.*

SHOW ME   Media 10.5—Creating a Data Macro
Access this video file through your registered Web Edition at
my.safaribooksonline.com/9780132117128/media.

LET ME TRY IT

Creating a Drillthrough Macro

An exciting technique available with Access 2010 is the ability to easily create a drillthrough macro. With a drillthrough macro, you click an ID on a main form and it takes you to a detail form for the record associated with that ID. Here's how it works:

1. Click to select the parent table in the list of tables in the Navigation Pane. For this example, I will select the Orders table.

2. Select Datasheet from the More Forms drop-down in the Forms group on the Create tab of the Ribbon. Access creates a datasheet form based on the Orders table (as shown in Figure 10.23).

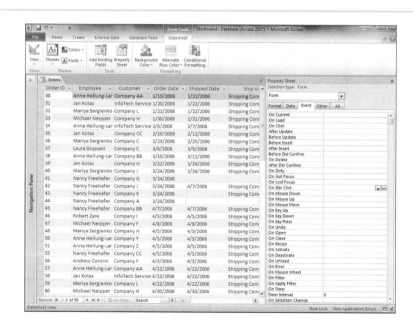

Figure 10.23   *The datasheet form displays all of the table's records in a datasheet.*

3. Save the form as frmOrdersDatasheet.

4. Select the Order ID column on the form. This may require using the Object drop-down in the Property Sheet.

5. Click the Build button for the On Dbl Click event of the text box. The Choose Builder dialog appears.

6. Select Macro Builder and click OK. The macro appears as in Figure 10.24.

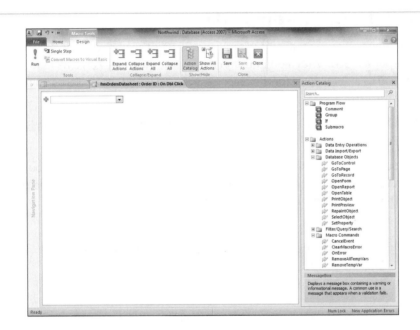

Figure 10.24   *The* On Dbl Click *event executes when the user double-clicks the designated object.*

7. Open the Action drop-down and select If from the list of available actions.

8. Enter the If action to only execute the action that follows it if the Order ID contains a value (see Figure 10.25).

9. Select the OpenForm action as the action you want to execute if the condition entered is true.

10. Fill in the arguments of the OpenForm action to open the Order Details form where the Order ID equals that on the frmOrdersDatasheet form (see Figure 10.26).

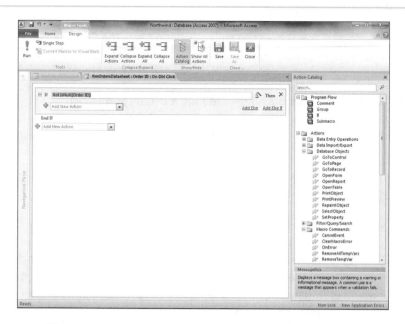

Figure 10.25   *The If action allows you to determine when the macro statements that follow it execute.*

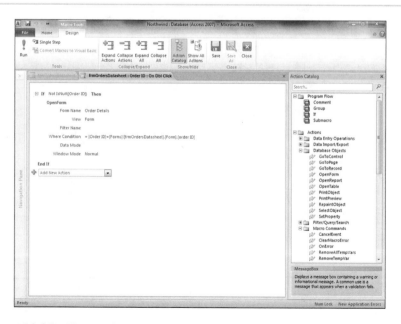

Figure 10.26   *The completed statement opens the Order Details form, displaying the detail items for the selected order.*

11. Save and close the macro.

12. Double-click the OrderID on the navigation form. The Order Details form should open, displaying data for the selected order.

SHOW ME   Media 10.6—Creating a Drillthrough Macro
Access this video file through your registered Web Edition at
my.safaribooksonline.com/9780132117128/media.

Other New Features Available in Macros

There were two major improvements introduced with Access 2007 macros. The first is the introduction of error handling, and the second is the introduction of variables. Notice the OnError macro action in Figure 10.27. The example branches to a macro named ErrorHandler in the case of an error. Unlike previous versions of Access, where error handling in macros was virtually nonexistent, the new OnError macro action provides similar error handling to that of VBA code (the programming language for Microsoft Access).

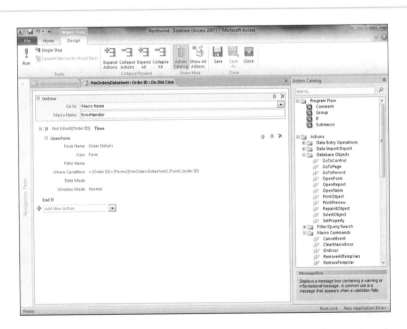

Figure 10.27   *The OnError macro action provides similar error handling to that of VBA code.*

Another exciting addition to Access 2007 macros was the introduction of variables. The new SetTempVar macro action enables you to create a variable and assign it a value. Figure 10.28 provides an example. Notice in the figure that the macro uses the SetTempVar action to create a variable called CurrentDate and assign it the value returned from the built-in Date() function.

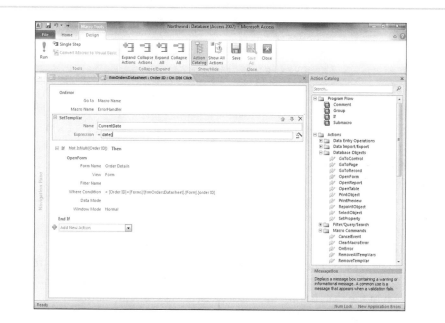

Figure 10.28 *You use the* SetTempVar *action to create a temporary variable in a Microsoft Office Access 2010 macro.*

 LET ME TRY IT

Testing a Macro

Although Access doesn't offer very sophisticated tools for testing and debugging your macros, it does give you a method for stepping through each line of a macro:

1. Open the macro in Design view.

2. Click Single Step in the Tools group of the Design tab.

3. To execute the macro, click Run. The first line of the macro is executed, and the Macro Single Step dialog box appears, showing you the Macro Name,

Condition, Action Name, and Arguments, as in Figure 10.29. In the figure, the macro name is mcrPersonalInfo, and the condition evaluates to false. The action name and arguments are not available.

Figure 10.29   *In the Macro Single Step dialog box, you can view the macro name, condition, action name, and arguments for the current step of the macro.*

4. To continue stepping through the macro, click the Step button on the Macro Single Step dialog box. If you want to halt the execution of the macro without proceeding, click the Stop All Macros button. To continue normal execution of the macro without stepping, click the Continue button.

The Single Step button in the Tools group of the Design tab is a toggle. After you activate Step Mode, it's activated for all macros in the current database and all other databases until you either turn off the toggle or exit Access. This behavior can be quite surprising if you don't expect it. You might have invoked Step mode in another database quite a bit earlier in the day, only to remember that you forgot to click the toggle button when some other macro unexpectedly goes into Step mode.

SHOW ME   Media 10.7—Testing a Macro
Access this video file through your registered Web Edition at
my.safaribooksonline.com/9780132117128/media.

Determining When You Should Use Macros and When You Shouldn't

Macros aren't always the best tools for creating code that controls industrial-strength applications because they're limited in some functionality. Access macros are limited in the following ways:

- You can't create user-defined functions by using macros.

- Access macros don't allow you to pass parameters.

- Access macros provide no method of processing table records one at a time.

- When using Access macros, you can't use object linking and embedding automation to communicate with other applications.

- Debugging Access macros is more difficult than debugging VBA code.

- Transaction processing can't be done with Access macros.

- You can't call Windows API functions by using Access macros.

- Access macros don't allow you to create database objects at runtime.

 LET ME TRY IT

Converting a Macro to VBA Code

Sometimes you will create a macro, later to discover that you want to convert it to VBA code. Fortunately, Access 2010 comes to the rescue. You can easily convert an Access macro to VBA code; after the macro has been converted to VBA code, the code can be modified just like any VBA module. Follow these four steps to convert an Access macro to VBA code:

1. Open the macro you want to convert in Design view.

2. Select Convert Macros to Visual Basic in the Tools group on the Macro Tools Design tab of the Ribbon. The Convert Macro dialog appears (see Figure 10.30).

3. Determine where you want to add error handling and comments to the generated code, and then click Convert. Access informs you that the conversion finished and places you in the Visual Basic Editor - VBE (see Figure 10.31).

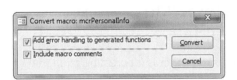

Figure 10.30 *The Convert Macro dialog box allows you to save a macro as a Visual Basic module.*

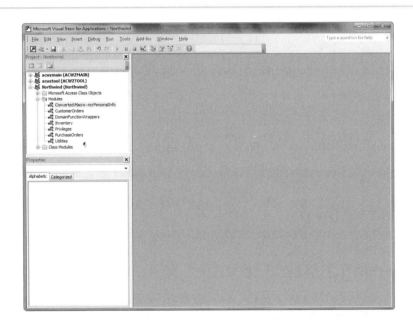

Figure 10.31 *The Visual Basic Editor allows you to view and modify the programming code that you generated.*

4. The converted macro appears under the list of modules with Converted Macro: followed by the name of the macro. Click Design to view the results of the conversion.

Figure 10.32 shows a macro that's been converted into distinct subroutines, one for each macro name. The macro is complete with logic, comments, and error handling. All macro conditions are converted into If...Else...End If statements, and all the macro comments are converted into VBA comments. Basic error-handling routines are automatically added to the code.

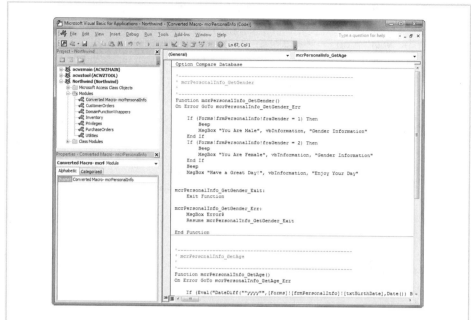

Figure 10.32   *A converted macro as a module.*

 SHOW ME   Media 10.8—Converting a Macro to VBA Code
Access this video file through your registered Web Edition at
my.safaribooksonline.com/9780132117128/media.

When you convert a macro to a Visual Basic module, the original macro remains untouched. Furthermore, all the objects in your application will still call the macro. To effectively use the macro conversion options, you must find all the places where the macro was called and replace the macro references with calls to the VBA function.

Creating an AutoExec Macro

With Access 2010, you can use either an AutoExec macro or Startup options to determine what occurs when a database is opened. Using an AutoExec macro to launch the processing of your application is certainly a viable option.

Creating an AutoExec macro is quite simple; it's just a normal macro saved with the name AutoExec. An AutoExec macro usually performs tasks such as hiding or minimizing the Navigation Pane and opening a Startup form or switchboard. The macro shown in Figure 10.33 hides the Navigation Pane, displays a welcome message, and opens the Home form.

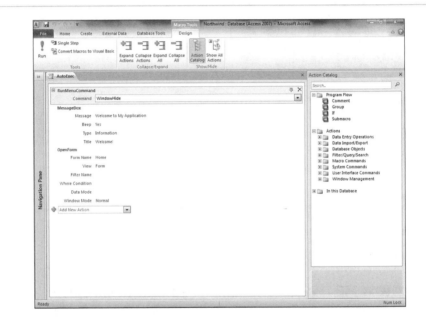

Figure 10.33   *An example of an AutoExec macro.*

When you're opening your own database to make changes or additions to the application, you probably won't want the AutoExec macro to execute. To prevent it from executing, hold down your Shift key as you open the database.

SHOW ME   Media 10.9—Creating an AutoExec Macro
Access this video file through your registered Web Edition at
***my.safaribooksonline.com/9780132117128/media**.*

TELL ME MORE   Media 10.10—When Should You Use Macros and When Shouldn't You?
Access this audio recording through your registered Web Edition at
***my.safaribooksonline.com/9780132117128/media**.*

One of the strengths of Access 2010 is its ability to share data with other applications.

11

Sharing Data with Other Applications

Microsoft Access is very capable of interfacing with data from other sources. It can use data from any OLE DB or ODBC (Open Database Connectivity) data source, as well as data from FoxPro, dBASE, Paradox, Lotus, Excel, and many other sources. In this chapter, you will learn how to interface with other Access databases, Excel, ASCII text files, and ODBC data sources.

What Is External Data?

External data is data that is stored outside the current database. External data may be data that you store in another Microsoft Access database, or it might be data that you store in a multitude of other file formats—including ISAM (Indexed Sequential Access Method), spreadsheet, ASCII, and more.

Access is an excellent *front-end* product, which means that it provides a powerful and effective means of presenting data—even data from external sources. You might opt to store data in places other than Access for many reasons. You can most effectively manage large databases, for example, on a back-end database server such as Microsoft SQL Server. You might store data in a FoxPro, dBASE, or Paradox file format because a legacy application written in one of those environments is using the data. You might download text data from a mainframe or midrange computer. Regardless of the reason the data is stored in another format, it is necessary that you understand how to manipulate this external data in Access applications. With the capability to access data from other sources, you can create queries, forms, and reports.

When you're accessing external data, you have two choices: You can import the data into an Access database or you can access the data by linking to it from an Access database. Importing the data is the optimum route (except with ODBC data sources), but it is not always possible. If you can't import external data, you should link to external files because Microsoft Access maintains a lot of information about these linked files. This optimizes performance when manipulating the external files.

Importing, Linking, and Opening Files: When and Why

When you import data into an Access table, Access makes a copy of the data and places it in the Access table. After Access imports the data, it treats the data like the data in any other native Access table. In fact, neither you nor Access has any way of knowing from where the data came. As a result, imported data offers the same performance and flexibility as any other Access table data.

Linking to external data is quite different from importing data. Linked data remains in its native format. By establishing a link to the external data, you can build queries, forms, and reports that present the data. After you create a link to external data, the link remains permanently established unless you explicitly remove it. The linked table appears in the Navigation Pane just like any other Access table, except that its icon is different. In fact, if the data source permits multiuser access, the users of an application can modify the data as can the users of the applications written in the data source's native database format (such as FoxPro, dBASE, or Paradox). The main difference between a linked table and a native table is that you cannot modify a linked table's structure from within Access.

Determining Whether to Import or Link

It is important that you understand when to import external data and when to link to external data. You should import external data in either of these circumstances:

- If you are migrating an existing system into Access.

- If you want to use external data to run a large volume of queries and reports, and you will not update the data. In this case, you want the added performance that native Access data provides.

When you are migrating <$Imigration;importing tables>an existing system to Access and you are ready to permanently migrate test or production data into an application, you import the tables into Access. You might also want to import external data if you convert the data into ASCII format on a regular basis and you want to use the data for reports. Instead of attempting to link to the data and suffering the performance hits associated with such a link, you can import the data each time you download it from the mainframe or midrange computer.

You should link to external data in any of the following circumstances:

- The data is used by a legacy application that requires the native file format.

- The data resides on an ODBC-compliant database server.

- You will access the data on a regular basis, making it prohibitive to keep the data up-to-date if you do not link to it.

Often, you won't have the time or resources to rewrite an application written in FoxPro, Paradox, or some other language. You might be developing additional applications that will share data with the legacy application, or you might want to use the strong querying and reporting capabilities of Access rather than develop queries and reports in the native environment.

If you link to the external data, users of existing applications can continue to work with the applications and their data. Access applications can retrieve and modify data without concern for corrupting, or in any other way harming, the data.

If the data resides in an ODBC database such as Microsoft SQL Server, you want to reap the data-retrieval benefits provided by a database server. By linking to the ODBC data source, you can take advantage of Access's ease of use as a front-end tool and also take advantage of client/server technology.

Finally, if you intend to access data on a regular basis, linking to the external table provides you with ease of use and performance benefits. After you create a link, in most cases, Access treats the table just like any other Access table.

Although this chapter covers the process of importing external data, this is essentially a one-time process and doesn't require a lot of discussion. It is important to note, however, that after you import data into an Access table, you can no longer use the application in its native format to access the data.

Looking at Supported File Formats

Microsoft Access enables you to import and link to files in these formats:

- Microsoft Access databases (including versions earlier than Access 2010)
- ODBC databases
- HTML (Hypertext Markup Language) documents with <table> tags
- XML (eXtensible Markup Language) documents (import and open only)
- Microsoft Exchange and Outlook
- dBASE III, dBASE IV, and dBASE 5.0
- Paradox 3.x, 4.x, and 5.x
- Microsoft Excel spreadsheets, versions 3.0, 4.0, 5.0, and 8.0
- Lotus WKS, WK1, WK3, and WK4 spreadsheets (import and open only)
- ASCII text files stored in a tabular format

LET ME TRY IT

Exporting to Another Access Database

You can easily export Access tables and queries to another Access database. The following is the required process:

1. Right-click the object you want to export and select Export from the context menu. (Alternatively, you can select Access from the Export group on the External Data tab of the Ribbon.) The menu appears as in Figure 11.1.

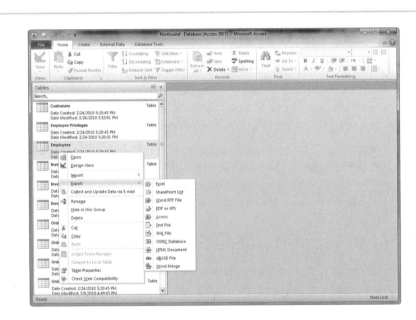

Figure 11.1   *After selecting Export, you can designate the type of file you want to export to.*

2. Select Access. The Export – Access Database dialog appears (see Figure 11.2).

3. Select the Access database to which you want to export the object and then click OK. The Export dialog box appears (see Figure 11.3).

4. In the Export dialog box, select Definition and Data or Definition Only, depending on whether you want to export just the structure or the structure and the data. Click OK.

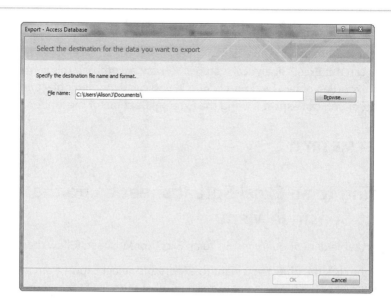

Figure 11.2   *The Export - Access dialog box allows you to designate the destination database.*

Figure 11.3   *The Export dialog box allows you to designate whether you want to export the definition and data or the definition only.*

When you export an object to another database, Access exports a copy of the object. When you choose Definition Only, Access copies just the object's structure (no data) to the receiving database.

SHOW ME   Media 11.1—Exporting to Another Access Database
Access this video file through your registered Web Edition at
my.safaribooksonline.com/9780132117128/media.

Exporting to an Excel Spreadsheet

You might want to export table data or query results to an Excel spreadsheet so that you can use Excel's analytical features. You can accomplish this in many ways. You can export an object by right-clicking it, you can export an object using drag and drop, or you can export it using the External Data tab of the Ribbon.

 **LET ME TRY IT**

Exporting to an Excel Spreadsheet Using the Context-Sensitive Menu

To export table data or query results to an Excel spreadsheet, follow these steps:

1. Right-click the object you want to export and select Export from the context menu. The menu expands to show all of the valid Export formats.

2. Select Excel from the menu. The Export – Excel Spreadsheet dialog appears (see Figure 11.4).

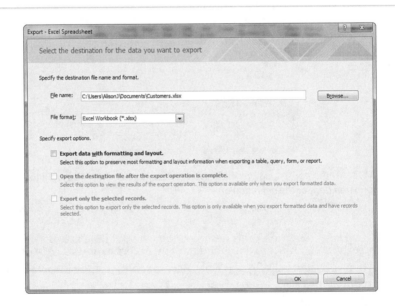

Figure 11.4 *The Export – Excel Spreadsheet dialog box allows you to designate the specifics for the export process to Excel.*

3. Designate the file name and file format.

4. Specify the desired export options (for example, if you want to export the data with formatting and layout and whether you want Excel to launch when the process is complete).

5. Click OK to complete the process.

 LET ME TRY IT

Exporting to an Excel Spreadsheet Using Drag and Drop

You can export a table or query to Microsoft Excel by dragging and dropping it directly onto an Excel spreadsheet. This whiz-bang technology makes the integration between these two powerful products virtually seamless. Here are the steps involved:

1. Arrange the Access and Excel application windows so that both are visible.

2. Drag the object (that is, the table or query) from the Access Navigation Pane onto the Excel spreadsheet. The results of dragging and dropping the Customers table from the Access Navigation Pane to Microsoft Excel appear in Figure 11.5.

 LET ME TRY IT

Exporting to an Excel Spreadsheet by Using the External Data Tab of the Ribbon

You can use the External Data tab of the Ribbon to export an Access table or query to Microsoft Excel, as follows:

1. Select the object you want to export.

2. Select Excel from the Export group on the External Data tab of the Ribbon. The Export – Excel Spreadsheet dialog appears.

3. Select the destination location and file format, as well as the export options, and click OK. The export process completes.

 SHOW ME   Media 11.2—Exporting to an Excel Spreadsheet
Access this video file through your registered Web Edition at
my.safaribooksonline.com/9780132117128/media.

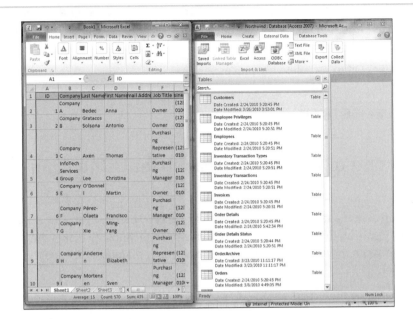

Figure 11.5 *Dragging and dropping an object directly from the Access Navigation Pane onto an Excel spreadsheet.*

Exporting to ASCII

ASCII is a standard file format that many programs can work with. Exporting to the ASCII format allows you to make the data in an Access database available to other applications.

LET ME TRY IT

Export Tables and Queries to the ASCII File Format

It is easy to export Access tables and queries to the ASCII file format. Here's how it works:

1. Right-click the object you want to export and select Export from the context menu. (Alternatively, you can select Text File from the Export group on the External Data tab of the Ribbon.) The Export menu expands.

2. Select Text File from the fly-out menu. The Export – Text File dialog appears (see Figure 11.6).

3. Select the destination folder and name for the text file.

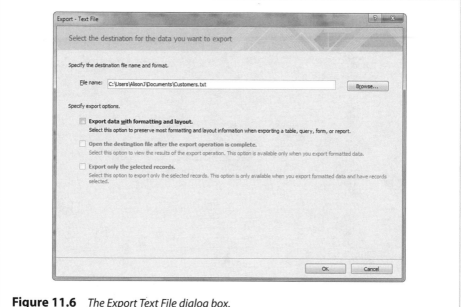

Figure 11.6   *The Export Text File dialog box.*

4. Designate the export options and click OK. If you opt to export the data
    with formatting and layout, the Encode dialog appears (see Figure 11.7).

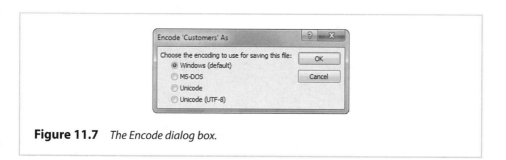

Figure 11.7   *The Encode dialog box.*

5. Select the desired encoding and click OK. The process completes, and the
    file appears as in Figure 11.8.

6. If you do not opt to export the data with formatting and layout, the Export
    Text Wizard appears (see Figure 11.9). This step allows you to select the
    export format that you want to use. You must select between Delimited
    and Fixed Width. These are two different text file formats that you may
    output to. The dialog provides samples of the output to help you make
    your selection.

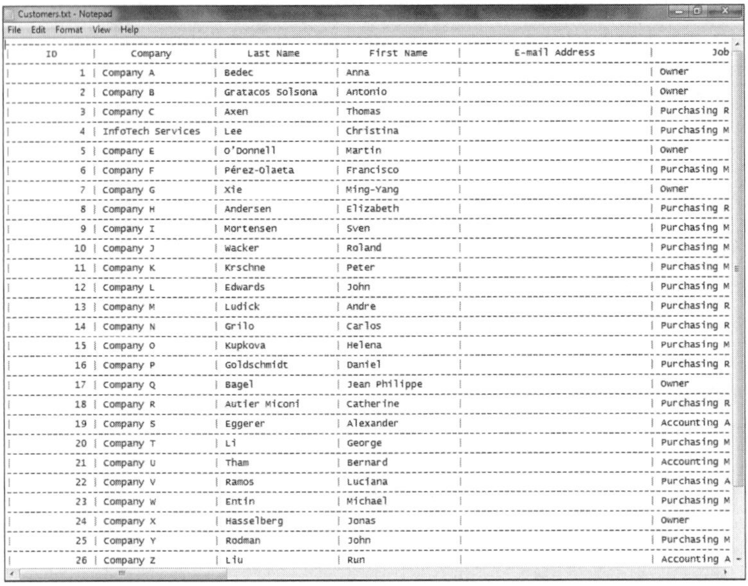

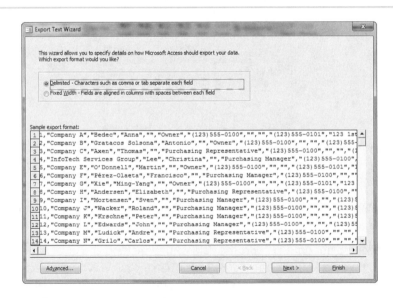

Figure 11.8   *An exported file when export the data with formatting and layout is selected.*

Figure 11.9   *The Export Text Wizard: step 1.*

7. If you select Delimited and then click Advanced, the Text Export Specification dialog box appears (see Figure 11.10). Here you can designate the field delimiter, text qualifier, language, date order, and other specifics about the file you are exporting. You will modify these options to meet the specifications of the consumer of the file you are creating.

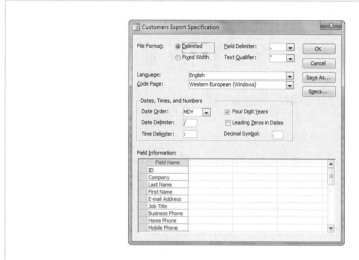

Figure 11.10   *The Text Export Specification dialog box.*

8. Select the desired settings, and then click OK.

9. Click Next.

10. Select the delimiter (see Figure 11.11).

11. If you select Include Field Names on First Row, the output file will include all the field names in the first row. Click Next. The final step of the Export Text Wizard appears.

12. Type the *appropriate* destination in the Export to File text box.

13. Click Finish to complete the process, and then click Close to close the wizard.

Importing from Another Access Database

You can import objects (for example, tables, queries, reports) from one Access database into another. When you import an object, you are making a copy of the

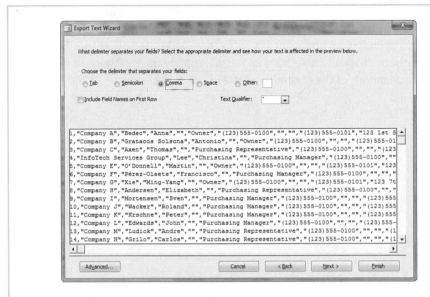

Figure 11.11 *The Export Text Wizard: step 2.*

object. Any changes you make to the imported object do not affect the original object.

 LET ME TRY IT

Import an Access Table

To see how to import an Access table object, follow these steps:

1. Open the database into which you want to import the table.

2. While viewing the list of tables, right-click anywhere within the Navigation Pane and select Import. (Alternatively, you can select Access from the Import & Link group on the External Data tab of the Ribbon.)

3. Select Access Database from the flyout menu. The Get External Data – Access Database dialog box appears (see Figure 11.12).

4. Select the folder where the Microsoft Access database you want to import is located.

5. Double-click the database file that contains the object you want to import.

6. Specify how and where you want to store the data in the current database (whether you want to import or link to the table).

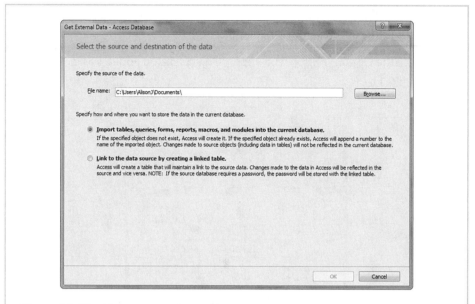

Figure 11.12   *The Get External Data – Access Database dialog box.*

7. Click OK. The Import Objects dialog appears (see Figure 11.13).

Figure 11.13   *The Import Objects dialog box.*

8. Select the Table tab.

9. Select the table from the list of tables.

10. Click the Options button. The Import Objects dialog appears as in Figure 11.14.

Figure 11.14   *The Import Objects dialog box after selecting the Options button.*

11. Select the desired options. Options include whether you want to import relationships, menus and toolbars, and import and export specifications. You can also designate whether you want to import just the table defini-tions, or the table definitions and the data. Finally, you can opt to import the queries as either queries, or as tables (the result of executing the queries). Generally, you will leave all these options at their default values, although you might want to modify them for specific applications.

12. Click OK to complete the process.

SHOW ME   Media 11.3—Importing from Another Access Database
Access this video file through your registered Web Edition at
my.safaribooksonline.com/9780132117128/media.

LET ME TRY IT

Importing Spreadsheet Data

You can easily import an Excel spreadsheet into an Access database. To do so, follow these steps:

1. Open the database into which you want to import the spreadsheet.

2. With Tables selected as the object type, right-click anywhere in the Navigation Pane and choose Import from the context menu. (Alternatively, you can select Excel from the Import & Link group on the External Data tab of the Ribbon.) The flyout menu appears.

3. Select Excel from the flyout menu. The Get External Data – Excel Spreadsheet dialog appears (see Figure 11.15).

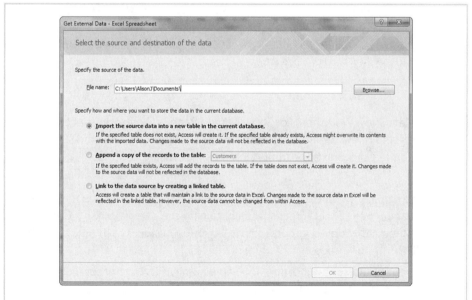

Figure 11.15   *The Get External Data – Excel Spreadsheet dialog allows you to select the file you want to import.*

4. Use the Browse button to select the Excel file that you want to import.

5. Specify how and where you want to store the data in the current database (for example, Import the Source Data into a New Table in the Current Database).

6. Click OK. The Import Spreadsheet Wizard appears (see Figure 11.16).

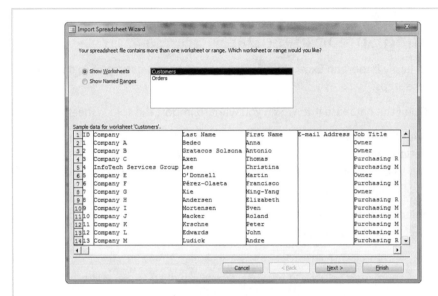

Figure 11.16   *The Import Spreadsheet Wizard enables you to designate whether you want to import a worksheet or a named range.*

7. Select Show Worksheets or Show Named Ranges (Access does not display this step of the wizard if the spreadsheet contains only one worksheet), and then click Next. The Import Spreadsheet Wizard continues.

If you plan to import spreadsheet data on a regular basis, it is helpful to define a named range in the Excel spreadsheet, containing the data you wish to import. You can then easily opt to import the named range in step 6 each time that you execute the import process.

Finally, you shouldn't give a control the same name as its control source. Access gives a bound control the same name as its field, and you need to change this name to avoid problems. If you fail to do so, and you reference the field in a formula for the control, #error# will appear on the report in the place of the data for that field. Following these simple warnings will spare you a lot of grief!

8. Select First Row Contains Column Headings, if appropriate (see Figure 11.17). Notice in the figure that the first row appears as column headings rather than data. Click Next. The wizard appears as in Figure 11.18.

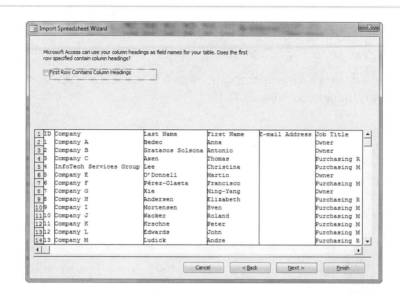

Figure 11.17   *Designate whether the first row of the spreadsheet contains column headings.*

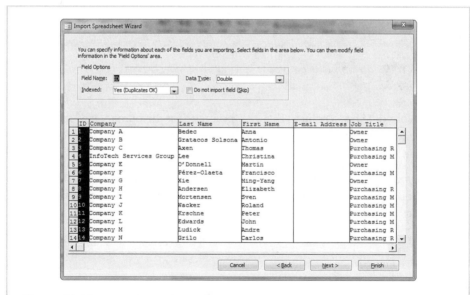

Figure 11.18   *Designate the specifics of each field that you are importing.*

9. Type the field name in the Field Name text box, if necessary.

10. Select whether you want Access to index the field.

11. Indicate whether to import a field by selecting the Do Not Import option for that field, if desired.

12. Click in the field list to select the next field.

13. Repeat steps 9–12 as appropriate for each field, and then click Next. The wizard appears as in Figure 11.19.

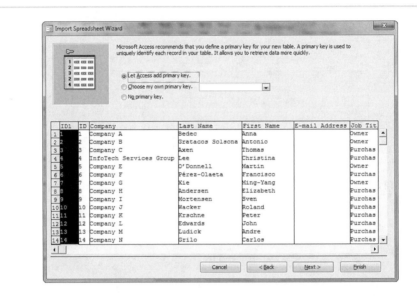

Figure 11.19   *The wizard allows you to designate a primary key field.*

14. If your data has a column that is appropriate for the primary key, select Choose My Own Primary Key. Otherwise, select Let Access Add a Primary Key.

15. If you opted to choose your own primary key, select the field from the drop-down box that you want Access to use as the primary key, and then click Next.

16. Type the table name in the Import to Table text box.

17. Click Finish.

18. Click OK.

SHOW ME   Media 11.4—Importing Spreadsheet Data
Access this video file through your registered Web Edition at
my.safaribooksonline.com/9780132117128/media.

Importing ASCII Data

Mainframes and minicomputers often export data in the ASCII file format. When you import ASCII data, you often need to make some changes for Access to handle the data properly.

 LET ME TRY IT

Import ASCII Data into Access

To import ASCII data into Access, follow these steps:

1. Open the database into which you want to import a table.

2. With Tables selected in the list of object types, right-click anywhere in the Navigation Pane and select Import from the context menu. (Alternatively, you can select Text File from the Import & Link group on the External Data tab of the Ribbon.) A flyout menu appears.

3. Select Text File from the flyout menu. The Get External Data – Text File dialog appears (see Figure 11.20).

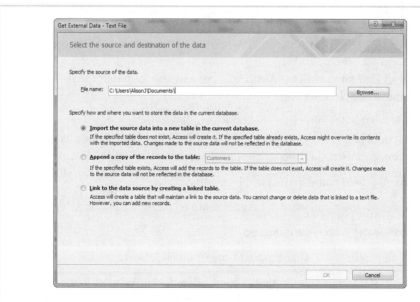

Figure 11.20   *The Get External Data – Text File dialog allows you to designate the location and name of the file that you want to import.*

4. Click Browse to locate the file you want to import.

5. Indicate how and where you want to store the data in the current database and click OK. This launches the Import Text Wizard (see Figure 11.21).

Figure 11.21   *The Import Text Wizard allows you to designate important information about the format of the file you are importing.*

6. Select Delimited or Fixed Width, to designate the format of the file you want to import. Click Next.

7. Indicate the delimiter that separates your fields (for instance, comma), the text qualifier, select or deselect First Row Contains Field Names, as appropriate, and then click Next. The wizard appears as in Figure 11.22.

8. Type the field name in the Field Name text box.

9. Select whether you want Access to create an index for the field.

10. Change the data type, if desired.

11. Repeat steps 8–10, as appropriate, and then click Next.

12. If your data has a column that is appropriate for the primary key, select Choose My Own Primary Key. Otherwise, select Let Access Add Primary Key.

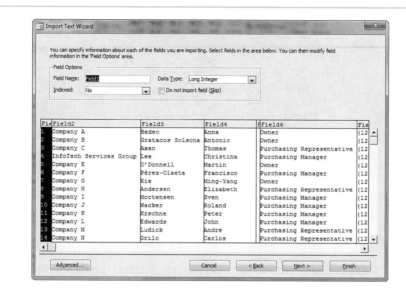

Figure 11.22   *The wizard allows you to supply field names and other important information about the fields you are importing.*

13. If you opted to choose your own primary key, select the field from the drop-down box that you want Access to use as the primary key, and then click Next.

14. Type the table name in the Import to Table text box.

15. Click Finish, and then click OK.

When working with ASCII data, you should be aware of a few things that can save you lots of time and effort in working with the imported data, as follows:

- After you import a table, you should open it and view its data. You might want to modify some of the field types to make them the appropriate Access data types. For example, the table you imported from might not have had a currency type.

- You can click the Advanced button anytime in the wizard to change the import specifications for each field (see Figure 11.23).

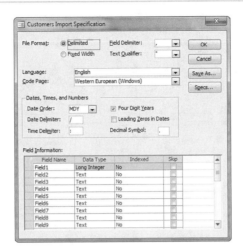

Figure 11.23 *The Advanced button enables you to change the import specifications for each field.*

 **LET ME TRY IT**

Linking to Tables in Another Access Database

When you link to data in another database, the data remains in its source location. Access simply creates a pointer to the data. To practice linking to data in different types of databases, follow these steps:

1. Open the database that will contain the link.

2. With Tables selected in the list of object types, right-click within the Navigation Pane and choose Import and then Access Database from the context menu. (Alternatively, you can select Access from the Import & Link group on the External Data tab of the Ribbon.)

3. Click Browse to locate the database that contains the table that you want to link to.

4. Click Link to the data source by creating a linked table (see Figure 11.24), and then click OK. The Link Tables dialog appears (see Figure 11.25).

5. Select the tables you want to link to.

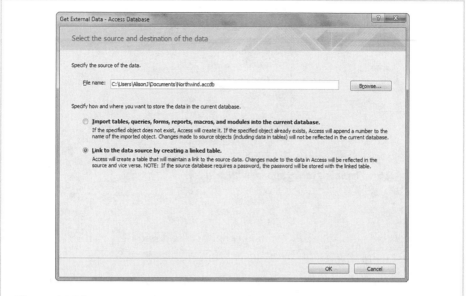

Figure 11.24   *You must designate that you want to link to the data source.*

Figure 11.25   *The Link Tables dialog box allows you to select the tables you want to link*

6.   Click OK. Figure 11.26 shows the results of such an operation.

Figure 11.26   *The linked tables appear with an arrow.*

When working with linked tables in another Access database, you need to remember a few important things, including the following:

- When you link a table to the source, you cannot change some properties in the linked table. The descriptions of these properties appear in red when in Design view of the table.

- If you make a change to any data in a linked table, the change will be reflected in the underlying table.

- Any relationships established between tables in the source are reflected in the linked tables.

- When working with data that needs to be kept on a file server, you should keep the data (that is, the tables) in one database and the other objects (for example, forms, reports) in another database. You then link from the application database to the data database.

 SHOW ME   Media 11.5—Linking to Tables in Another Access Database
Access this video file through your registered Web Edition at
my.safaribooksonline.com/9780132117128/media*.*

Linking to Another Type of Database

Even if you're not ready to actually import data from a database management system (such as FoxPro), you still might want to make changes to it by using Access. You can link to other types of databases and to Excel spreadsheets.

LET ME TRY IT

Link to Excel Spreadsheets

Linking to Excel spreadsheets involves the following steps:

1. Open the database that will contain the link.

2. With Tables selected as the object type, right-click in the Navigation Pane and select Import and then Excel from the context menu. (Alternatively, you can select Excel from the Import & Link group on the External Data tab of the Ribbon.) The Get External Data – Excel Spreadsheet dialog appears.

3. Click Browse to locate the spreadsheet whose data you want to link to.

4. Designate that you want to Link to the data source by creating a linked table.

5. Click OK. The Link Spreadsheet Wizard appears.

6. Select Show Worksheets or Show Named Ranges, as appropriate, and then click Next.

7. Click to select First Row Contains Column Headings, if appropriate.

8. Click Next.

9. Type a name for the linked table.

10. Click Finish, and then click OK. An icon associated with the linked table appears (see Figure 11.27).

LET ME TRY IT

Link to Other Databases

In addition to linking to Access tables and Excel spreadsheets, you might want to link to dBASE, FoxPro, Paradox, and other database files. Here are the required steps:

1. Open the database that will contain the links.

2. With Tables selected in the object list, right-click in the Navigation Pane and select Link Tables from the context menu. (Alternatively, you can

Figure 11.27 *Access associates an Excel icon with the link.*

select the appropriate data type [for example, dBASE] from the More drop-down in the Import & Link group on the External Data tab of the Ribbon.)

3. Click Browse and locate the file containing the data you want to link to.

4. Select Link to the data source by creating a linked table.

5. Click OK. The table appears in the Navigation Pane with the appropriate icon (for example, dBASE).

When working with linked tables in other databases, you need to remember a few important things, including the following:

- When you link a table to the source, there are some properties that you cannot change in the linked table. The descriptions of these properties appear in red while in Design view of the table.

- Any data you change in a linked table changes in the source table, too.

SHOW ME   Media 11.6—Linking to Another Type of Database
Access this video file through your registered Web Edition at
my.safaribooksonline.com/9780132117128/media.

Linking to SQL Server Databases

In a system where you store your data solely in Access tables, the Access Database Engine supplies all data retrieval and management functions and handles security, data validation, and enforcement of referential integrity.

In a system where Access acts as a front end to client/server data, the server handles the data management functions. It's responsible for retrieving, protecting, and updating data on the back-end database server. In this scenario, the local copy of Access is responsible only for sending requests and getting either data or pointers to data back from the database server. If you're creating an application in which Access acts as a front end, capitalizing on the strengths of both Access and the server can be a challenging endeavor.

You might ask why you would want to convert your database to a client/server application. The reasons include the following:

- Greater control over data integrity
- Increased control over data security
- Increased fault tolerance
- Reduced network traffic
- Improved performance
- Centralized control and management of data

Scenarios in which you *may* need to upsize include the following:

- Large number of simultaneous users (more than 10–15)
- Large volume of data (tables with more than approximately 100,000 rows)
- Increased need for security (payroll data and such)

 LET ME TRY IT

Link to SQL Server Data

If you store your data in SQL Server, you will need to link to it from your Access database. The steps that follow show you how to link from an Access database to a table stored on a SQL Server:

1. Select ODBC Database from the Import & Link group on the External Data tab of the Ribbon. The Get External Data – ODBC Database dialog appears.

2. Select Link to the data source by creating a linked table and click OK. The Select Data Source dialog appears.

3. Select the Machine Data Source tab. The dialog appears as in Figure 11.28.

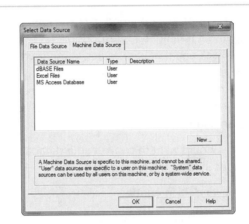

Figure 11.28   *The Machine Data Source tab of the Select Data Source dialog.*

4. Click New. A warning may appear indicating that you are unable to create System DSNs. If the warning appears, click OK to dismiss the dialog. The Create New Data Source Wizard appears (see Figure 11.29).

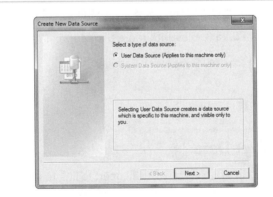

Figure 11.29   *The first step of the Create New Data Source Wizard.*

5. Click Next. The wizard appears as in Figure 11.30.

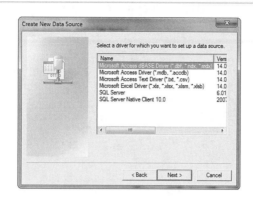

Figure 11.30 *The second step of the Create New Data Source Wizard.*

6. Select SQL Server or SQL Server Native Client 10.0 (depending on which version of SQL Server you are accessing), and then click Next.

7. Click Finish to launch the Create a New Data Source to SQL Server Wizard (see Figure 11.31).

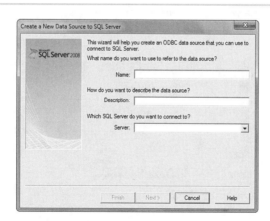

Figure 11.31 *The first step of the Create a New Data Source to SQL Server Wizard prompts you to name the data source and to designate the source server.*

8. Supply a name and optional description for the data source.

9. Designate the name of the SQL Server you want to connect to. (You might need to contact your system administrator to obtain this information.)

10. Click Next. The wizard appears as in Figure 11.32.

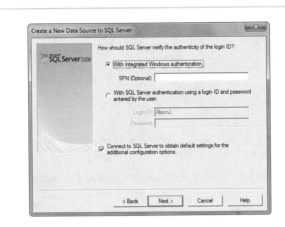

Figure 11.32 *Indicate the type of security you will use to log on to the server.*

11. Indicate the type of security you will use to log on to the server. (Again, you might need to contact your system administrator for this information.)

12. Click Next. The wizard appears as in Figure 11.33.

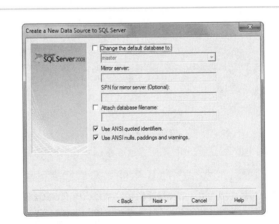

Figure 11.33 *Designate the default database that you want to connect to.*

13. Change the default database to point at the SQL Server database that you want to link to.

14. Click Next. The final step of the wizard appears. You can generally leave all these settings at their default values.

15. Click Finish. A dialog appears showing you all of the settings you have selected (see Figure 11.34).

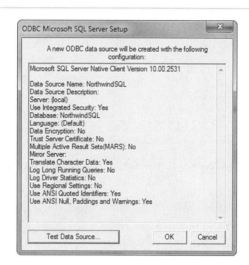

Figure 11.34 *Click Test Data Source to ensure that the settings you have selected are correct.*

16. Click Test Data Source to test your connection to the SQL Server database. A dialog appears confirming that the test was successful.

17. Click OK to close the dialog, and OK again to close the wizard. Your data source appears in the list of available data sources.

18. Click OK to select the new data source and begin the process of linking to the tables within it. The Link Tables dialog appears (see Figure 11.35).

19. Select the tables you want to link to and click OK. The process completes and the tables appear in the Navigation Pane with globes (see Figure 11.36), indicating that they are using ODBC to connect to the SQL Server. You can now treat the tables like any other linked tables.

SHOW ME Media 11.7—Linking to SQL Server Databases

Access this video file through your registered Web Edition at
my.safaribooksonline.com/9780132117128/media.

Figure 11.35 *The Link Tables dialog enables you to designate the tables you want to link to.*

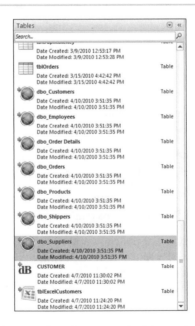

Figure 11.36 *The tables you selected appear with globes in the Navigation Pane.*

The Linked Table Manager

The Linked Table Manager is an important tool for working with linked tables. It allows you to move tables to another folder or another drive and then update the link to that table.

 **LET ME TRY IT**

Move and Update Table Links

To move and update table links, follow these steps:

1. Choose Linked Table Manager from the Import & Link group on the External Data tab of the Ribbon. The Linked Table Manager appears (see Figure 11.37).

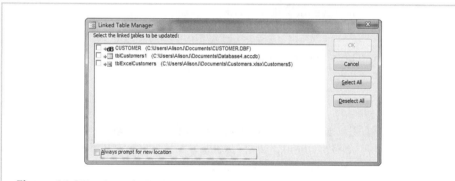

Figure 11.37   *The Linked Table Manager.*

2. Select the linked tables you want to update.

3. Select the Always Prompt for New Location check box.

4. Click OK.

5. Select the folder or drive to which you have moved the table.

6. Select the table, and then click Open.

7. Click OK.

You might at some time have a link that you no longer need. For example, you might import data because it is no longer necessary to use the legacy system that you have in place. The following are the steps necessary to remove such a link:

1. Select the link you want to remove.

2. Press the Delete key. The dialog box shown in Figure 11.38 appears.

Figure 11.38 *Access prompts you to remove the link.*

3. Click Yes to remove the link. The link is removed.

It is important to note that this process does not remove the linked object. It just removes the link.

SHOW ME **Media 11.8—The Linked Table Manager**
Access this video file through your registered Web Edition at
my.safaribooksonline.com/9780132117128/media.

TELL ME MORE **Media 11.9—Practical Applications of Working with External Data**
Access this audio recording through your registered Web Edition at
my.safaribooksonline.com/9780132117128/media.

Working with Web Databases

Microsoft Access 2010 enables you to create web databases. Using a web database, you can create an application where many of the database objects can be viewed in a browser. In this chapter, you learn how to create and work with a web database. You learn about how to create and use application parts and how to create server objects. You will then see how your completed application can run in a web browser. It is important to note that this new and exciting technology requires that you have access to a SharePoint 2010 server. Furthermore, SharePoint Foundation 2010 requires a 64-bit version of Windows Server 2008. If you do not have a SharePoint 2010 server available to you, you will only be able to follow along with this chapter until the section entitled "Publishing Your Database to Access Services." You will not be able to complete that section of the text.

Working with Web Databases

As its name implies, a web database is a database whose objects can be published to the Web and viewed in a browser. Creating and working with a web database is simple. Here's what's involved:

1. Designate Blank web database as the type of file you want to create.

2. Create objects that are publishable to the Web.

3. Publish the database to Access Services.

4. View your application in a browser.

The sections that follow cover all these steps in detail.

LET ME TRY IT

Creating a Blank Web Database

The process of creating a web database is similar to that of creating a standard Access database. Here are the steps:

1. Click the File tab on the Ribbon. Your screen appears as in Figure 12.1.

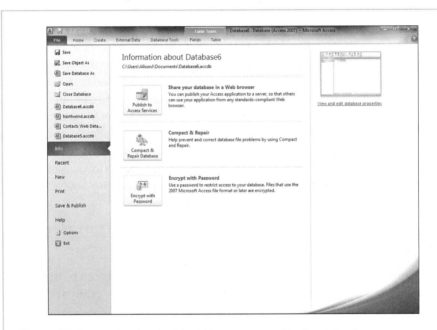

Figure 12.1   *Use the File tab of the Ribbon to create a blank web database.*

2. Select New. Your screen appears as in Figure 12.2.

3. Select Blank web database from the list of available templates.

4. Supply a folder location and file name for the new database.

5. Click Create to complete the process. The new database appears as in Figure 12.3. Notice that it appears almost like a standard database, except for the icon for Table1, indicating that it resides on the server.

If you click the Create tab, you will immediately notice some differences between the web database and standard databases (see Figure 12.4). For example, you can create application parts, client queries versus server queries, client forms versus

Figure 12.2   *You must select Blank web database as the available template for your new database.*

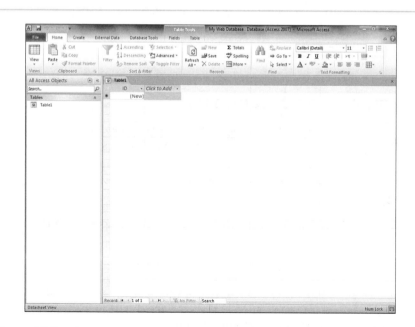

Figure 12.3   *The web database appears almost identical to a standard Access database.*

Figure 12.4   *The Create tab allows you to create client and server objects.*

server forms, client reports versus server reports, and client objects. The text that follows covers all of these objects, including how and when you should use them.

 SHOW ME   Media 12.1—Creating a Blank Web Database
Access this video file through your registered Web Edition at
my.safaribooksonline.com/9780132117128/media.

Creating Publishable Objects

When you work with a web database, you can create both publishable and non-publishable objects. If you create client objects, those objects remain in the Access database and cannot be published to the Web. All other objects can be published to the Web. The text that follows covers how to create publishable objects.

 LET ME TRY IT

Working with Application Parts

Application parts enable you to easily create objects that are publishable to the Web. The Application Parts drop-down, shown in Figure 12.5, shows you that you can use application parts to quickly create standard web forms and standard web applications. Let's take a look at a couple of examples of how you can easily work with application parts.

1. Select the Application Parts drop-down from the Templates group on the Create tab of the Ribbon.

2. You may be prompted to close open objects. If so, click Yes.

3. The Navigation Pane appears with a new form whose name varies depending on the application part you selected. In Figure 12.6, the form created is called SingleOneColumnRightLabels.

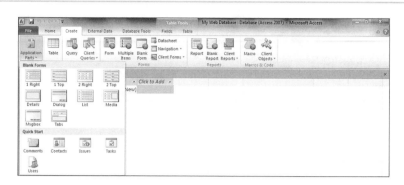

Figure 12.5   *The Application Parts drop-down allows you to quickly create web applications.*

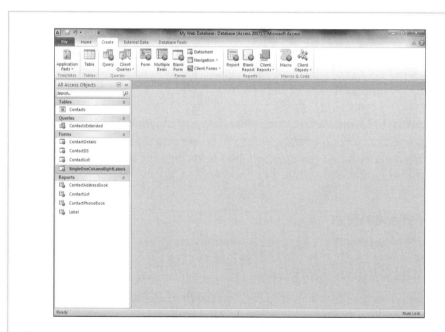

Figure 12.6   *The new application part that you create appears in the Navigation Pane.*

4. Double-click to open the form. It appears as in Figure 12.7. Notice that it is complete with placeholders for four fields, a Save button, and a Save & Close button.

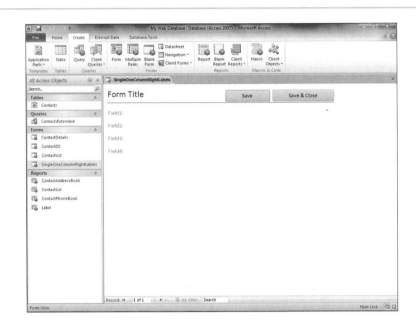

Figure 12.7   *The form created using the Application Parts drop-down.*

5. Switch to Layout View to modify the design of the form (see Figure 12.8). The process of working with the web form is similar to that of working with a standard form. You can drag and drop fields onto the form and then modify the properties of the objects on the form.

 LET ME TRY IT

Creating Server Queries

Creating server queries is similar to creating standard queries. The process is as follows:

1. Select Query from the Queries group on the Create tab of the Ribbon. The Show Table dialog appears.

2. Select the tables you want to add to the query and click Add.

3. Click Close to close the Show Table dialog. (A new query appears as in Figure 12.9.)

4. Add fields and expressions to the query, just as you would add them to any other query. An example of a completed query appears in Figure 12.10.

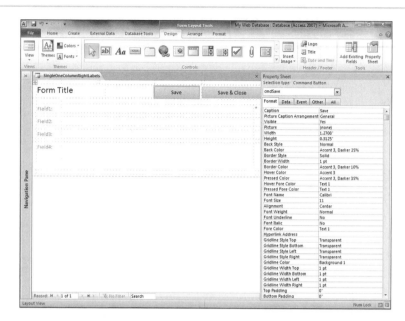

Figure 12.8 *You use Layout view to modify the forms you create within the Application Parts drop-down.*

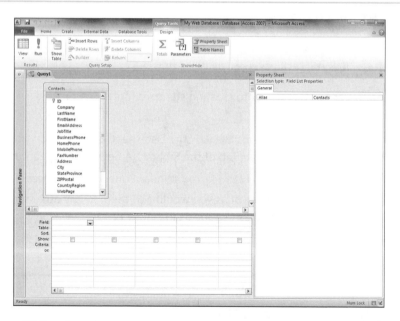

Figure 12.9 *Like its client counterpart, a new query appears with the tables at the top half of the query grid.*

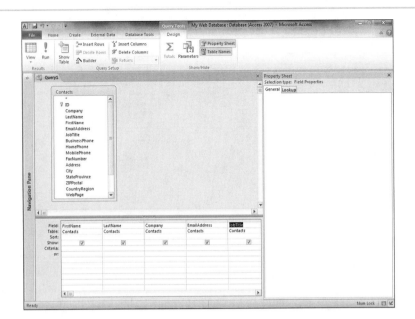

Figure 12.10   *The completed web query looks almost like its client counterpart.*

LET ME TRY IT

Creating Server Forms

Creating server forms is similar to creating standard forms. The process is as follows:

1. Select Form, Multiple Items, Blank Form, Datasheet, or Navigation from the Forms group on the Create tab of the Ribbon. (A new form appears as in Figure 12.11.)

2. Add objects to the form, just as you would add them to any other form. An example of a completed form appears in Figure 12.12.

LET ME TRY IT

Creating Server Reports

Creating server reports is similar to creating standard reports. The process is as follows:

Figure 12.11   *The multiple items form, shown in Layout view.*

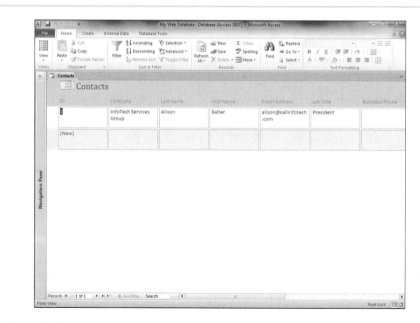

Figure 12.12   *The multiple items form, shown in Form view.*

1. Select Report or Blank Report from the Reports group on the Create tab of the Ribbon. (A new report appears as in Figure 12.13.)

Figure 12.13   *A web report, shown in Layout view.*

2. Add objects to the report, just as you would add them to any other report. An example of a completed report appears in Figure 12.14.

 SHOW ME   Media 12.2—Creating Publishable Objects
Access this video file through your registered Web Edition at
my.safaribooksonline.com/9780132117128/media.

 **LET ME TRY IT**

Publishing Your Database to Access Services

Before you can view your application in a browser, you must first publish it to Access Services. You must use a SharePoint server running Access Services. Once you have your SharePoint server set up properly, the process is simple:

1. Click the File tab. Your screen will appear as in Figure 12.15.

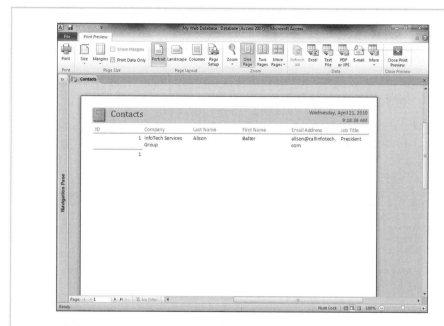

Figure 12.14   *A web report, shown in Print Preview.*

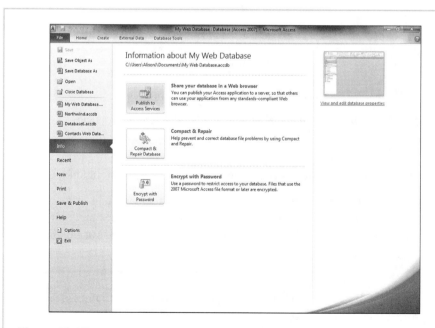

Figure 12.15   *Click the File tab to begin the publishing process.*

2. Click the Run Compatibility Check button to ensure that the objects in your database are supported on the Web.

3. Select Publish to Access Services.

4. Fill in the Server URL with the name of the SharePoint server you are publishing to.

5. Fill in the Site Name field with a descriptive name of your choice. Your screen should appear as in Figure 12.16.

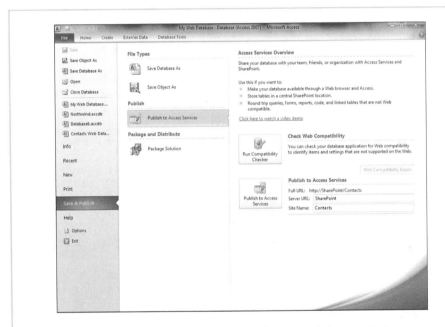

Figure 12.16   *You must enter the server URL and site name before continuing.*

6. Click Publish to Access Services. The publishing process should begin.

7. If the process is successful, all tables are moved to SharePoint lists, and your forms, reports, and macros become objects stored on the SharePoint server. A message appears indicating that the database published successfully. You are now ready to view your application in a browser.

SHOW ME   Media 12.3—Publishing Your Database to Access Services

Access this video file through your registered Web Edition at
my.safaribooksonline.com/9780132117128/media.

Viewing Your Application in a Browser

After you have published your database to Access, you are ready to view it in a browser. The dialog that appears when the publishing process is complete contains a link to the published site. Simply click the link and Access takes you into your browser, showing your startup form within the browser window.

It is very important that you include a startup form in all of the databases that you will publish to the Web. Otherwise, your application will appear with a complete list of all the forms and reports contained in the database.

 TELL ME MORE   Media 12.4—The Pros and Cons of Using a Web Database

Access this audio recording through your registered Web Edition at ***my.safaribooksonline.com/9780132117128/media***.

index

Symbols

(pound sign), 30
* (asterisk), 30
< (less than) operator, 144
<= (less than or equal to)
operator, 144
<> (inequality) operator, 144
= (equal to) operator, 144
> (greater than) operator, 144
>= (greater than or equal to)
operator, 144
? (question mark), 30

A

Access Services, publishing web
databases to, 318-320
Action queries
Append queries, 163-165
Delete queries, 161-162
Make Table queries, 165-167
Update queries, 158-161
actions
action arguments, 247-250
macro actions
adding, 244-245, 257
copying, 258-259
deleting, 257
moving, 258
aggregate functions, 167-169
Align feature (Ribbon), 178
Align tools, 178
aligning controls, 178-180
Allow Additions property
(forms), 190
Allow AutoCorrect property
(controls), 199
Allow Deletions property (forms),
190
Allow Design Changes property
(forms), 191
Allow Edits property (forms), 190
Allow Filters property
forms, 190
reports, 240

Allow Zero Length property
(fields), 113-114
AND operator, 43-45, 144
Append queries, 163-165
application parts, 312-314
applications
corporation-wide applications,
15-16
departmental applications, 15
enterprise-wide client/server
applications, 16
personal applications, 13-14
small-business applications, 14
ASCII
exporting data to, 282-285
importing, 293-296
asterisk (*), 30
Auto Center property
forms, 189
reports, 238
Auto Resize property
forms, 189
reports, 238
Auto Tab property (controls), 199
AutoExec macros, creating,
273-274
AutoForm feature, 73-75
AutoLookup feature, 150-153
AutoNumber fields, 103
AutoReport feature, 85-86

B

Back Color property (controls),
193, 218
Back Style property (controls),
193, 218
Between operator, 145
Border Color property (controls),
194, 219
Border Style property
controls, 194, 219
forms, 189
reports, 239
Border Width property (controls),
194, 219

browsers, viewing web databases
in, 321
buttons. *See specific buttons*
By Entire Value setting
(sorting/grouping), 234

C

calculated fields, 153-154
Can Grow property
controls, 217
group headers/footers, 237
Can Shrink property
controls, 217
group headers/footers, 237
Cancel property (controls), 199
Caption property
controls, 193, 216
fields, 110
forms, 188
reports, 238
Cascade Delete Related Records
option, 134-135
Cascade Update Related Fields
option, 133-134
changes, undoing, 22-23
Choose Builder dialog box,
259-260
Close Button property (forms),
189
Close command (File menu), 21
closing
forms, 72-73
queries, 54
reports, 89
tables, 21
Combo Box Wizard, 201-205
combo boxes, 201-205
Command Button Wizard,
206-208
commands. *See specific
commands*
comparison operator, 47-48
conditional formatting,
78-79, 185-186
Conditional Formatting dialog
box, 78